Teaching Girls o

Teaching Girls on Fire

*Essays on Dystopian Young Adult
Literature in the Classroom*

Edited by SARAH HENTGES *and*
SEAN P. CONNORS

McFarland & Company, Inc., Publishers
Jefferson, North Carolina

LIBRARY OF CONGRESS CATALOGUING-IN-PUBLICATION DATA

Names: Hentges, Sarah, 1976– editor. | Connors, Sean P., 1969– editor.
Title: Teaching girls on fire : essays on dystopian young adult literature
   in the classroom / edited by Sarah Hentges, Sean P. Connors.
Description: Jefferson : McFarland & Company, Inc., Publishers, 2020. |
   Includes bibliographical references and index.
Identifiers: LCCN 2020016522 | ISBN 9781476679297 (paperback : acid free paper ∞)
   ISBN 9781476638904 (ebook)
Subjects: LCSH: Young adult fiction, American—21st century—History and
   criticism. | Young adult fiction, American—Study and teaching. | Dystopias
   in literature. | Teenage girls in literature.
Classification: LCC PS374.Y57 T44 2020 | DDC 813/.60992827—dc23
LC record available at https://lccn.loc.gov/2020016522

BRITISH LIBRARY CATALOGUING DATA ARE AVAILABLE

ISBN (print) 978-1-4766-7929-7
ISBN (ebook) 978-1-4766-3890-4

Front cover image © 2020 Shutterstock

Printed in the United States of America

McFarland & Company, Inc., Publishers
   Box 611, Jefferson, North Carolina 28640
   www.mcfarlandpub.com

To all the teachers—inspiring action
and creating consciousness,
in and out of the classroom.

Table of Contents

Preface   1

Introduction: Girls on Fire: "Off the Page and Into the World"
SEAN P. CONNORS *and* SARAH HENTGES   3

**Part One: Exploring New Ground
for Girls on Fire**

Athletic Girls on Fire: Representations of the Female Athlete
in *The Hunger Games* and Sports-Related Media
WENDY J. GLENN   19

From Girls on Fire to Historical Bad Girls: A Framework
for Critiquing Postfeminism and Neoliberalism
in YA Literature
SEAN P. CONNORS *and* LISSETTE LOPEZ SZWYDKY   35

Teaching Feminisms: Triumphs and Failures in The Hunger
Games Trilogy
ROBERTA SEELINGER TRITES   51

**Part Two: #MeToo: Sexual Realities,
Activism and Empowerment**

Young Adult Literature and Girls on Fire as Fuel for Teaching
the #MeToo Movement
ARIANNA BANACK, CAITLIN METHENY *and* AMANDA RIGELL   71

Say Something, Do Something: Creating Allies and Agents
Through *The Nowhere Girls* on Fire
KATIE SLUITER *and* GRETCHEN RUMOHR   92

Troubling Girls on Fire in Young Adult Literature: A Critical
Examination of Systemic Violence and Sexual Trauma
in *Asking for It*
  KATE LECHTENBERG, JENNA SPIERING, AMANDA HAERTLING
  THEIN *and* NICOLE ANN AMATO   105

Part Three: The Girl on Fire
in the University Classroom

On Teaching Girls Who Want to Burn: The Problems
and Possibilities of Feminist Education
  TESSA PYLES   123

It Starts with a Book: An Exemplary "Girl on Fire" and Her
Undergraduate Thesis on Racial Social Justice
  KATIE RYBAKOVA *and* SYDNI COLLIER   141

Teaching Octavia Butler's Diverse Body of Speculative Fiction:
Genre, Race and the Radical Imaginary
  BRYAN YAZELL   154

Teaching/Learning YA Dystopia's Girls on Fire in Denmark's
Educational System and International Community
  SARAH HENTGES, ELAINE BRUM, PETRA ILIC
  and ROMAINE BERRY   171

Conclusion: "[Girls on Fire]: Tear This Wall Down!"
International and Imaginative Contexts for Teaching
Girls on Fire
  SARAH HENTGES   191

About the Contributors   207

Index   211

Preface

The last decade has seen an explosion of female protagonists—on the page, on the screen, and in the world. This collection of essays provides examples of how teachers in a variety of contexts can—and do—harness the cultural power of the Girl on Fire. Each essay provides both theoretical inquiries and practical applications, and collectively, they challenge us to think about how we can make our classrooms dynamic spaces for critical inquiry, creative application, and activism. Some essays provide a new lens on cherished texts, some pair young adult texts with canonical texts, and some examine young adult texts that open spaces for inquiry and dialogue regarding some of the enduring issues, such as reproductive rights, climate change, and movements against racism, sexism, homophobia, and violence. Through these collected essays, we hope our readers will join this conversation about teaching and the critically active role that educators play in shaping the future. We, as editors, have certainly been inspired by the ideas and passion of the authors whose work was selected for *Teaching Girls on Fire*.

Several years ago, in April 2015, Sean attended a conference presentation that Sarah gave on her work on Girls on Fire. Inspired by her presentation, he approached her afterward, and the two of them talked about their shared passion for young adult dystopian literature. Although we did not know it at the time, the seeds for this book were planted during that chance encounter. We gave further fuel to our collaborative fire through our contributions to a special issue of *SIGNAL Journal* that Sean edited. In the years that followed, we remained in touch, occasionally sharing projects we happened to be working on and exchanging ideas for future projects we could potentially collaborate on. When Sarah proposed the idea for this book of essays, Sean readily accepted, and together they reached out for essays to other educators whose work challenges and inspires them. The realization of this book thus speaks to the inspirational power of the Girl on Fire. Moreover, it exemplifies a number of qualities that we associate with this figure, including the value of collaboration, ingenuity, and persistence. Above all else, though, this collection of essays reflects our contributors' shared commitment to provide students with tools and resources they can draw on to usher in a world that is more equitable and just than the one their predecessors have left for them. To that end, we hope the odds truly are in their favor! And we also know that together we burn brighter.

In the time between the completion of this book and the final edits, the world has changed. The COVID-19 pandemic has made dystopia all the more real. *Teaching Girls on Fire*—teaching about empowered female heroines in fiction and in the real world—could never be more important or more timely. Resiliency, community, agency, and self-care are just some of the Girls on Fire lessons we can teach our youth and ourselves. As Katniss reminds the powers that be in her world, and many memes remind us in our world, "If we burn, you burn with us!" This is a promise as much as it is a threat. We're all in this together and the future is bright when we help our girls burn brighter.

Introduction

Girls on Fire: "Off the Page and Into the World"

SEAN P. CONNORS *and* SARAH HENTGES

In the wake of yet another mass shooting, this one at Marjory Stoneman Douglas High School in Parkland, Florida, teacher Jennifer Ansbach, responding to the birth of the youth-led #NeverAgain movement, tweeted, "I'm not sure why people are so surprised that the students are rising up—we've been feeding them a steady diet of dystopian literature showing teens leading the charge for years. We have told teen girls they are empowered. What, you thought it was fiction? It was preparation" (@JenAnsbach). Implicit in Ansbach's characterization of YA dystopian fiction as an empowering genre that inspires young people—and young women, in particular—to rise up and act as agents of social change is a tacit acknowledgment of the strong female protagonists that populate these books, the Girls on Fire that combat structural and systemic oppression and strive to transform their communities into more just, more equitable places.

From #NeverAgain to #MeToo to #BlackLivesMatter to #StudentsStrike4 Climate, a growing number of young people around the globe are rising up and working together to address problems they perceive as threatening their social futures. Often, teenage girls are at the front of these movements. While it is hard to know whether YA dystopian fiction is, as Ansbach suggests, responsible for inspiring large-scale youth activist movements, a growing number of educators share her belief in the genre's potential to capture the political imagination of young readers. Indeed, these books are arguably most impactful when students read them in school, as teachers can strategically frame their study of them, calling their attention to themes they might otherwise overlook and creating opportunities for them to exercise their voice in the service of calling attention to issues they recognize as problematic in their local communities. Sean, for example, describes how he capitalizes on pre-service teachers' interest in YA dystopian fiction by inviting them to undertake assignments that require them to build on the political themes and social justice topics they encounter in these books. From asking students to use YA dystopian novels as the basis for short films that call viewers' attention to different social justice topics ("Looking Deeper") to examining how the design of YA book covers can marginalize or exclude some groups of people, Sean aims to position students as real-life "Mockingjays—empowered agents capable of using reading and writing to act on, and transform, the world" ("Becoming Mockingjays" 18–19).

Sarah also asks students to put the ideas from their classes into action in their lives and in their communities, noting the archetypal and symbolic power of the Girl on Fire and students' ability to "make personal and structural connections" (206, 207). Students create lesson plans, social media campaigns, pamphlets, fliers, and library displays and pathfinders. They host film showings and discussions, write fiction and children's stories, and fashion art projects and activist interventions—all while they also work through their personal traumas (209–10).

Amber Simmons, a high school English teacher, explains how she uses books like Suzanne Collins's The Hunger Games trilogy as a vehicle to support students' examining violence and injustice in the world. Arguing for the importance of this work, Simmons asserts, "Like an ember that fuels a fire, reading can stoke our students into becoming socially responsible citizens, causing them to spit and blaze in the face of injustice and spread their fire throughout the community" (31).

At the center of instructional assignments like these is the Girl on Fire, a figure that is understood in all kinds of ways. As Sarah describes in her work, in popular culture, the Girl on Fire shines through Alicia Keys's powerful voice; we dance and sing along. She is, more so, Katniss Everdeen, the protagonist of The Hunger Games books and films and pop culture propaganda. Katniss is the "girl who *was* on fire" (our emphasis), and she continues to burn. The Girl on Fire is, to paraphrase Britney Spears's words, young enough to still be a girl, but not quite old enough to be considered a woman. She is a fictional character in young adult dystopia who has a variety of influences on the real world. She questions the way things are and works toward change. She struggles, she fights, she explores, she loves, she nurtures, she challenges. She comes of age and comes to consciousness. She is often the last or only defense for those who cannot fight for themselves. She is intersectional and multidimensional. She is a story and a symbol.

Sara K. Day, Miranda A. Green-Barteet, and Amy L. Montz, in *Female Rebellion in Young Adult Fiction*, argue that "the female protagonists of contemporary young adult dystopias … seek to understand their places in the world, to claim their identities, and to live their lives on their own terms." Further, they credit these young women with striving "to recreate the worlds in which they live, making their societies more egalitarian, more progressive, and, ultimately, more free" (3). In this way, Girls on Fire are political and transformative figures. Faced with inequality and injustice, they seek to redress them. While they are independent, they are also community-minded. Capable of great ferocity, these girls exude empathy and compassion, often aligning themselves with people who are vulnerable or socially marginalized. As such, it is not surprising that the Girl on Fire serves as a model for the sort of person many educators aspire for students to emulate.

In her book *Girls on Fire: Transformative Heroines in Young Adult Dystopian Literature*, Sarah traces the Girl on Fire from the "Original Girl on Fire," Lauren Olamina, the adolescent protagonist of Octavia E. Butler's *Parable of the Sower*, and the "quintessential" Girl on Fire, Katniss Everdeen, but she also explores the very ordinary and almost always "Othered" Girls on Fire across young adult dystopian literature's hundreds of texts featuring this strong female protagonist. She begins on the margins and has to accept responsibility, and take action, to make her world more just. Sarah further makes the argument for centering Girls on Fire stories that feature girls of color and challenge the structures of dominant culture, including white supremacy, patriarchy, and heteronormativity. But there are many ways for Girls on Fire—and their allies—to challenge interlocking structures of oppression and re-make the world in more just and egalitarian ways. Both fictional girls and real-life girls do this work every day, and in *Teaching Girls on Fire* we want to not only bring attention to these Girls on Fire—we want to provide tools that teachers of all kinds can use to create consciousness and inform action and help to foster students who want to burn. Without burning out.

This book of essays, *Teaching Girls on Fire: Essays on Dystopian Young Adult Literature in the Classroom*, constitutes a companion piece to Sarah's book, and reflects our shared belief in the Girl on Fire's potential to stir young people's interest in social and political topics, awaken their civic imagination, and inspire them to work for change in their schools and local communities. Lest our vision appear overly idealistic, there is a basis for it in scholarship that examines how activist groups are using popular culture as a resource to engage fans in working to combat social and economic injustice. As one example, Henry Jenkins chronicles the work of the Harry Potter Alliance, a non-profit organization that strives to tap into the enthusiasm that millions of readers have for J.K. Rowling's Harry Potter books and use it to unite fans in addressing different activist causes. To date, the Harry Potter Alliance has, among other things, donated $123,000 in rescue supplies to the people of

Haiti in the wake of a devastating earthquake, donated approximately 390,000 books to communities in need as part of its Accio Book Campaign, and successfully leveraged the Warner Bros. corporation to ensure that its Harry Potter licensed chocolate products are Fair Trade certified. Building on the excitement surrounding The Hunger Games books and films, the Harry Potter Alliance also launched the "Odds in Our Favor" campaign, which aspires to heighten people's awareness of economic inequality. In these ways, the Harry Potter Alliance aspires to "chang[e] the world by making activism accessible through the power of story" (Harry Potter Alliance).

At the heart of the Harry Potter Alliance's quest to use stories to transform the world is the concept of cultural acupuncture. As defined by Andrew Slack, the organization's founder, cultural acupuncture involves "finding where the psychological energy is in the culture, and moving that energy toward creating a healthier world" (para. 4). We regard the Girl on Fire as embodying the sort of energy that Slack has in mind. Girls on Fire create energy not only in their respective storyworlds, where they inspire other people to follow their lead in dismantling oppressive social structures, but also for the millions of readers that enthusiastically devour the books, films, and television shows in which they appear. The Girl on Fire is consequently rife with possibility as a resource that educators can draw on to engage students in examining social, political, and economic problems and imagining more egalitarian ways of living together.

This book is comprised of essays that embody, model, and extend the idea of the Girl on Fire. Not only do our authors write about teaching the idea of the Girl on Fire, many of them also embody the fire of this cultural symbol. As educators, we have found that this image resonates with our students across all kinds of contexts. The Girl on Fire is a character in books as much as she is a figure and symbol in popular culture. This symbol resonates with students who connect themselves to the trials and triumphs of the Girl on Fire as well as girls and women in their lives who they regard as strong or resilient. The definition of the Girl on Fire is thus meant to be open rather than exclusive, inspirational rather than literal.

In most every presentation that Sarah gives on her Girls on Fire work, she includes (or concludes with) a quote from her book that sums up her optimistic argument:

> Girls on Fire not only challenge the past to live up to the future, they also challenge the future to live up to our collective visions and the unrealized fantasies of the past. America is romantic, idealistic, and conflicted, but our strengths are reflected in these texts that dare to imagine the American dream "deferred" and renewed. We want better; we want justice. That idea, that hope, that ability to remake "institutions, values, norms, and activities" [through oppositional consciousness], means that there is still hope for us through the collective power of Girls on Fire [240].

We hope that this collection of essays on teaching Girls on Fire helps to stoke this collective power and elucidate a variety of texts from canonical literature to young adult literature, and from popular cultural texts to the social and cultural texts that literature helps us to unpack and redefine. Most of all, we hope that the book serves as both a source of inspiration and a resource for educators interested in creating consciousness in students and motivating them to take social action.

* * *

Like the Girl on Fire, who elides boundaries and resists simple categorization, this collection of essays constitutes an interdisciplinary project that was born of Sarah and Sean's shared interest in young adult dystopian fiction. As such, it brings together authors from a range of backgrounds, disciplines, and fields. To challenge the authors whose work appears in this book to think about the possible roles the Girl on Fire can play in educational settings, we asked them to consider a range of questions, including the following:

- To what extent has the Girl on Fire changed or evolved over time, and how is her presence felt in other media and genres beyond YA dystopian fiction?
- What is it about the Girl on Fire that inspires young readers to engage in social activism?
- How are educators and activists using YA dystopian fiction, and more specifically, the Girl on Fire, to motivate students to address problems in their school or local communities?
- How do real-life girls exemplify the spirit of the Girl on Fire, either in confronting injustice or working to transform their communities?
- What are the limitations of the Girl on Fire, and what does acknowledging them contribute to our understanding of this figure?

The essays in the sections that follow consequently aim for both theoretical explorations and practical, hands-on teaching tools. They highlight the Girl on Fire in the classroom—both as topic and as practitioner. We find it fitting that so many of these essays are co-authored, and that so many students' voices are included. Some authors are seasoned academics while others are making their publishing debut. While each essay describes different texts, critical lenses, and teaching approaches, they all embody the passion that we have as teachers, and the desire that we possess to help our students not only understand literary texts or current events, but also to understand themselves and their agency.

In "Part One: Exploring New Ground for Girls on Fire," we offer three new lines of inquiry. In "Athletic Girls on Fire: Representations of the Female

Athlete in *The Hunger Games* and Sports-Related Media," Wendy J. Glenn provides us with a lens for considering both fictional characters and real-life athletic girls. As Glenn demonstrates, athletic Girls on Fire combine the symbolic power of Katniss with the real-life accomplishments of women in the world of sports—an arena where girls and women are too often belittled and exploited, a microcosm of culture-at-large. As Glenn notes, "That stoic, serious young woman, framed by flames and holding a raised bow in a poised moment of impending action, sparked a movement, one that has the potential to evoke, challenge, and reshape assumptions about girls and sport." Glenn makes connections to literary texts, contemporary issues in sports, and a variety of supplemental texts, all of which provide tools for teachers who wish to engage students through topics familiar and important to them. Because athletics often dominate many cultural spaces, the Girl on Fire can help us to better understand and challenge the patriarchal structures that shape girls' experiences and representations of girls in sports.

In the second essay, "From Girls on Fire to Historical Bad Girls: A Framework for Critiquing Postfeminism and Neoliberalism in YA Literature," Sean P. Connors and Lissette Lopez Szwydky examine how the Girl on Fire is represented in young adult genres beyond dystopian fiction, specifically, neo–Victorian young adult novels. In doing so, they consider not the future, but the past, reminding us of the power of the female protagonist and the danger of reimagining historical contexts in ways that erase the struggles of girls and women. As they remind us in their essay, the Girl on Fire is not the first or only incarnation of the strong girl protagonist, though Sarah would argue that the category of Girl on Fire contains and supersedes all of the previous incarnations—the Smart Girl, the Historical Bad Girl, the Future Girl. Connors and Szwydky's essay not only connects young adult literature and the Girl on Fire to the canonical text of *Frankenstein*, it also offers a framework that teachers and students can use to examine how seemingly progressive representations of girls in popular culture texts can participate in discourses that are actually injurious to girls and women, one example being postfeminism.

In the final essay in this section, "Teaching Feminisms: Triumphs and Failures in The Hunger Games Trilogy," Roberta Seelinger Trites challenges us to continue to think critically about the Girl on Fire, as well as the ways in which feminism must be considered in multidimensional ways, embracing and unpacking contradictions and critiquing the ways in which feminism sometimes fails to live up to its potential. To do so, Trites draws on different feminist methodologies to critically examine Collins's The Hunger Games books. In doing so, she identifies a series of questions and reading strategies that she suggests teachers and students can profitably apply to works of young adult dystopian fiction for the purpose of interpreting the Girl on Fire. While

Trites acknowledges the Girl on Fire as a leader, she argues that to be a *feminist* leader, this figure must "recognize the agency of those around her, support others, listen thoughtfully … [and] work for the greater good, rather than her own personal gain." This vision of the Girl on Fire is particularly important as we see more and more women entering into leadership roles in politics. Alexandria Ocasio-Cortez, for instance, has lit a fire beneath the feet of the status quo and has given hope to many girls interested in a career in politics.

In the current socio-political climate, it is no surprise that the #MeToo movement would speak to the idea of teaching the Girl on Fire—what better symbol to inspire personal and collective struggles for social justice? In this book, the collective nature of the #MeToo movement is, in part, animated through the collaborative writing that shapes the three essays that comprise "Part Two: #MeToo: Sexual Realities, Activism and Empowerment." Each of these essays is co-authored, and they reflect the contributions of nine women. Further, they remind us that, as educators, we cannot ignore what is going on in the world outside of our classrooms; as feminist scholars have long noted, the personal is political, and what girls and their male counterparts see around them will inevitably come with them into our classrooms. The three essays in Part Two explore specific young adult texts that deal with the topic of sexual assault—*Asking for It, Shout, Speak, Moxie,* and *The Nowhere Girls*—as well as the larger structures surrounding the politics of the #MeToo movement.

In "Young Adult Literature and Girls on Fire as Fuel for Teaching the #MeToo Movement," Arianna Banack, Caitlin Metheny and Amanda Rigell present a multilayered instructional unit complete with pre-reading and post-reading activities as well as guides to teaching about the #MeToo movement using four works of young adult realist fiction: *Shout, Speak, Moxie,* and *The Nowhere Girls.* In doing so, Banack, Metheny and Rigell examine the different ways in which the female protagonists in these books embody the spirit of the Girl on Fire. Their essay provides a variety of tools, instructional activities, and creative approaches that teachers can draw on to engage students in examining issues connected to the #MeToo movement, including suggestions for community action projects that are designed to support students' putting the spirit of the Girl on Fire into action. As Banack, Metheny and Rigell note, "Because the Girl on Fire spirit can represent degrees of inner strength, advocacy, bravery, and resilience, pairing her character with women in the #MeToo movement illustrates how individuals can come to exhibit these characteristics gradually over time, moving through their trauma to develop inner strength and serve as a role model for others."

In "Say Something, Do Something: Creating Allies and Agents Through *The Nowhere Girls* on Fire," Katie Sluiter and Gretchen Rumohr offer an array of instructional activities and assignments that they suggest educators can enact in order to to engage students in examining issues related to sexual assault and harassment. In addition to identifying a diverse assortment of supplemental texts that students can productively put in conversation with the young adult novel *The Nowhere Girls*, Sluiter and Rumohr highlight different activities that students can undertake to call attention to the issue of sexual assault in either their school or local communities. As Sluiter and Rumohr note, the pedagogical resources they share in their essay can serve as "kindling for a fire, helping students familiarize themselves with sexual assault, connect with literary characters who've experienced it and advocated for change, consider real-world research and applications, and write for change with these new discoveries and experiences."

In "Troubling Girls on Fire in Young Adult Literature: A Critical Examination of Systemic Violence and Sexual Trauma in *Asking for It*," Kate Lechtenberg, Jenna Spiering, Amanda Haertling Thein and Nicole Ann Amato ask what it means to be a Girl on Fire in the face of anxiety and depression brought on by sexual trauma. Taking Louise O'Neill's young adult novel *Asking for It* as their case study, the authors raise a series of important questions that they argue teachers and students who are interested in examining representations of systemic violence and sexual trauma in young adult literature would do well to consider. These questions include: "What does the trope of the Girl on Fire suggest about girls who don't 'catch fire' when they experience sexual violence?" And, "what happens when the fire burns out and things don't end happily?" In working through these questions, Lechtenberg, Spiering, Haertling Thein, and Amato are careful to remind us that "no single Girl on Fire can repair historically entrenched systems of patriarchy and misogyny, and that protagonists who are survivors of sexual assault exhibit forms of voice and agency that defy traditional expectations for strong female characters." They highlight a series of questions that they suggest teachers and students can ask in the service of attending respectfully, and sensitively, to representations of young women responding to sexual trauma in popular culture texts.

Part Three, the final section in this book of essays, considers "The Girl on Fire in the University Classroom" and, like Part One, it provides a variety of strategies for approaching this figure in instructional spaces. At the same time, however, it also speaks to some of the challenges that are associated with teaching the Girl on Fire, particularly through the lenses of feminism and social justice, including how we address themes of the social construction of race and international contexts, for instance. In "On Teaching Girls Who Want to Burn: The Problems and Possibilities of Feminist Education," Tessa Pyles draws from her experience in the women's studies classroom at different universities and offers several examples of the ways in which her students have struggled to "burn" when faced with a number of intersecting oppressions. In doing so, she describes how she endeavors to foster a classroom environment in which her female students "feel heard, respected, and safe to speak or write aloud what they might not have before," and how she aims to "support them as they begin to question and challenge the legitimacy of a system that has always told them they are powerful and yet makes them feel incredibly powerless."

While Tessa has more than earned her own place in the world of university teaching and scholarship, as she demonstrates in her essay, it is worth noting that she was once a student in Sarah's first course at the University of Maine at Augusta a decade ago: "Race, Class, Gender, and Sexuality in American Culture." Tessa's educational journey—from an undergraduate major in liberal studies with specializations in American studies and women's and gender studies; to a master's degree in English with a women's, gender, and sexuality studies specialization; to a Ph.D. in American culture studies (all while raising her son as a "single mother")—speaks to her passion, commitment, intellect, talent, perseverance, and overall Girl on Fire spirit in addition to the transformative nature of critical interdisciplinary education.

Tessa's journey also speaks to the power of mentoring, a power that Katie Rybakova and Sydni Collier illustrate in "It Starts with a Book: An Exemplary 'Girl on Fire' and Her Undergraduate Thesis on Racial Social Justice." So many of our Girl on Fire characters lack female mentors, but many of them also have female mentors who make a significant difference in their lives, like Raven for Lena in the *Delirium* series, Lydia for Fen in *Orleans*, Gaia's mother in *Birthmarked*, and Madda for Cassiopeia in *Shadows Cast by Stars*. As teachers, we are also always mentors and models, a fact that Rybakova and Collier invite us to hold in mind. In these roles, we stoke the fires that help Girls on Fire to burn without burning out.

In "Teaching Octavia Butler's Diverse Body of Speculative Fiction: Genre, Race and the Radical Imaginary," Bryan Yazell offers us several examples and contexts for teaching the diverse works of Octavia E. Butler through the lens of genre. His examples not only speak to the importance of teaching Butler's works, but also expand the Girl on Fire symbol across Butler's texts, beyond the *Parables* books that Sarah considers in her *Girls on Fire* book. Further, Yazell offers us strategies for talking about literature across difference. As he explains, "a given classroom may comprise people of various backgrounds or interests, but discussions about how a given character or author—the Girl on Fire in this case—challenges social conventions asks us to imagine ourselves as part of a larger reading community. In other words, teaching Girls on Fire also necessarily involves discussions about genre." As we see in all these essays, whether we are considering speculative fiction, science fiction, dystopian fiction, young adult fiction, canonical literature, or realist fiction, the Girl on Fire continues to be a figure that resonates with readers across difference.

In the final essay in this section, Sarah models a mentoring opportunity as she and three of her students—Elaine Brum, Petra Ilic and Romaine Berry—collaborate on "Teaching/Learning YA Dystopia's Girls on Fire in Denmark's Educational System and International Community." In this essay, Sarah frames a master's-level course she taught, "Girls on Fire: Young Adult Dystopian Literature and American Futures," highlighting several assignments and providing space for her students to reflect on this Girls on Fire–focused course within the context of their classroom work as well as within the larger scope of their educations. While all three of these students have completed the MA program in American studies at the University of Southern Denmark, none of them are Danish students. Thus, while this essay provides some insights into the Danish educational system—and the educational systems of their home countries in Britain, Serbia, and Brazil—it also illuminates the experiences of students involved in international educational contexts that require cultural negotiations.

* * *

Throughout these three parts and ten essays, the authors provide a rich variety of ideas, texts, critical approaches, models, and prompts that can be used in specific kinds of classrooms—like university courses or high school classes. At the same time, however, they also provide ideas toward teaching in all kinds of spaces and to all kinds of students. Toward these ends, we want to be sure to point out that while we are focusing on the *Girl* on Fire, we do not want to imply that this educational intervention is somehow only for girls. In fact, we want to argue that education around the Girl on Fire is at least as important for boys and men. Several essays highlight the ways in which teaching Girls on Fire to male students is key to our goals of transformative teaching. For instance, Wendy J. Glenn's essay includes a section entitled "Boys, Men and the Athletic Girl on Fire." Sean and his co-author, Lissette Lopez Szwydky, unpack the love triangle between the Frankenstein brothers and their adopted cousin Elizabeth in Kenneth Oppel's *This Dark Endeavor*, elucidating the ways in which Elizabeth more than holds her own in her competitive dynamic with her male cousins while questioning how this depiction of a historical figure skews our understanding of the historical period even as it creates a Girl on Fire as a central character. And, as Arianna Banack, Caitlin Metheny and Amanda Rigell argue in "Young Adult Literature and Girls on Fire as Fuel for Teaching the #MeToo Movement," the novel "*Moxie* opens the door for conversations about educating male allies, a critical part of ending rape culture and toxic masculinity, and teaching boys that the spirit of the Girl on Fire isn't just for girls." In addition to helping us understand the cultural dynamics, Banack, Metheny and Rigell also share examples of "editorials, profiles, essays, and articles that might facilitate discussions of male allyship." These are the kinds of classroom interventions we hope will temper toxic masculinity and allow boys to explore themselves as multidimensional beings as much as feminism has given girls the tools to empower themselves despite patriarchy's corsets.

No collection of essays can cover the entirety of a subject, especially one as rich as Girls on Fire. That being said, we have tried to cover as much ground as we can, but there are a few omissions that are, perhaps, instructive to our collective and ongoing work. While a couple of essays address climate change, this collection lacks an essay that specifically engages with strategies for teaching about climate change in relation to YA dystopian texts and Girls on Fire. Related, "Alimentopia: Utopian Foodways," a research project undertaken by scholars at the University of Porto, provides another interesting line of inquiry for further considerations of Girls on Fire texts. As they describe on their Facebook page, "This Project (Pj) aims to offer a multi-disciplinary approach to the discussion about future conditions of food production and consumption through holistic and prospective utopian thinking, thus aiding the implementation of the emerging field of Food Studies (FS) in Portugal." The role food plays in utopian and dystopian futures, and the role it plays in current struggles for social justice, can be a fruitful classroom tool that might be connected with the young adult novel *Green Valentine*, for instance, and discussions of food deserts, community organizing, and guerrilla gardening (Hentges 200–1). Sarah made some of these connections to *Green Valentine* in a one-credit collaboratively taught course with the theme of climate change in the spring of 2017, just one more incarnation of teaching Girls on Fire.

In the MA class highlighted in the tenth essay, one student taught a lesson based upon her BA thesis work in relation to the Girls on Fire material, highlighting the book *Jane Eyre's Sisters: How Women Live and Write the Heroine's Story*, and providing another interesting way of considering these texts through the idea of the heroine as having a different story and trajectory from the classical male hero. This teaching moment connects with the classical Greek texts that are often canonical in compulsory education and were, she noted, often repeated throughout her Danish education. As she argued, the male hero is expected to go away, save the world, and then return home to live out his life and feast on the fruits of his battles. This is not the path that female heroines follow. This is but one important lens as mainstream American culture makes more room for girls and women to be heroes, increasingly on their own terms. Finally, another interesting connection that is not made in this collection of essays is the relationship between the Girl on Fire symbol and the contemporary world of politics. Here, there is certainly the beginning of a controlled burn.

Perhaps the most glaring omission is the underrepresentation of Othered Girls on Fire. With the exception of Bryan Yazell's essay about the works of Octavia E. Butler, Sarah's discussion with her students about the texts they read that focused largely on texts about girls of color, and a few other mentions that are often connected to wider social justice issues, this collection of essays also suffers from a lack of inclusion of the most marginalized of Girls on Fire—girls of color. While we do think that many of the lessons and strategies included in this collection of essays are universally applicable across classrooms of all kinds and across diverse groups of students, there are no single essays that focus on, for instance, Black Girls on Fire or Indigenous Girls on Fire or Latinx Girls on Fire. (Nor do any essays take up the subject of LGBTQA Girls on Fire.) At the same time, we think it is problematic to expect to divide girls into socially constructed categories of race when so many of our real and fictional girls transcend race. However, we also recognize that we have not yet reached a state of cultural equilibrium where we can explain away a lack of engagement with race and racism. Looking at a future where race doesn't exist means that we fail to recognize the impacts that race and racism continue to have in American culture in the present and the ways in which the present has been shaped by the past. The omission here—like everywhere—speaks to the structures of white supremacy that continue to divide us. But these same factors that divide also unite when we consider our world in more critical and intersectional ways. We become a coalition rather than random fragments, the elements that—like oxygen, a fuel source, and an ignitor—must all be present to create and sustain fire. (See Chapter 6 as well as pp. 48–49 and 70–71 of *Girls on Fire* for more discussions of structural racism and 227–34 for discussions of developing critical consciousness.)

Given this lack of explicit engagement with race, Sarah addresses some of the structural reasons for this deficiency in the conclusion, "'[Girls on Fire]: Tear This Wall Down!' International and Imaginative Contexts for Teaching Girls on Fire." In doing so, she provides several examples of interventions we might make as teachers and scholars to ensure that our classrooms and our scholarly work are providing diversity as well as intersectionality. In the conclusion, Sarah also offers reflections on the ways in which her presentation of her Girls on Fire work during her Fulbright year in Denmark resonated with students as well as with lifelong learners in a variety of international contexts, and with two young women of color, specifically. These international contexts join the diverse range of teaching spaces, "teachable" moments, and pedagogical interventions that are featured throughout this book. Some of these contexts further reveal important holes in this *Teaching Girls on Fire* book as well as the kinds of omissions that may happen, consciously or unconsciously, in predominantly white classroom spaces more generally. These contexts also provide a variety of jumping off points for teaching Girls on Fire, taking them off the page and into the world. Better yet, they empower us and our students to burn without burning ourselves out as we work together to realize the better world we are all striving toward.

Works Cited

"Alimentopia: Utopian Foodways." *Facebook.* Accessed 1 July 2019. https://www.facebook.com/Alimentopia-Utopian-Foodways-1076482925767618/.

Bower, Jody Gentian. *Jane Eyre's Sisters: How Women Live and Write the Heroine's Story.* Quest Books, 2015.

Connors, Sean P. "Becoming Mockingjays: Encouraging Student Activism Through the Study of YA Dystopia." *The ALAN Review,* vol. 44, no. 1, 2016, pp. 18–29.

_____. "An Invitation to Look Deeper Into the World: Using Young Adult Fiction to Encourage Youth Civic Engagement." *The ALAN Review,* vol. 45, no. 1, 2017, pp. 12–21.

_____, ed. *SIGNAL Journal,* vol. 39, no. 1, Fall 2015/Winter 2016.

Day, Sarah K., and Miranda A. Green-Barteet and Amy L. Montz. "Introduction: From 'New Woman' to 'Future Girl': The Roots and the Rise of the Female Protagonist in Contemporary Young Adult Dystopias." *Female Rebellion in Young Adult Dystopian Fiction.* Day, Green, and Montz, eds. Ashgate Studies in Childhood, 1700 to the Present. Ashgate, 2014.

Hentges, Sarah. *Girls on Fire: Transformative Heroines in Young Adult Dystopian Fiction.* McFarland, 2018.

@JenAnsbach. "I'm Not Sure Why People Are So Surprised That the Students Are Rising Up—We've Been Feeding Them a Steady Diet of Dystopian Literature Showing Teens Leading the Charge for Years. We Have Told Teen Girls They Are Empowered. What, You Thought It Was Fiction? It Was Preparation." *Twitter,* 18 Feb. 2018, 6:42 p.m., https://twitter.com/JenAnsbach/status/965385962925813761.

Jenkins, Henry. "'Cultural Acupuncture': Fan Activism and the Harry Potter Alliance." In "Transformative Works and Fan Activism," edited by Henry Jenkins and Sangita Shresthova, special issue, *Transformative Works and Cultures,* no. 10, 2012. doi:10.3983/twc.2012.0305.

Simmons, Amber. "Class on Fire: Using the Hunger Games Trilogy to Encourage Social Action." *Journal of Adolescent & Adult Literacy,* vol. 56, no. 1, 2012, pp. 22–34.

Slack, Andrew. "Cultural Acupuncture and a Future for Social Change." *The Huffington Post,* 25 May 2011, http://www.huffingtonpost.com/andrew-slack/cultural-acupuncture-and_b_633824.html. Accessed 25 June 2019.

Primary Sources

Anderson, Laurie Halse. *Speak.* SPEAK, 1999.

_____. *Shout.* Viking, 2019.

Bower, Jody G. *Jane Eyre's Sisters: How Women Live and Write the Heroine's Story.* Quest Books, 2015.

Butler, Octavia E. *Parable of the Sower.* Warner Books, 2000.

Collins, Suzanne. *Catching Fire.* Scholastic, 2009.

_____. *The Hunger Games.* Scholastic, 2008.

_____. *Mockingjay.* Scholastic, 2009.

Knutsson, Catherine. *Shadows Cast by Stars.* Atheneum Books, 2013.

Mathieu, Jennifer. *Moxie.* Roaring Brook Press, 2017.

O'Brien, Caragh M. *Birthmarked.* Roaring Brook Press, 2010.

Oliver, Lauren. *Delirium.* HarperCollins, 2011.

_____. *Pandemonium.* HarperCollins, 2012.

_____. *Requiem.* HarperCollins, 2013.

O'Neill, Louise. *Asking for It*. Quercus, 2016.
Oppel, Kenneth, *This Dark Endeavor*. Simon & Schuster, 2011.
Reed, Amy. *The Nowhere Girls*. Simon Pulse, 2017.
Smith, Sherri L. *Orleans*. Penguin, 2013.
Wilkinson, Lili. *Green Valentine*. Allen & Unwin, 2015.

PART ONE

Exploring New Ground for Girls on Fire

Athletic Girls on Fire

Representations of the Female Athlete
in The Hunger Games
and Sports-Related Media

WENDY J. GLENN

A Google search of images for "Katniss Everdeen," the protagonist of Suzanne Collins's 2008 novel, *The Hunger Games*, reveals image after image of a stoic, serious young woman wearing a pack of arrows on her back or holding a raised bow in a poised moment of impending action, hearkening the stone portrayals of Greek athletic forms in ancient sculpture. Across several images, Katniss is framed by flames. She is the athletic Girl on Fire, a trope grounded in her story of rebellion and taken up in contemporary media to describe young female athletes. Fictional and real representations of the athletic Girl on Fire invite consideration of the gendered ideologies of sport. Such considerations include both whether and how young adult (YA) fiction and media featuring athletic female protagonists reflect, support, and/or challenge these ideologies and the implications this might suggest for young people as readers of these texts.

The positioning of female athletes in YA literature suggests reinforcement of a socially constructed, gendered binary. As noted by Glenn and King-Watkins, if female protagonists are athletes, they are also expected to be feminists, role models, or pioneers who resist hegemonic masculinity; they cannot be feminine and must adhere to traditionally masculine expectations; and they have to choose one identity or the other—athlete or female ("Being an Athlete *or* Being a Girl"). Even when some semblance of choice exists, the rules of existing across the binary require the athletes to hold identities that fail to challenge gender expectations. When a young woman is permitted to be both an athlete and a girl, there are clear stipulations around how this must be done. Research suggests, too, that empowerment narratives commonly associated with successful female athletes in YA literature provide only surface-level advocacy for young women and instead mask and sometimes reaffirm the very structures that limit their opportunities in sport. In their exploration of two YA fiction series that center on female athletes, Pretty Tough and Dairy Queen, Whiteside et al. engaged in an analysis guided by poststructuralist perspectives on identity, specifically the emergence of a girlhood subjectivity. Their analysis argued that the discourse of empowerment obscures how girls are directed toward an ideology of sport that undermines their ability to experience sports on their own terms.

Beyond the pages of story, "girl power" rhetoric has the potential to placate rather than inspire critical thinking on behalf of young women and girls in the world. Recent popular discourse has resulted in narratives that promote assertiveness and strength as possible, desirable traits in young women and girls. Such narratives are evidenced in the 1990s program "Girl Power!" sponsored by the United States Department of Health and Human Services and designed to empower girls and challenge stereotypes (Giardina and Metz) and the 1999 *Newsweek* magazine cover that features Brandi Chastain wearing a sports bra and includes the headline "Girls Rule!" As noted by Whiteside et al., "girls today have grown up in an era where they are encouraged in both institutional settings as well as in popular discourse to 'be all they can be'... [, but] girl power rhetoric ultimately functions to depoliticize women's issues and advocacy efforts" (417–18). Although this rhetoric positions young women as agentic and empowered, the language of "girl power" ignores how a gendered hierarchy in sport remains intact. Young women have the opportunity to prove their skill and find success in the world of sport, but the measure of this success is aligned with a male standard, doing little to challenge hegemonic ideologies of sport culture.

To examine the presentation of female athletes in fiction and in life, this essay employs positioning theory to explore the portrayal of Katniss as an athlete, particularly how her positioning, by herself and others, is linked to power. Although these ideas have resonance across the series, this discussion focuses on the first novel in the series, *The Hunger Games*. In addition, the essay uses positioning theory to examine how the athletic Girl on Fire has been taken up outside of fiction by marketers, schools, teams, and girls themselves as a tool for social activism, and to explore how students and teachers might examine, critique, and revise the storylines attributed to young female athletes.

Positioning Theory

Positioning theory allows readers to think carefully and critically about the interactions between characters and systems and structures within a text.

It invites consideration of how such interactions are always influenced by the roles of those involved and the associated powers and privileges they possess—or do not possess—and how individuals make sense of themselves and others in response. According to Moghaddam and Harré, positioning theory centers on "how people use words (and discourse of all types) to locate themselves and others" (2). Such locating happens in particular ways in particular contexts. As argued by Tan and Moghaddam, positioning involves the process of ongoing construction of the self through talk, particularly through "the discursive construction of personal stories that make a person's actions intelligible and relatively determinate as social acts and within which the members of conversations have specific locations" (183).

Given the role of location and context that shapes any interaction, the positions that exist within these storylines are not fixed, but fluid, and participants in social settings can both position and be positioned by others (Barnes). Positioning theory, then, is inherently interactional, such that positional identities are not only self-ascribed but assigned to individuals by co-participants in any given social practice (Harré and van Langenhove). This, then, suggests that the ways in which a person makes sense of the self and others are also dynamic and open to change through experience; our identities are in a state of flux as we engage with others in the world. As Davies and Harré explain, "An individual emerges through the processes of social interaction, not as a relatively fixed end product but as one who is constituted and reconstituted through the various discursive practices in which they participate" (35).

Because individuals in any interactional encounter possess varying levels of power and privilege, positioning theory attends explicitly to issues of equity and morality. Harré argues that positioning theory is "based on the principle that not everyone involved in a social episode has equal access to rights and duties to perform particular kinds of meaningful actions at that moment and with those people" (193). Being positioned in a certain way carries obligations or expectations about how one should behave and/or constraints on what one may meaningfully say or do (Barnes, Buehler), obligations and expectations that cannot or will not be met by all involved in the exchange. When people who possess limited power in a particular moment and context are positioned in ways that fail to capture their identities and associated values and beliefs, they are subject to the values and beliefs of those who do hold the power in this exchange and context.

The construction of storylines about the self and others growing from interactional moments associated with positioning theory has additional resonance when considered in the analysis of fictional texts, particularly given the relationship between the reader, text, and author. Authors, wittingly or not, create stories grounded in certain assumptions, biases, and norms connected to the cultural communities they inhabit in the world outside of fiction. As a result, institutional structures and localized ways of doing, thinking, and being are inherently woven into the stories that they create and influence how the protagonists are positioned by themselves and by other characters. This becomes increasingly complicated when we consider how readers also bring their own assumptions, biases, and norms to a text. They, too, are shaped by the cultural communities they inhabit. In the process of literary analysis, then, our attendance to the authorial presentation of the protagonists' personal characteristics, merits, or flaws; their perceived status in comparison to others; and how they locate their own or others' experiences within a moral context, for example, can reveal the assumptions that an author brings to the development of a character. And our attention to our own and others' sensemaking around these positionings can reveal readers' assumptions.

Because positioning theory is concerned with storylines, roles, and resulting identities, it provides a useful lens for analyzing literature, particularly the narrative construction of a protagonist as revealed through interactions with other characters and institutional structures. In the case of *The Hunger Games*, we can use positioning theory to better understand how Katniss is presented as an athletic Girl on Fire, a savior to her people but also a teen girl in the process of determining her own values and resulting identities. The sections below delineate how the application of positioning theory to the novel offers insight into Katniss as an athletic Girl on Fire and offer ideas for how educators might invite students into conversations around these ideas in both fictional texts and lived experiences.

Constructions of the Athletic Girl on Fire

Positioning theory can help us to consider what it means to be an athletic Girl on Fire. The author of *The Hunger Games*, Suzanne Collins, positions Katniss as an athlete with intention, centering on key definitional features of this identity. First, she presents a character whose physicality is a source of power, one that allows Katniss to engage as a fierce competitor in the arena. We see this in the ways that Katniss is described by, or positioned by, other characters in the story. In fact, when we look across these positionings, it is interesting to note that Katniss is characterized by others *only* in terms of her physicality. Gale tells her she will be a successful competitor, as she is the best hunter that he knows (40). Prim calls her fast and brave and subsequently capable of winning (36). Peeta affirms Prim's confidence in Katniss's abilities, telling Katniss that his mother says that she is a survivor and has a chance to win (89, 90); he later names her a "lethal" person in response to her fighting skills (258). And Haymitch, Katniss's coach, describes her as a fighter, fit, and not entirely hopeless (57–58).

In some ways, Collins presents Katniss as affirming of these physical positionings when she considers her own athletic identity in comparisons to or interactions with others. At several points in the narrative, Katniss articulates how her skills as a forager and hunter make her unlike her competitors. She constructs herself as clever with plants, able to climb swiftly, and having good aim with her bow and arrow (99); she is small in size but practiced at climbing trees to escape danger, something her larger competitors cannot achieve (181–82). When she is able to secure a bow and arrow, her preferred athletic equipment, she gains confidence and a new perspective on her ability to face her competitors, claiming: "The weapons give me an entirely new perspective on the Games. I know I have tough opponents left to face. But I am no longer merely prey that runs and hides or takes desperate measures" (197).

One moment in particular reveals Collins's focus on physicality in her positioning of Katniss as an athletic Girl on Fire. This occurs when Katniss faces the Gamemakers in a private session prior to the official start of the Games. The aim of this meeting is to allow the competitors to demonstrate their most impressive skills. Katniss's session is one of the last, after the Gamemakers have witnessed twenty-three other demonstrations and consumed ample amounts of food and wine. As Katniss shows off her athletic prowess with a bow and arrow, noting her own "excellent shooting" (101), she finds their lack of attention unsatisfactory. She explains, "Suddenly I am furious, that with my life on the line, they don't even have the decency to pay attention to me. That I'm being upstaged by a dead pig" (101). In response, she shoots an arrow straight at the Gamemaker's table, skewering the apple in the pig's mouth and pinning it to the wall behind. Soon after the display, she reaffirms her physical talent, noting, "I wasn't trying to kill one of them. If I were, they'd be dead!" (103).

These positionings challenge what Whiteside et al. found in their analysis of young adult texts that feature female athletes. Their work reveals protagonists who excel athletically but "also see their bodies as fundamentally different from a feminine ideal and, thus, sites of failure and social inadequacy…. [A]lthough all the main characters see their bodies as athletically useful, they also point out in overt ways how those same bodies fail them socially, often viewing their bodies through a heteronormative lens" (423). Collins creates a context in which Katniss's athletic body is never "less than," even when others attempt to define her body in gendered ways. For example, when Katniss, near the end of the novel, tries on the second dress that Cinna creates for her, she notices the padding over her breasts, "adding curves that hunger has stolen from [her] body" (354). She finds this disconcerting and frowns, ready to challenge Cinna's decision before he explains that the alternative provided by the Capitol was surgical alteration. She then notes how the dress is gathered at her ribs rather than her waist, eliminating "any help the padding would have given [her] figure" anyway (355). Here, her body, emaciated and far from the ideal held by those in positions of power, remains her own and is presented as it is rather than as others might want it to be.

However, as Collins unpacks her vision of the athletic Girl on Fire, we also see evidence of how physicality is necessary but not adequate for winning the Games. There are other elements of athleticism, such as resourcefulness and strategy and resilience, that play key roles in Katniss's success in the arena. We see this positioning when Katniss meets the other tributes at the training center. She describes herself as small but strong due to her life circumstances: "I may be smaller naturally, but overall my family's resourcefulness has given me an edge in that area. I stand straight, and while I'm thin, I'm strong" (94). While in the arena, Katniss helps Rue find hope by telling her that the two of them are strong in ways different from their Career competitors who have physical brawn but have never gone hungry. She tells Rue, "You can feed yourself. Can they? …. Say the supplies were gone. How long would they last? … I mean, it's the Hunger Games, right?" (206–7). This is a turning point in the novel, as Katniss determines that she and Rue will think strategically about how to destroy the food supply held and guarded by the Career competitors. She notes, "And for the first time, I have a plan. A plan that isn't motivated by the need for flight and evasion. An offensive plan" (207).

As the story progresses, we acquire additional evidence that suggests the limits to physical athleticism and the need for strategic thinking in the quest to win the Games. As she flees into the forest after facing a violent encounter with Clove and her knives, Katniss reports, "I crash into the trees, repeatedly swiping away the blood that's pouring into my eye, fleeing like the wild, wounded creature I am" (289). She barely makes it back to the cave she is sharing with Peeta before collapsing. Her body is exhausted, wounded, and incapable of allowing her to do more than rest and await recovery. And yet, although her body seems to have reached its useful end, her mind has not. It is strategic thinking that ultimately allows Katniss and Peeta to emerge victorious together, outsmarting the Gamemakers by threatening to eat the poisonous berries and leave the Games without a victor (345). Following the games, Katniss's body remains somewhat defeated; her mirrored reflection reveals "wild eyes, hollow cheeks, my hair in a tangled mat. Rabid. Feral. Mad" (348). Her mind, however, allows her to realize that she has not yet won and that her greatest challenge of the Games still remains: she must convince the Capitol that her love for Peeta, not a desire to embarrass the Gamemakers, was the motivating force behind the berry incident. Her body has survived, allowing her to make it through to this moment, but her political savvy is now the thing that can save her. The ways in which Collins positions Katniss as an athlete results in a storyline of self that names and values both physical and mental strength, athleticism of the body and mind. This serves to challenge binary constructions of males as physically strong and females as emotionally strong and instead offers a consideration of the role of strategy and smarts irrelevant of gendered norms.

To support adolescent readers in thinking strategically about definitions of the athletic Girl on Fire, educators might first ask them to read, examine, and critique the narratives used in sports media to define athletes more generally, considering how these narratives are written by people who have their own aims and intended audiences in mind. Students might engage, for example, in a process of information gathering centered on the history of Nike's advertising, particularly the ways in which the company has used various campaigns to address social issues. The article, "A Brief History of Nike Using Advertising to Address Social Issues" (Coffee), provides a useful overview of the history of Nike's advertising efforts, including specific ads that students might wish to view. Students might work in pairs or small groups to focus on a particular advertisement and consider the following guiding questions in preparation for a whole group sharing of their findings:

1. How would you describe the message this ad aims to convey?

2. What design elements are used to convey this message? What do you notice about the images, the voices, the text, the music, etc.? How effectively are these elements employed? What emotional response do you have in response to watching this ad?

3. For whom is this ad intended? Why might Nike believe this audience needs or might benefit from this ad?

4. What does Nike, as a corporation, stand to gain from the airing of this ad?

Students might then view the most recent Nike ad, "Dream Crazier," that aired during the 2019 Oscar Awards show. Narrated by decorated tennis player Serena Williams, the ad centers on the idea that female athletes have not been given access to or respect in sport in the same ways experienced by male athletes. Following this viewing, students might consider more explicitly this and other narratives that center on the experiences of female athletes on the courts, fields, and pitches (please see Table 1.1 for a list of articles that name strong female athletes in the community as "Girls on Fire").

Students might examine the text and paratext (images, links, authorship) within and across these articles to explore the questions:

1. How are these athletic Girls on Fire positioned by the authors of the articles, by those who describe them in the articles, and by themselves?

2. What role does physicality play in descriptions of their success? What about emotion? What about mental fitness? What else is noted as essential to the successful performance of these athletes?

3. Where do you see evidence of connection to the idea, "dream crazier," in the presentation of these athletes? What does this suggest about what it means to be an athletic Girl on Fire?

Winning as an Athletic Girl on Fire

Positioning theory can also help us to consider what it means for an athletic Girl on Fire to emerge victorious and how the concept of winning is complicated when we consider the roles and influence of power and morality. In the context of Collins's *The Hunger Games*, positioning theory offers a way of thinking about Katniss as an athlete whose performance influences not only her life but the lives of those in the larger community from which she hails and represents in the Games. As noted earlier, positioning theory centers on a process of ongoing construction of the self within and across particular contexts (Tan and Moghaddam). With this in mind, as a competitor from District 12, a district defined by hunger and hardship growing from the oppressive rule of the Capitol, Katniss can be seen as positioned as a savior-athlete, a competitor whose victory not only chastises those in power but provides material wealth to her family and neighbors. Collins's positioning of Katniss in this way makes transparent the role of power in sport, particularly in a dystopian world in which the Games are more than just a game, and the players are used by the Gamemakers as pawns for the entertainment of the masses and by the Capitol to maintain political power and the resulting status quo. Being positioned in certain ways comes with associated expectations for behavior that are not able to be met by everyone involved due to power inequities (Barnes). Some people, then, are subject to the values and beliefs of those who do hold the power in this exchange and context.

As a savior-athlete, however, Katniss ultimately makes moves to challenge (with intention and care) these values and beliefs. At the start of the novel, Katniss is ever-aware of the fact that the Capitol is watching and that she must play a particular role in order to remain in their favor and to survive. When Katniss steps forward to volunteer as tribute in place of her sister, Prim, she is attentive to the reality that the event is televised; in response, she refuses to cry out of concern that she will be "marked as an easy target. A weakling" (23). When she arrives at the Capitol and participates in the televised introduction of the victors, she sees her image, that of the Girl on Fire, on the big screen and grins widely and waves to the audience, knowing that there is an advantage to being recognized and thus supported by sponsors

(70). Although she is initially angry that Peeta's public declaration of his love for her makes her look weak, she soon realizes that it actually has the effect of building interest in her and her story and could lead to additional support (135). This trend continues throughout the Games when she says that she wants potential sponsors to see that she is a good hunter, a good bet (164); when she refuses to show weakness when she is severely burned (179); and when she fights against letting her fear show after the explosion of the food supply and her resulting bloody ear (223).

At the end of the novel, however, once Katniss has been named a victor, having beaten the Gamemakers by outsmarting them, she refuses to cater fully to the expectations of those in power. When she is rested and healed and free to rejoin her team, Katniss does not care that her behavior does not fit the expectations of the athletic victor: "Maybe a victor should show more restraint, more superiority, especially when she knows this will be on tape, but I don't care. I run for them and surprise even myself when I launch into Haymitch's arms first" (352). In this moment, she does not let the Capitol define her and instead constructs the role of victor for herself. In doing so, she works to rewrite her storyline, affirming the idea that individuals are shaped through a process of social interaction and that identities are not fixed but reshaped through discursive practices in which an individual participates (Davies and Harré).

Educators might support students in thinking about the presence of the savior-athlete in texts and situations beyond the realm of a dystopian novel like *The Hunger Games*. Students might, for example, explore the collection of poems housed on the ESPN-W website. This page includes pieces that center on various female athletes, including Maya Moore, Diana Taurasi, Simone Biles, and Serena Williams and examine the concept of what it means to be a winner, a victor, particularly as women in a patriarchal society, as women of color in a white-dominant society, and as young women in a society that affords them limited power. For example, students might read and reflect upon Natalie Diaz's poem, "What Could We Do with Victory but What She Has Done: An Ode to Maya Moore." Guiding questions might include:

1. How are athletes bound up with their histories? With their communities?
2. How are athletes at the mercy of those in positions of power (coaches, families, sponsors, etc.)?
3. How do athletes exert power themselves? What is the potential effect on those who are watching?
4. Are all athletic Girls on Fire saviors to someone in some way?

Relative to these same questions of what it means for the athletic Girl on Fire to be victorious, positioning theory also invites moral critique of

Table 1.1: Articles That Name Female Athletes in the Community as "Girls on Fire"

Article	Summary
Villa, Walter. "Why Michigan Recruit Boogie Brozoski Has Swagger in Her Step." *ESPN-W*, 16 Oct. 2014.	Features Lauren "Boogie" Brozoski, a 5-foot-5 senior basketball point guard who led Long Island Lutheran (Brook ville, New York) to three state titles in four years
Maconi, Caryn. "'Girl on Fire' Mackenzie Brown Aiming for the Podium in Rio as Team USA's Sole Female Archer." *Team USA*, 30 June 2016.	Features archer Mackenzie Brown, who made her Olympic Trials debut at age 16 and was a favorite at the Games in Rio
Grundy, William. "Grace Morris Injured and Out for the Entire Track Season—Still a Girl on Fire." *Mile Split*, 15 Feb. 2018.	Features cross country runner Grace Morris, who suffered a foot fracture but continued to fight for recovery and a chance to run again
Amorosano, Ken. "An Interview with Hailey Kinsel, Barrel Racing's 'Girl on Fire.'" *Cowgirl*, 30 Oct. 2018.	Features barrel racer Hailey Kinsel, who held the number one position heading into the 2018 National Finals Rodeo and has earned almost $200,000 in winnings

the idea of "winning at all costs." Within *The Hunger Games*, the athlete is constructed by those in power as one who assumes a lack of morality and instead possesses a willingness to compete at all costs; the winner is ultimately positioned as having to kill to survive. These ideas are taken up both philosophically and practically in the novel. On the night before the official start of the Games, Katniss and Peeta engage in conversation about the tension between survival and the preservation of one's moral identity. Peeta tells her, "I don't want them to change me in there. Turn me into some kind of monster that I'm not" (141). Katniss realizes that he "has been struggling with how to maintain his identity. His purity of self" (142) as he imagines the reality of the Games; there will emerge a victor, and all others will die. Katniss's struggle at this moment, however, centers on a desire for self-preservation. She tells Peeta, "Look, if you want to spend the last hours of your life planning some noble death in the arena, that's your choice. I want to spend mine in District Twelve" (142) and later thinks, "We will see how high and mighty he is when he's faced with life and death" (143).

When faced with such decisions herself, however, Katniss affirms Peeta's moral stance through her actions. Katniss survives the Games using her skill in sport to kill only two opponents directly. She shoots an arrow into the neck of a boy from District One after he captures and mortally wounds Rue, and after she shoots an arrow through Cato's hand to free Peeta and Cato falls to the muttations, Katniss eventually kills him out of mercy and pity (340–41). In both cases, the acts bring emotional weight; survival—and winning—come at a cost. After killing the boy from District One, Katniss notes that he "was the first person I knew would die because of my actions.... I killed a boy whose name I don't even know. Somewhere his family is weeping for him. His friends call for my blood. Maybe he had a girlfriend who really believed he would come back...." (243). After Cato has been shot and relieved of his suffering, Katniss tells Peeta, "Hurray for us," but Collins reveals that "there's no joy of victory in [her] voice" (341).

While the killing of another human is always fraught with moral complication, in this context, one of literal survival, Collins's decision to position Katniss as a victor who takes few lives serves as a challenge to the "winning at all costs" mentality assumed and celebrated by the Capitol and Gamemakers. Collins invites readers to consider, too, questions of equity and justice on a more systemic level when she describes Katniss's sadness around the deaths of Rue and, especially, Thresh. Katniss reflects upon these losses, realizing, "I have to bury the real pain because who's going to bet on a tribute who keeps sniveling over the deaths of her opponents. Rue was one thing. We were allies. She was so young. But no one will understand my sorrow at Thresh's murder. The word pulls me up short. Murder!" (308). Katniss behaves and begins to think in ways that serve to challenge the culture of power in her world.

Educators might invite students to reflect upon the "winning at all costs" narrative in their own lives and communities. They might first engage in a reading and analysis of the motivational speech, "Win at All Costs," by Nick Macri. Students might reflect individually in writing on whether or not success in sport, and in life, is a matter of a personal decision-making. Is effort enough to succeed, or are there other forces, structures, barriers, and/or supports at play when we set out to achieve our goals? They might also consider whether success is something we deserve. If only one person deserves to win, how does this position the non-winners? Students might then engage in a small group inquiry activity that asks them to consider positioning "in the wild" around the idea of "winning at all costs." After working together to gather 8–10 images from an online search for "motivational quotations sport," students might analyze what they find, asking such questions as: How is athletic success positioned within and across these images? What is valued? What is not? Do morality, ethics, and values play a role in these positionings? Students might capture and share their findings in a visual format of their choosing.

Boys, Men and the Athletic Girl on Fire

Positionality can help us examine the gendered power relationships that are often inherent in the narratives of female athletes. As evidenced by UNESCO's World Radio Day series on radio and sport, the stories of female athletes often include reference to the fathers and coaches who made their success possible. Other scholars have identified this pattern of positioning in young adult novels that feature female protagonists. Whiteside et al., for example, found in their analysis of books in the Pretty Tough and Dairy Queen series that the male characters, particularly the fathers, play a central role in shaping the protagonists' sporting experiences and that "in many ways, sport is constructed as a means through which to gain male approval and attention" (426). Gaining male attention and approval can be seen as evidence of emotional labor, or the practice of activating or suppressing "feelings in order to sustain the outward countenance that produces the proper state of mind in others" (Hochschild 7). Offering encouragement or appreciation, listening, and providing empathic feedback are often seen as inherently feminine, and females are subsequently judged as individuals by their ability to successfully engage in this type of work.

One might argue that Katniss is dependent upon men for her survival (she receives medicine for her burn as a result of Haymitch's efforts, and Peeta helps nurse her back to health after she risks her life to get him medicine for his fever). However, it could also be claimed that she is ultimately responsible for saving herself and Peeta through strategic thinking that comes with great risk given the accompanying rebuke of the Capitol's Games. This might suggest that the novel offers a challenge to the narrative of self-sufficient victor. Here, any suggestion of Katniss's emotional labor is not centered on people pleasing but on survival itself in that her communal act of saving both her and Peeta disrupts the social order established by the Capitol.

To explore whether and how these ideas manifest in *The Hunger Games*, educators might encourage students to consider how Katniss is positioned by the men in her life. Guiding questions could include:

1. What role does Peeta play in Katniss's definition of/enactment of herself as an athlete? Does her dependence upon him as she recovers in body and spirit make her less strong? How does the romantic relationship she nurtures with Peeta while on camera influence her athletic identity and our perception of her as a competitor? As a female?

2. What is Haymitch's role as Katniss's mentor and coach? Is her success as an athlete connected to his mentorship or support?

3. How does the death of Katniss's father and his lack of physical presence in the novel affect Katniss as an athlete?

4. Who is ultimately responsible for Katniss's victory in the Games? What and/or who saves her and allows her to win?

Relative to the men, boys, and the athletic Girl on Fire, positionality can also help us to consider how sport is often defined by gender—and what happens when this barrier to access is removed. Football, for example, is often constructed as a male sport, while softball is identified as more suitable for female athletes. Scholars have noted how these divisions have been evidenced in fiction for young adult readers, even those books that are written with a female audience in mind. In her analysis of titles in the Pretty Tough series, Heinecken noted that the descriptions of strong female athletes in these books "disrupt stereotypes of girls as physically weak and passive" but their "focus on female teamwork does little to disrupt the male dominance of sport, as girls' sporting achievements mostly occur against other girls, … enforcing the idea that men's activities and men's power are the real thing and women's are not" (37).

However, even in young adult titles that examine the experiences of female athletes who choose to play on historically male teams, disparities persist. In an analysis of ten young adult titles, Glenn and King-Watkins found that as the fictional female athletes move into male-dominated spaces, they are forced to reconceptualize their identities within either/or binaries that reaffirm gendered expectations and that these binaries ignore the complicated multiplicity of identities and their associated privileges and oppressions ("Fictional Girls Who Play with the Boys"). In a related study, these same scholars found that the protagonists are positioned as engaging in a process of enculturation that asks them to navigate between their existing and newly experienced gendered subjectivities ("Being an Athlete *or* Being a Girl"). Their identities are challenged as they encounter new norms, expectations, characters, and communities, and their ability to resolve this threat is limited by societal norms that devalue females as athletes.

The Hunger Games provides a unique textual site in which to explore these ideas, as the story not only disrupts stereotypes of girls as physically weak and passive but also seems to disrupt the male dominance of sport by offering a narrative that features a female not only competing with males but ultimately defeating them. Although the novel reaffirms binary constructions of gender, it does raise opportunities to consider some barriers to access to sport in the context of fiction. In addition to considering these ideas in the text, educators might suggest that students learn more about the real-world game of Quidditch, which has its origins in story, too. The sport is constructed as non-gendered and has specific rules about who can be on the field, rules that are aimed with intention at creating inclusive opportunities for all athletes (Wynne Davis, U.S. Quidditch).

Extending the Athletic Girl on Fire

Educators interested in expanding this work might invite students to engage with other young adult titles that feature female athletes as protagonists to examine the presence of the athletic Girl on Fire, particularly the ways in which the trope is constructed and how conceptions of winning—and the influence of men and boys—influence this construction (please see Table 1.2 for suggested titles).

Table 1.2: Young Adult Novels
That Feature Female Athletes as Protagonists

Novel	Summary
Esckilsen, Erik E. *The Outside Groove.* Houghton Mifflin Harcourt, 2006.	Casey LaPlante has grown up around the track given her older brother's success as a local racecar driver. Tired of being ignored by her family, despite her own academic and athletic successes, and believing that racing can't really be that hard, Casey takes up the sport herself.
Gibney, Sharon. *See No Color.* Carolrhoda Lab, 2015.	At seventeen, Alex Kirtridge knows that she is an amazing baseball player and that she is adopted. What she doesn't fully understand is how to make sense of her identity as a biracial child in a white family that professes not to see color. Playing baseball is simple; navigating life off of the diamond is not.
Heldring, Thatcher. *The Football Girl.* Penguin Random House, 2017.	Tessa plays flag football with the guys for fun during the summer and plans to run cross country when the school year begins. However, upon losing the last game of the summer season, Tessa wants redemption and is surprised to discover how much she loves the game of football. Despite opposition from her teammates and family, she decides to go out for the team.

Although Katniss Everdeen, the athletic Girl on Fire, lives in the dystopian world of Collins's creation, her identity has been taken up as a trope in other fiction for young adult readers and in media framings of young female athletes who live beyond the pages of story. How Katniss and her fictional and nonfictional designees of this identity marker are positioned can invite students into thoughtful consideration of representation relative to the gendered ideologies of sport. That stoic, serious young woman, framed by flames and holding a raised bow in a poised moment of impending action, sparked a movement, one that has the potential to evoke, challenge, and reshape assumptions about girls and sport.

WORKS CITED

Amorosano, Ken. "An Interview with Hailey Kinsel, Barrel Racing's 'Girl on Fire.'" *Cowgirl*, 30 Oct. 2018, https://cowgirlmagazine.com/hailey-kinsel-interview/.

Barnes, Mary. "The Use of Positioning Theory in Studying Student Participation in Collaborative Learning Activities." Session presented at the Annual Meeting of the Australian Association for Research in Education, Melbourne, Australia, 28 Nov.–2 Dec. 2004. Retrieved from https://www.aare.edu.au/data/publications/2004/bar04684.pdf.

Buehler, Jennifer. "Positioning Theory: Exploring Power, Social Location, and Moral Choices of the American Dream in *American Street*." *Engaging with Multicultural YA Literature in the Secondary Classroom: Critical Approaches for Critical Editors*, edited by Ricki Ginsberg and Wendy J. Glenn, Routledge, 2019, pp. 11–21.

Coffee, Patrick. "A Brief History of Nike Using Advertising to Address Social Issues." *AdWeek*, 4 Sept. 2018, https://www.adweek.com/agencies/a-brief-history-of-nike-using-advertising-to-address-social-issues/.

Collins, Suzanne. *The Hunger Games*. Scholastic, 2008.

Davies, Bronwyn, and Rom Harré. "Positioning and Personhood." *Positioning Theory: Moral Contexts of Intentional Action*, edited by Rom Harré and Luk Langenhove, Blackwell, pp. 32–52.

Davis, Wynne. "There May Not Be Flying, but Quidditch Still Creates Magic." *National Public Radio*, 3 June 2017, https://www.npr.org/2017/06/03/531044118/there-may-not-be-flying-but-quidditch-still-creates-magic.

Diaz, Natalie. "What Could We Do with Victory but What She Has Done: An Ode to Maya Moore." ESPN-W, 7 Apr. 2017, http://www.espn.com/espnw/voices/article/19092941/what-do-victory-has-done-ode-maya-moore.

Esckilsen, Erik E. *The Outside Groove*. Houghton Mifflin Harcourt, 2006.

Giardina, Michael D., and Jennifer L. Metz. "Women's Sports in Nike's America: Body Politics and the Corporo-Empowerment of Everyday Athletes." *Sport, Culture, and Advertising: Identities, Commodities, and the Politics of Representation*, edited by Steven J. Jackson and David L. Andrews, Routledge, 2005, pp. 60–82.

Gibney, Sharon. *See No Color*. Carolrhoda Lab, 2015.

Glenn, Wendy, and Danielle King-Watkins. "Fictional Girls Who Play with the Boys: Barriers to Access in the Transition to Male-Dominated Sports Teams." *Children's Literature in Education*, 2019 online preview, print forthcoming. https://doi.org/10.1007/s10583-019-09384-7.

_____, and Danielle King-Watkins. "Being an Athlete *or* Being a Girl: Selective Identities Among Fictional Female Athletes Who Play with the Boys." *Children's Literature Association Quarterly*, in press.

Grundy, William. "Grace Morris Injured and Out for the Entire Track Season—Still a Girl on Fire." *Mile Split*, 15 Feb. 2018, https://tx.milesplit.com/articles/233251/gracie-morris-injured-and-out-for-the-entire-track-season-still-a-girl-on-fire.

Harré, Rom. "Positioning Theory: Moral Dimensions of Social-Cultural Psychology." *The Oxford Handbook of Culture and Psychology*, edited by Jaan Valsiner, Oxford University, 2012, pp. 191–206.

_____, and Luk van Langenhove, eds. *Positioning Theory: Moral Contexts of Intentional Action*. Blackwell, 1999.

Heinecken, Dawn. "Pretty Tough Sports and the Promotion of Female Empowerment in Young Adult Sports Fiction." *The Lion and the Unicorn*, vol. 39, no. 1, 2015, pp. 23–41.

Heldring, Thatcher. *The Football Girl*. Penguin Random House, 2017.

Hochschild, Arlie Russell. *The Managed Heart: Commercialization of Human Feeling*. University of California Press, 1983.

Maconi, Caryn. "'Girl on Fire' Mackenzie Brown Aiming for the Podium in Rio as Team USA's Sole Female Archer." *Team USA*, 30 June 2016, https://www.teamusa.org/US-

Olympic-and-Paralympic-Foundation/News/2016/June/30/Girl-on-Fire-Mackenzie-Brown-aiming-for-the-podium-in-Rio-as-Team-USAs-sole-female-archer.

Macri, Nick. "Win at All Costs." *Fearless Motivation*, 29 Sept. 2015, https://www.fearlessmotivation.com/2015/09/29/win-at-all-costs-sports-motivational-speech/.

Moghaddam, Fathali, and Rom Harré. "Words, Conflicts and Political Processes." *Words of Conflict, Words of War: How the Language We Use in Political Processes Sparks Fighting*, edited by Fathali Moghaddam and Rom Harré, Praeger, 2010, pp. 1–30.

Nike. "Dream Crazier." *YouTube*, 24 Feb. 2019, https://www.youtube.com/watch?v=whpJ19RJ4JY.

Tan, Siu-Lan, and Fathali Moghaddam. (1999). "Positioning in Intergroup Relations." *Positioning Theory: Moral Contexts of Intentional Action*, edited by Rom Harré and Luk van Langenhove, Blackwell, 1999, pp. 178–194.

"UNESCO Calls for Fairer Media Coverage of Sportswomen." UNESCO, 8 Feb. 2018, https://en.unesco.org/news/unesco-calls-fairer-media-coverage-sportswomen.

US Quidditch. "Title 9¾." *USQ*, 2019, https://www.usquidditch.org/about/title-9-3-4.

Villa, Walter. "Why Michigan Recruit Boogie Brozoski Has Swagger in Her Step." *ESPN-W*, 16 Oct. 2014, http://www.espn.com/espnw/news-commentary/article/11709953/why-michigan-recruit-boogie-brozoski-swagger-step.

Whiteside, Erin, Marie Hardin, Lauren J. DeCarvalho, Nadia Martinez Carillo, and Alexandra Nutter Smith. "'I Am Not a Cow': Challenging Narratives of Empowerment in Teen Girls' Sports Fiction." *Sociology of Sport Journal*, vol. 30, no. 4, 2013, pp. 415–434.

From Girls on Fire
to Historical Bad Girls

A Framework for Critiquing Postfeminism
and Neoliberalism in YA Literature

SEAN P. CONNORS *and*
LISSETTE LOPEZ SZWYDKY

Although she was not the first strong girl in popular culture, the 2008 introduction of Katniss Everdeen, the bow-and-arrow-wielding rebel of Suzanne Collins's The Hunger Games series, occasioned a transformational moment in the young adult (YA) publishing market. Not only was The Hunger Games trilogy commercially successful, spawning a lucrative four-film franchise and eventually surpassing the Harry Potter series to become the best-selling books on Amazon (Haq), but it also signaled the arrival of what some voices in the media regarded as a new type of female character: the Girl on Fire. In subsequent years, YA dystopias featuring strong female heroines who fought injustice and advocated for oppressed peoples in their communities became commonplace on bookstore shelves. Commenting on this trend, Sonya Sawyer Fritz argues: "Female protagonists have taken center stage in YA dystopias as girls who resist the forces of their broken and corrupt societies to create their own identities, shape their own destinies, and transform the worlds in which they live" (17).

Many teachers and librarians have been no less enthusiastic in celebrating these books, which they credit with allowing teenage girls to explore new subjectivities. Barbara Ward and Terrell Young, for example, argue that when selecting literary texts for girls, "Care should be taken to find books that feature strong female literary role models, allowing girls to explore their own identities, claim their own voices, and gain confidence, particularly during

35

the adolescent years" (257). Others, like Roberta Seelinger Trites, caution against cataloguing books as "'feminist,' simply because they feature a strong female protagonist" (85). As Trites notes, texts that portray progressive female characters can also reproduce narratives that undermine or problematize feminist discourses.

In YA dystopian fiction, the Girl on Fire constitutes one manifestation of a figure that Anita Harris (2004) calls "the Future Girl." In other genres, the Future Girl takes other forms. As we will argue, in YA adaptations of nineteenth-century novels (henceforth, YA neo–Victorian novels), the Future Girl often takes the form of a close "ancestor" of the Girl on Fire: the Historical Bad Girl. Like the Girl on Fire, the Historical Bad Girl also appears to resist her society's conservative gender ideologies and binaries. An exceptional individual, she is intelligent, competitive, sexually desirable, and (in some cases) athletic. However liberating these portrayals may be, we argue that like the Girl on Fire, the Historical Bad Girl is capable of reproducing narratives associated with postfeminism, which holds that in a world where men and women compete on a level playing field, feminism is no longer necessary.

In the sections to follow, we present a critical framework that we suggest teachers can use with students to support their investigating of whether YA novels engage in or resist postfeminist and neoliberal discourse. We then apply our framework to a YA neo–Victorian novel, *This Dark Endeavor* (2011), the first book in Kenneth Oppel's two-volume The Apprenticeship of Victor Frankenstein series. In doing so, our intention is to demonstrate how, by depicting the character of Elizabeth Lavenza as a Historical Bad Girl, Oppel's novel inadvertently engages in narratives associated with postfeminism, despite actively trying to rewrite Elizabeth as a strong, female lead for twenty-first-century readers. Although our focus in this essay is on the genre of YA neo–Victorian novels, our framework is applicable to other genres of YA literature, including realistic dystopian fiction. To conclude, we examine the implications of students' interrogating representations of Historical Bad Girls and Girls on Fire in YA literature.

Future Girls, Girls on Fire and Historical Bad Girls

In her book *Future Girl: Young Women in the Twenty-First Century,* Anita Harris demonstrates how Western corporations co-opted the concept of girl power, which originated with the Riot Grrrl movement in the early 1990s, and used it to construct an image of the Future Girl, a figure that Harris describes as "self-inventing, ambitious, and confident" (17), and which she argues is celebrated as ideally equipped to address the challenges of the new global economy. Unlike her predecessors, who were subject to gender discrimination, the Future Girl is depicted as a beneficiary of feminism's hard-won victories. An exceptional individual, she is capable of achieving personal and financial success, provided she is willing to compete in the marketplace and capitalize on her talents. Thus, despite evidence that suggests gender discrimination is a persistent problem for women in social, political, and economic contexts, the Future Girl fosters the impression that feminism, having achieved its intended purpose of providing access to these political and economic spaces, is no longer needed. As Angela McRobbie observes, "elements of contemporary popular culture are perniciously effective in regard to this undoing of feminism" (27).

In contemporary YA literature, the Future Girl takes different forms. In some cases she is what Shauna Pomerantz and Rebecca Raby call the "Post-Nerd Smart Girl," a figure they describe as:

> attractive, capable, and sexually desirable. She is clever and sexy, brainy and beautiful, and though she may not always be popular, she has the power and confidence to build her own world. This smart girl can also be athletic, tough, and cool, showcasing a range of possibilities that were previously presented as antithetical to smart girls of the past. In short, this smart girl has it all, including a bright future, dates with boys, and a "can-do" attitude [287].

Social constructs such as gender and race never pose obstacles for the Post-Nerd Smart Girl, who appears to succeed on the basis of her own merits. For this reason, Pomerantz and Raby argue that the Post-Nerd Smart Girl is implicated in postfeminist and neoliberal discourses that emphasize individualism, competition, and meritocracy at the explicit expense of intersectional feminist identities

Dawn H. Currie, Deirdre M. Kelly, and Shauna Pomerantz identify another manifestation of the Future Girl in popular culture: "butt-kicking girls" who "stand up for themselves and the greater good" (42). As they describe her, the butt-kicking girl "has a moral compass and is trying to do the right thing" (42). An example of the butt-kicking girl is the Girl on Fire, a figure that Sarah Hentges argues is "complex, intelligent, brave, and a triumphant survivor of impossible situations" (5). Like the Post-Nerd Smart Girl, the Girl on Fire also has the potential to perpetuate postfeminist and neoliberal discourses, as we see in Marie Lu's dystopian novel *Legend* (2011), which features a multi-talented female prodigy, June, who is believed to have received the only perfect score on a government-administered standardized test used to identify exceptional individuals (Connors and Trites). Gender, race, or class never pose obstacles for June, who is depicted as succeeding purely on the basis of her own merits in a system that is ostensibly devoid of race and gender-based discrimination.

While Girls on Fire are contemporary character-types often used to project future images of female empowerment, equivalent characters are found in texts that look backward in time to (fictional) historical predecessors. Having read a number of YA neo–Victorian novels (particularly those that adapt or extend canonical literary works), we have come to recognize yet another manifestation of the Future Girl: the Historical Bad Girl. Although neo–Victorianism continues to be redefined and renegotiated as both an aesthetic and a genre that cross various forms and media, we use the term here to refer to contemporary texts that are not only set in the nineteenth century, but which also engage, even if superficially, with the period's literature, politics, or social conventions. Attractive and intelligent, confident and strong-willed, competitive and occasionally athletic, the Historical Bad Girl is seemingly unaffected by her society's traditional gender norms and binaries, leading to widely inaccurate depictions of the historical settings that are supposed to inform historical fiction. Instead of following period-specific historical norms, the Historical Bad Girl competes against boys and uses her talents to secure not only her independence, but also to earn the affections of her (male) love interest(s). On the surface, such a narrative seems to advance at least some feminist goals.

Upon closer scrutiny, however, we argue that the Historical Bad Girl, like other incarnations of Future Girls, is prone to paradox. McRobbie argues that postfeminism is subject to "double-entanglement," as it "comprises the coexistence of neoconservative values in relation to gender, sexuality, and family life … with processes of liberalization in regard to choice" (28). The same can be said of the Historical Bad Girl, who despite resisting some of her society's conservative gender ideologies, also reproduces others: for example, the stereotype that girls are naturally nurturing. Like the Post-Nerd Smart Girl and the Girl on Fire, the Historical Bad Girl can mask the role that structural inequalities play in privileging some groups of people and oppressing others.

In the next section, we present a three-part critical framework that teachers can use with students to investigate how YA novels reproduce or resist narratives associated with postfeminism and neoliberalism. We apply our framework to Kenneth Oppel's Frankenstein-inspired YA prequel *This Dark Endeavor,* attending closely to how the novel positions the character of Elizabeth Lavenza, Victor Frankenstein's cousin, as a Historical Bad Girl. Although we focus on a YA neo–Victorian novel, we argue that teachers and students can apply our framework to other genres of YA literature, including dystopian fiction, to interrogate when other manifestations of the Future Girl or Girl on Fire participate in postfeminist and neoliberal discourses.

A Framework for Critiquing Postfeminism and Neoliberalism in YA Literature

Although the meaning of the term postfeminism is debated in academia, we understand it to refer to a set of assumptions that regard society as having progressed to a point when gender no longer poses an obstacle for educational, professional, and social advancement. Steeped in a belief that contemporary girls and women are free to do or become whatever they choose, postfeminism emphasizes choice and individual exceptionalism while mitigating, if not erasing, the role that sexism, racism, classism, and other forms of oppression play in creating structural inequalities that impact personal, professional, and political opportunities for women, people of color, and individuals who are in some way marginalized via any combination of intersectional identities.

Postfeminism is influenced by neoliberalism, a political economic theory that emerged in the late 1970s and early 1980s, gaining momentum under Ronald Reagan's administration in the United States and Margaret Thatcher's government in the United Kingdom. As the prefix "neo" implies, neoliberalism is a "new" form of classical liberalism, which advocated for individual freedom and *laissez faire* (or free market) economics. According to Julie Wilson, neoliberalism is characterized by a belief that the "government's charge is not the care and security of citizens, but rather the promotion of market competition" (2). Underlying neoliberalism is an assumption that all of society benefits when businesses compete against each other, as competition is thought to foster ingenuity, thus ensuring that consumers have access to the best goods at the lowest cost. As a result, neoliberalism rigorously opposes government regulation of business, along with other social institutions that are perceived as prohibiting businesses and corporations from exercising their full talents. Neoliberalism may have begun as an economic theory, but today it structures other domains of human life. For example, proponents of neoliberalism oppose social safety-net programs such as unemployment, social security, and Medicare, as they are thought to breed government dependency. Instead, it celebrates the talented individual, and holds each and every person accountable for what they become in life.

Postfeminism and neoliberalism are both steeped in an ideology of individual exceptionalism, and we see this phenomenon explicitly in the rising popularity of YA heroines and multiple manifestations of Future Girls, including Girls on Fire, Post-Nerd Smart Girls, and Historical Bad Girls. Harris connects the two ideologies, arguing that "the neoliberal discourse that has accompanied deregulation and deindustrialization merges well with a version of girlpower that emphasizes self-invention and individual economic empowerments" (10). For this reason, as seen in Figure 2.1, our critical framework for interrogating whether individual YA novels reproduce or resist narratives associated with postfeminism and neoliberalism begins with the question: *Does the text emphasize individual exceptionalism or strength through collective relationships?*

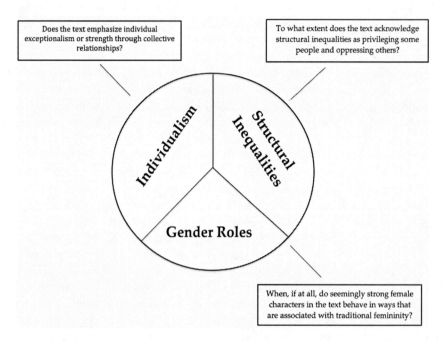

Figure 2.1. Framework for Critiquing Postfeminism and Neoliberalism

In celebrating the talented individual, postfeminism, like neoliberalism, is premised on an assumption that people compete against each other on a level playing field, and that they have access to the same opportunities, material resources, and life chances. In this way, both postfeminism and neoliberalism discipline girls and women to take personal responsibility for their successes or failures in life. Yet as Harris and other critics argue, these discourses also erase the role that structural problems such as racism, sexism, classism, and so on play in producing inequalities that favor the interests of some groups of people (e.g., white, middle-class, heterosexual girls and women) while oppressing or sidelining others. With this in mind, a second question that teachers and students can ask in the service of assessing whether YA novels reproduce or resist discourses associated with postfeminism and neoliberalism is: *To what extent does the text acknowledge structural inequalities as privileging some people and oppressing others?*

Currie, Kelley, and Pomerantz link neoliberalism to classical liberalism, a political philosophy that sought to free individuals "to pursue their best interests, based on reason as a guide to morality and values" (202). Whereas the quality of reason was historically attributed to men, Currie and her colleagues credit first-wave feminism with having called attention to "women as moral equals to men" (202), the result of which has implications for how they are conceptualized within a neoliberal framework. "Transformed into neoliberalism, the ideal Subject embodies a mix of both masculine and feminine traits: independence, competition, and risk-taking are accompanied by the feminine propensity for flexibility, conscientiousness, and reflexivity" (202). Yet as McRobbie argues, postfeminism is subject to "double-entanglement" insofar as it tends to commingle "processes of liberalization in regard to choice and diversity" with "neoconservative values" associated with "gender, sexuality, and family life" (28). In literary texts that reproduce postfeminist narratives, this can result in portrayals of female characters that on the one hand appear to perform a new subjectivity, but which on the other hand reproduce conservative gender ideologies. Recognizing this tension, a third question that teachers and students can ask in the service of investigating when works of YA fiction reproduce postfeminist and neoliberal narratives is: *When, if at all, do seemingly strong female characters in the text behave in ways that are associated with traditional femininity?*

By attending closely to the topics and related questions that comprise the critical framework we have presented in this section (see Figure 2.1), teachers and students can investigate when works of YA fiction reproduce or resist discourses that are associated with postfeminism and neoliberalism. In doing so, they can critique whether texts that depict seemingly strong female characters—be they Girls on Fire, Post-Nerd Smart Girls, or Historical Bad Girls—are as progressive in their representation of teenage girls as they appear to be. In the next section, we apply our critical framework to Kenneth Oppel's *This Dark Endeavor*. In doing so, we demonstrate how the figure of the Historical Bad Girl, a close relative of the Girl on Fire as she appears in contemporary YA neo–Victorian novels, is complicit in reproducing discourses associated with postfeminism and neoliberalism.

Critiquing Postfeminism and Neoliberalism in Kenneth Oppel's This Dark Endeavor

This Dark Endeavor is the first book in Kenneth Oppel's two-volume The Apprenticeship of Victor Frankenstein series, which serves as a prequel to Mary Shelley's (1818) *Frankenstein* insofar as it imagines Victor, his cousin, Elizabeth Lavenza, and their poet friend, Henry Clerval, as teenagers. The series also adds a major character, giving Victor a twin, Konrad, with whom he endlessly competes. In many ways, the Frankenstein twins are mirror-images of each other: Victor is impulsive and brooding, Konrad is sensible and kind. However, Oppel is careful not to write all of the redeemable qualities into flat character types. In his version, Victor tends to be the more politically radical and liberated figure, with Konrad often voicing paternalistic viewpoints that somewhat undercut the character's likability, despite his being Elizabeth's main love interest in the first book of the series. Konrad's existence in the series is important not only because he serves as a character foil for the teenage Victor, but also because his presence informs one of the biggest tensions in this YA series: a love triangle between the Frankenstein brothers and their adopted cousin Elizabeth.

Unlike its historical predecessor, which contains no magical or supernatural elements, Oppel's vision of the Frankenstein story fuses magic, adventure, and traditional gothic elements. While there are obvious intentions of exploring the ancient alchemy that serves as a historical point of reference in Shelley's 1818 novel, modern readers will also see the influence of contemporary YA literature, especially magic-focused series such as the Harry Potter books as well as tropes popularized by gothic television series such as *Buffy the Vampire Slayer*, *The Vampire Chronicles*, and other shows that feature a core group of teenagers investigating and battling monsters and other forces of evil.

Although the Konrad storyline represents a major departure from the cast of characters and plot of Shelley's novel, the most notable way that Oppel's series rewrites the storyworld that Shelley created two-hundred years ago is through its reenvisioning of Elizabeth. Unlike her nineteenth-century counterpart in Shelley's novel, who is mostly confined to the domestic sphere and forced to be submissive to her male counterparts, Oppel's updated character reflects the expectations of a contemporary audience that has benefited from more than two centuries of feminist philosophy and social movements. In the twenty-first century YA series, Elizabeth is intelligent, fearless, competitive, and athletic, and these qualities lead Victor, Konrad, and Henry to regard her as an equal. She rivals and often exceeds their knowledge of cultural customs and current events. She has access to all of the same spaces as the boys. She is much more courageous than the bookish Henry, bolder than Victor, and savvier than Konrad. She also steals most of the scenes. When the teens conduct research in the Dark Library, Elizabeth demonstrates equal and often greater intellectual abilities in research and interpretation of ancient texts—despite the fact that girls and women did not have access to formal education during the historical period in which the series is set. Elizabeth's exceptionalism also extends to her physical abilities. She accompanies the boys on all of their physical adventures. She climbs trees, explores caves, and fights wild creatures, and never misses the opportunity for a well-placed verbal jab at her male peers whenever they underestimate her talents. In all of these ways, she is an exceptional individual in every sense of the word—a twenty-first century Girl on Fire teleported into a historical setting.

Individual Exceptionalism

Our framework for critiquing the role that individual works of YA fiction play in reproducing or resisting narratives associated with postfeminism and neoliberalism begins with the question: *Does the text emphasize individual exceptionalism or strength through collective relationships?* By updating the gender roles that Shelley imagined for her characters in her 1818 novel, *This Dark Endeavor* appears to offer contemporary readers a more progressive set of gender politics. In doing so, however, the novel positions the character of Elizabeth as an exceptional individual, the first quality that we associate with the figure of the Historical Bad Girl as she exists in YA neo–Victorian literature.

In eighteenth- or nineteenth-century society, Oppel's Elizabeth would have either been impossible or, at the very least, socially ostracized for her regular challenging of gender norms. However, as she is described by Oppel's Victor, the novel's narrator and focalizer, Elizabeth is intelligent, courageous, and fiercely independent, refusing to shy away from competition or accept differential treatment. When the Frankenstein family first adopts her, Victor recalls that she was like a "feral cat" who "hissed and snarled and hit. Sometimes bit" (10), even biting him on one occasion when he "suggested girls' brains were smaller than boys" (11). From the outset, the novel thus positions Elizabeth as a strong female character who openly competes with her male cousins.

As a member of the socially and politically progressive Frankenstein family, Elizabeth's feminist sensibilities are openly encouraged and supported by her adoptive parents. When Alphonse hopes that, following the horrors of the French Revolution, the French people will embrace a government that acknowledges all men as equals, his wife, Caroline, responds, "And all women, too." In this scene and others, Caroline Frankenstein channels the early feminist philosopher Mary Wollstonecraft (Mary Shelley's mother), whose *A Vindication of the Rights of Woman* (1792) famously proposed a system of national education aimed at providing young girls the same education as their male counterparts in the service of newly formed democratic systems of government in America and France. Caroline continues, "It would come sooner … if the education of girls was not designed to turn them into meek, weak-minded creatures who waste their true potential." When Elizabeth replies, "Not in this house," the novel implicitly establishes her as exceptional in the late eighteenth-century setting, a century (or more!) before women were granted the right to vote in any nation.

The novel further emphasizes Elizabeth's exceptionality when she and Victor embark on a quest to retrieve the ingredients needed to mix an elixir they assume will restore a gravely ill Konrad to health. When Victor expresses reservation about Elizabeth accompanying him in climbing a massive tree under cover of darkness to recover a lichen that is only visible by moonlight, she angrily reminds him that she once rescued him from a tree he had gotten stuck in, noting: "You needed me then, and you need me now" (105). Pointing out that feminine garments would impede her ability to climb the tree, Elizabeth changes into a tunic and pair of trousers borrowed from Victor, which heightens his desire for her. Watching her climb with "no sign of hesitation or fear," he is both "filled with admiration" and moved by a "powerful and savage pounding through [his] veins" (114), and he immediately follows her. As they later make their way back down the tree they encounter three roosting vultures, and Elizabeth rescues Victor once again. Seizing one of the birds from a branch, she sinks her teeth into its throat, both astonishing and exciting Victor. Later, when they apprise Konrad of their exploit, he scolds Victor for exposing Elizabeth to risk, prompting her to angrily reply, "I'm quite capable of taking care of myself, Konrad, I can assure you" (127).

By emphasizing her courage, intelligence, and desirability, *This Dark Endeavor* positions Elizabeth as an exceptional individual. Throughout the novel, she competes with, and sometimes bests, Victor, who respects her for her "sweetness and goodness and good humor and intelligence," as well as her "power and fury and passion" (269). Unimpeded by the conservative gender norms that characterize the book's historical setting, Elizabeth instead leverages her many talents to rise above them. In doing so, she reproduces the emphasis that neoliberalism and postfeminism place on meritocracy. However, as we argue in the next section, by failing to acknowledge the impact of social constructs such as gender and class, *This Dark Endeavor* inadvertently papers over structural inequalities that advantage some groups of people over others.

Structural Inequalities

Our second essential framing question for critiquing postfeminism and neoliberalism in YA literature is: *To what extent does the text acknowledge structural inequalities as privileging some people and oppressing others?* Set in eighteenth-century Geneva amidst the backdrop of the French Revolution, there are moments when *This Dark Endeavor* acknowledges the role that patriarchal structures would have historically played in disadvantaging women. Although Victor identifies the city of Geneva as a republic, he also clarifies that only male citizens are elected to its General Council (25). Likewise, though he describes his parents as "exceedingly liberal" people with progressive gender politics, he concedes that in Genevan society, his "home was a most peculiar one," as does his mother, who characterizes it as an "exception to the rule" (26). The Frankenstein household, therefore, acts as yet another form of exceptionalism in the book.

In one particularly telling scene, Elizabeth shares her dream of becoming a writer with the group, and Konrad immediately recommends that she adopt a pen name, as "the idea of a woman writing a novel [is] scandalous" (34). Elizabeth brushes off the idea: "'Perhaps I will shock the world with my own,' she said. 'Elizabeth Lavenza has such a literary flair, don't you think? It would be a shame to waste it'" (34). Somewhat flustered, Konrad turns to the subject of marriage, which is met with a similar response. The scene poses an interesting moment for a historical intervention and discussion. Although women were already writing novels by the late eighteenth century, usually publishing them anonymously but on limited occasions under their own names, there were significant barriers to getting published as a woman writer during the eighteenth and nineteenth centuries that went well beyond simple "scandal" or social propriety. Most women who did find a way to publish their work did so because they were extremely well-connected and moved in social circles that afforded them unconventional privileges that did not extend to the vast majority of women. Yet despite such opportunities for exploring the real-world historical barriers that women faced during this period, the novel seldom acknowledges gender as posing obstacles for Elizabeth, who succeeds at everything she does.

Like the male characters in the book, Elizabeth enjoys considerable freedom. When Victor and Konrad practice fencing, she competes against Henry (37). She accompanies Victor and Henry on their midnight excursion to the Sturmwald forest, and ventures below ground with Victor and Konrad on their quest to find an ancient fish needed for their magic elixir. When Victor and Henry first visit the disgraced John Polidori's apothecary shop in a section of Geneva populated by sailors and prostitutes, Elizabeth is with them, and she participates in the novel's climactic battle against Polidori and his lynx. At no point do Victor's parents (or any other adult, for that matter) intervene or question the propriety of a young woman's engaging in such risky adventures. Instead, Elizabeth's ability to do so is taken for granted, and she is given free reign of not only domestic and public spheres, but also secret spaces and forbidden territories. In these ways, the novel reproduces a postfeminist narrative that regards sexism as an individual, rather than structural, problem, given that no authority figures ever question or limit what Elizabeth can or cannot accomplish.

If *This Dark Endeavor* erases obstacles that Elizabeth would have faced as a young woman living at the turn of the nineteenth century, it also papers over the ways that her upper class status would have advantaged her. The series follows Shelley's characterization of Elizabeth as orphaned by her mother and having a disinterested father, which under normal circumstances could have made a young child very vulnerable, especially during the historical time in which Oppel's series is set. After her mother's death, Elizabeth's remarried father "promptly abandoned her to an Italian convent" (10). Taking pity on the girl, the patriarch of the Frankenstein family adopts Elizabeth and raises her as a member of his own family, offering her access to the same opportunities he affords his sons. Thus, like Victor and Konrad, Elizabeth studies "Greek, Latin, literature, science, and politics" (27). Without a kind and generous male patron, a young orphaned child in her position would have either died or fallen into a life of prostitution or other dangerous living conditions. Fortunately, Elizabeth has a well-to-do, kind uncle in Alphonse, and this connection to the middle-to-upper class of respectable Genevan society grounds the character's subject position in the series.

By neglecting to acknowledge how Elizabeth's upper-class standing would have privileged her, or depict social obstacles she would have faced as a result of her gender, *This Dark Endeavor* inadvertently depicts sexism as an individual, rather than a structural, problem. In doing so, it perpetuates the emphasis that neoliberalism and postfeminism place on individualism, while ignoring "individuals as subject to pressures, constraints, or influence from outside themselves" (Gill and Scharff 7). Written to appeal to a twenty-first-century sensibility, Elizabeth's exceptionalism, thus, comes at the cost of accurate depictions of both gender and class and the importance of understanding identity as intersectional.

Progressive Versus Traditional Representations of Femininity

As we have argued, it is necessary to attend closely to how literary texts that feature seemingly strong girls (whether in the form of Girls on Fire, Historical Bad Girls, or Post-Nerd Smart Girls) represent these characters, because these texts often intermix progressive and conservative gender politics, a tension that can lead to productive interpretations and conversations. Recognizing this, teachers and students interested in critiquing postfeminism and neoliberalism in YA literature can ask: *When, if at all, do seemingly strong female characters in the text behave in ways that are associated with traditional femininity?*

Unlike most teenage girls living at the turn of the nineteenth century, Elizabeth enjoys almost unlimited, unrestricted access to spaces and situations typically associated with male characters, especially when considering the historical setting of Oppel's series. Konrad is the only character in the novel who questions the appropriateness of Elizabeth engaging in traditionally masculine activities, leading her to dismiss him. When he reprimands Victor for allowing Elizabeth to climb a tree in the middle of the night, she angrily replies, "I'm quite capable of taking care of myself, Konrad, I can assure you," thus ending the argument (127). On the surface, interactions such as this one (and there are several in *This Dark Endeavor*) paint Elizabeth as a strong-willed, independent character who has no interest in fulfilling stereotypical gender roles. However, this interpretation is problematized by the fact that Konrad is eventually revealed to be Elizabeth's chosen love interest, suggesting that heterosexual romance outweighs women's independence at the end of the day—hardly a feminist narrative despite all of the freedoms that Elizabeth enjoys throughout the book.

Through the relationship between Elizabeth and Konrad, as well as her later relationship with Victor, the series most closely participates in postfeminist discourses, particularly as they appear in neo–Victorian popular culture across form and media. As Antonija Primorac, building on the work of scholars such as Rosalind Gill and Diane Negra, explains, postfeminism and neo-Victorianism emerged hand-in-hand in the 1990s as part of a larger cultural narrative that emphasized the dream of "having-it-all" (education, marriage, family, career, independence) without serious discussion of the structural limitations that society places on working mothers (Primorac 5). Elizabeth fully exemplifies this neoliberal, postfeminist narrative throughout the series. She sees herself both as an independent young woman, a faithful partner, and a potential mother. She imagines herself as achieving success as a novelist, while at the same time confidently seeing her future self as fulfilled in a traditional, heterosexual marriage: "No doubt. I will have a fabulous husband and many, beautiful talented children" (35). This confident tone dominates the first book of Oppel's series.

Although Oppel's Elizabeth typifies the Historical Bad Girl through various examples of exceptionalism, she is also characterized as a maternal figure who is devoted to family and God. She is sometimes described in conventional or conservative terms that seem out of character for this Girl on Fire in historical costume. In one scene, for example, the reader learns that although Elizabeth goes everywhere with her male peers, she requires a chaperone to attend church services. Either Konrad or Victor typically take her; however, they never participate in prayer or services. Here, Elizabeth stands out as the only devoutly religious member of the Frankenstein family, all of whom are atheists.

A similar conservatism characterizes the love triangle between Konrad, Elizabeth, and Victor, which is one of the series' central tensions. At first glance, Elizabeth's love and devotion to Konrad is odd, or at least initially surprising, since he is the more politically moderate Frankenstein twin—a far cry from Elizabeth's otherwise progressive politics. As a plot device in the twenty-first century novel, the pairing of Elizabeth and Konrad functions more directly to advance Victor's storyline, as his jealousy toward his brother and his increasing sexual attraction to Elizabeth become a focal point for giving readers access to Victor's most intimate thoughts. When Victor makes a considerable sacrifice in order to save his brother (while simultaneously impressing Elizabeth with his bravery), he describes Elizabeth in overly domestic and idealized terms: "When I regained consciousness, Elizabeth was standing over me, mopping my forehead with a cool cloth. I just stared at her, and thought her the most beautiful thing in all the wide world. If only I could be allowed to stare at her like this, I would be a happy man" (245). Here, Oppel's series reproduces one of the most pervasive tropes of nineteenth-century fiction, as Elizabeth becomes an updated version of the Victorian "angel in the house," only slightly modified for twenty-first-century readers in true neo–Victorian aesthetic style.

It is worth noting as well that although the novel reproduces many conservative narratives that somewhat undermine its more progressive intentions, there are also several moments in the book that offer opportunities for productive discussions about toxic masculinity and sexual consent. The reader is given access to Victor's most passionate thoughts, including the extent to which he resists numerous temptations to take advantage of Elizabeth, especially when she sleepwalks into his room and climbs into his bed (212). Victor also spends considerable time describing his overwhelming desires for Elizabeth while fighting back urges to "steal a kiss" or otherwise transgress sexual boundaries despite her repeated rejections of his advances. Overall, the series offers a complex view of gendered relations and individualism that can provide productive sites of conversation in the classroom.

Conclusion

As critical educators, we are encouraged by the growing number of strong female characters that have taken center stage in YA literature over the course of the past decade. Whether they are Girls on Fire, Historical Bad Girls, or Post-Nerd Smart Girls, these female characters are often depicted as taking ownership of their stories and advocating for themselves and their communities. Perhaps it is not surprising, then, that some educators have begun to regard literary texts that feature the Girl on Fire and her protégés as powerful resources they can use to engage young adults in addressing activist causes. Amber Simmons, for example, explains how she harnesses the spirit of the Girl on Fire to engage high school students in tackling social action projects that target problems in their local communities. Reflecting on the importance of this work, Simmons explains, "Like an ember that fuels a fire, reading can stoke our students into becoming socially responsible citizens, causing them to spit and blaze in the face of injustice and spread their fire throughout the community" (31).

While we share Simmons's vision and applaud the idea of using literature as a vehicle to engage students in working for change in their local communities, we argue that it is also important for teachers and students to interrogate representations of strong girls in literary texts, as these representations are sometimes deceptive and not necessarily as empowering as they appear to be. Consider, for example, the figure of the Historical Bad Girl in YA neo–Victorian novels. While there are certainly many historical examples of women who challenged the social norms and gendered conventions of their day (including Mary Shelley and her mother), the level of freedom and agency afforded to the character of Elizabeth in Oppel's series is notably anachronistic and might lead contemporary young adult readers to think that girls and women have *always* been able to challenge social conventions freely and without consequences.

With this in mind, neo–Victorian fiction for young adult readers offers a particularly productive genre to explore neoliberal and postfeminist discourses given the genre's double displacement of history through a present-day lens. As Nadine Boehm-Schnitker and Susanne Gruss explain, neo–Victorianism:

> looks into the desires and contexts that tinge and shape the perspectives of our contemporary construction of memory; moreover, it explores the changing purposes with which we fashion the past—and with it, ourselves. The process of fashioning the neo–Victorian … entails a self-fashioning, which implies that the phenomenon of neo–Victorianism can be understood in the context of concerns of twentieth- and twenty-first-century identity politics [1].

When literary texts for adolescents—whether neo–Victorian or dystopian—reproduce postfeminist and neoliberal narratives that emphasize individualism at the expense of the collective, they not only erase the role that social structures play in disadvantaging girls and women, but they also make it harder for girls and women to work together to address them. In doing so, they risk undermining the beliefs, values, and motivations that drive social activism in the first place.

As educators, we are familiar with the influence that popular culture texts can have on students' understanding of feminism and its relevance to contemporary society. It is not unusual for some of our students to distance themselves from feminism, which they associate with negative portrayals of angry and/or undesirable women, and which they sometimes regard as discriminating against males. However, when pressed on this point of view through historically based questions—for example, *Without feminism, what would the makeup of this classroom look like? Who would be able to make legal, professional, or even personal decisions?*—it becomes clear that many teenagers and college students have not considered how much their current positions benefit from the hard-earned feminist victories of earlier generations because contemporary media has largely impressed a neoliberal understanding of identity and success. Here, productive comparisons between Girls on Fire and Historical Bad Girls can serve as a bridge to develop a critical sense of history and its relationship to contemporary identity politics.

WORKS CITED

Boehm-Schnitker, Nadine, and Susanne Gruss, eds. *Neo-Victorian Literature and Culture: Immersions and Revisitations*. Routledge, 2014.

Connors, Sean P., and Roberta Seelinger Trites. "*Legend*, Exceptionalism, and Genocidal Logic: A Framework for Reading Neoliberalism in YA Dystopias." *The ALAN Review*, vol. 45, no. 3, 2018, pp. 31–41.

Currie, Dawn H., Deirdre M. Kelly, and Shauna Pomerantz. *'Girl Power': Girls Reinventing Girlhood*. Peter Lang, 2009.

Fritz, Sonya Sawyer. "Girl Power and Girl Activism in the Fiction of Suzanne Collins, Scott Westerfeld, and Moira Young." *Female Rebellion in Young Adult Dystopian Fiction*, edited by Sara K. Day, Miranda G. Green-Barteet, and Amy L. Montz, Ashgate, 2014, pp. 17–31.

Gill, Rosalind. *Gender and the Media*. Polity Press, 2007.

_____, and Christina Scharff. "Introduction." *New Femininities: Postfeminism, Neoliberalism, and Subjectivity*, edited by Rosalind Gill and Christina Scharff, Palgrave Macmillan, 2011, pp. 1–17.

Haq, Husna. 'Hunger Games' passes 'Harry Potter' as bestselling Amazon series. *The Christian Science Monitor* (2012).<http://www.csmonitor.com/Books/chapter-and-verse/2012/0821/Hunger-Games-passes-Harry-Potter-as-bestselling-Amazon-series>

Harris, Anita. *Future Girl: Young Women in the Twenty-First Century*. Routledge, 2004.

Hentges, Sarah. *Girls on Fire: Transformative Heroines in Young Adult Dystopian Literature*. McFarland, 2018.

McRobbie, Angela. "Postfeminism and Popular Culture." *Interrogating Postfeminism: Gender and the Politics of Popular Culture*, edited by Yvonne Tasker and Diane Negra, Duke University Press, 2007, pp. 27–39.

Negra, Diane. *What a Girl Wants? Fantasizing the Reclamation of Self in Postfeminism*. Routledge, 2009.

Oppel, Kenneth, *This Dark Endeavor*. Simon & Schuster, 2011.

Pomerantz, Shauna, and Rebecca Raby. "Reading Smart Girls: Post-Nerds in Post-Feminist Popular Culture." *Girls, Texts, Cultures*, edited by Clare Bradford and Mavis Reimer, Wilfred Laurier University Press, 2015, pp. 287–311.

Primorac, Antonija. *Neo-Victorianism on Screen: Postfeminism and Contemporary Adaptations of Victorian Women*. Palgrave, 2018.

Shelley, Mary W., and Susan J. Wolfson. *Mary Wollstonecraft Shelley's Frankenstein, Or, the Modern Prometheus*. Pearson Longman, 2007. Originally published 1818.

Simmons, Amber. "Class on Fire: Using the Hunger Games Trilogy to Inspire Social Action." *Journal of Adolescent & Adult Literacy*, vol. 56, no. 1, 2012, pp. 22–34.

Trites, Roberta Seelinger. *Twenty-First Century Feminisms in Children's and Adolescent Literature*. University Press of Mississippi, 2018.

Ward, Barbara A., and Terrell A. Young. "Brave, Determined, and Strong: Books for Girls (and Sometimes Boys)." *Reading Horizons*, vol. 49, no. 3, 2009, pp. 257–268.

Wilson, Julie A. *Neoliberalism*. Routledge, 2018.

Wollstonecraft, Mary. *A Vindication of the Rights of Woman: An Authoritative Text Backgrounds and Contexts Criticism*. W.W. Norton, 1988. Originally published 1792.

Teaching Feminisms

Triumphs and Failures
in The Hunger Games Trilogy

Roberta Seelinger Trites

When the third book in Suzanne Collins's The Hunger Games trilogy
came out, one of the thirteen-year-old students at my university's laboratory
school finished reading *Mockingjay* and then cried for six hours, as her parents told me, because "Katniss married the wrong guy." This student was not
a sophisticated enough reader yet to notice that Collins textually encodes
Peeta as the "right" man throughout the series, precisely because he listens
to Katniss, is caring, and values her life so much. Peeta is a character constructed straight out of the values of "Third Wave" feminism. (In this context,
the term "wave" corresponds to the idea of an "era.")

During the era of Third Wave feminism, which began in the 1980s, feminists advanced the idea that women deserve to be cared for and nurtured as
much as men do. The young student at the lab school who believed Gale was
the "right" guy, however, had unconsciously internalized an old-school narrative in which the strong, silent man inevitably marries the princess. That
said, Peeta is himself another type of Prince Charming—just a gentler one
than Gale. But what bothers me most about this anecdote is that the thirteen-
year-old cis-female reader never doubted for one moment that Katniss would
end the series *married* heteronormatively—and to the right "type" of *guy*: a
masculine, strong, and silent cis-male. This eighth-grader was an astute, critically aware, highly advanced reader who self-identified as a feminist even at
her young age. Nevertheless, she didn't seem to understand the nuances of
feminism, so her response made me wonder, "How can I explain to readers
her age how to evaluate feminism in more sophisticated terms than she was
employing? How can I explain that feminism has developed in historical

51

waves and occurs in gradations and across a spectrum? How can I explain that feminism is not an off/on, yes/no, feminist/sexist binary switch?" My long-term reflection on these questions informs the rest of this essay. I believe teachers—and their students—who understand several different aspects of feminism are better prepared to understand the complexity of a trilogy such as The Hunger Games. They are also better prepared to evaluate various different forms and nuances of feminism in other Girl on Fire stories.

Thus, as I explore feminist readings of Collins's series in this essay, I organize my argument into an initial introduction that explains historically-oriented and conflicting public opinion about The Hunger Games trilogy and its feminist potential. I then offer specific questions and reading strategies designed to help scholars, teachers, students, and general readers alike understand various feminist methodologies for interpreting the Girl on Fire, as Collins characterizes her. In the first reading strategies section, I demonstrate Katniss as the Girl on Fire in terms of the literary feminism of the Second and Third Waves of feminism. Next, I examine Katniss in terms of material feminism, focusing specifically on embodiment and the myth of the mind/body split. Finally, I critique the inherent anti-feminism of the neoliberal theory to which many Girl on Fire series subscribe. In the conclusion of each of these sections, I provide questions designed to help educators guide their students' critical thinking about feminism. My goal is to complicate what it means to be a feminist reader, particularly of YA literature, because I believe students, educators, artists, and fans are all better served thinking about the Girl on Fire's feminist potential along a spectrum, rather than regarding her as a wholly feminist role model—or as a wholly sexist figure.

Feminism and the Girl on Fire

The internet is on fire with arguments about whether Katniss is a feminist or not. Rachel Stark, for example, argues that Katniss is a feminist because she is a smart, independent, bow-wielding warrior and also because she does something none of the other Tributes can do: she fosters and nurtures the relationships that help save her life. James Tilton considers the series feminist because Peeta and Katniss are allowed to switch gender roles. Rikita Trikha praises Katniss for modeling skills important to female success: teamwork, creative thinking, marketing, image management, paying it forward, capitalizing on her skills, and leadership. Anita Sarkeesian respects the way that Katniss experiences PTSD in the face of trauma, unlike many male slayers in suspense thrillers: "Because of her compassion, empathy, cunning, resourcefulness, and intelligence, she embodies many feminist values."

Sarah Thaller, on the other hand, refers to the "bait and switch" in the series: Katniss is strong and independent, but she ultimately succumbs to "hetero- and repronormativity" in marrying Peeta and reproducing two children. A blogger on Fandomentals—Nancy—analyzes how male-dominated and male-determined the series is; she counts how many times characters other than Katniss are mentioned throughout the series: aside from Katniss, the top four characters listed are male (in order, Peeta, Gale, Haymitch, Finnick); Prim comes in fifth place, while Snow and Cinna have more mentions than Rue, and Plutarch is referenced more often than Effie. According to Nancy, the series is male-dominated in that males hold so much more power in Panem than women do. Along similar lines, Kyndall Williams bluntly expresses frustration that the only way Katniss can be empowered is if she is coded as masculine.

This is only a small sample of the voices on the internet arguing about the feminist status of these novels. Consistently, the points of contention seem to involve gender roles (and discrimination or disempowerment based on those roles), independence, and—above all else—power, especially in terms of who wields it and how. These were the core issues identified at the beginning of the Women's Rights Movement in the 1960s, also referred to as the "Second Wave" of feminism. (The Suffrage Movement, in which women fought to earn the right to vote, is considered the "First Wave.") In 1963, the Presidential Commission on the Status of Women, chaired by Eleanor Roosevelt, asserted that women were covered against discrimination by the Fourteenth Amendment—but the Commission nevertheless acknowledged how disempowering widespread discrimination was for women. That same year, Betty Friedan's *Feminist Critique* (1963) criticized American attitudes towards women and girls that were based on their "sex roles" (245). Also in 1963, Gloria Steinem—who later was among the founders of the National Women's Political Council and *Ms* Magazine—wrote an exposé on the widespread sexual objectification of women she observed when she worked undercover at the Playboy Club as a Playboy Bunny. Thus, in 1963, citizens of the United States were provided with ample evidence that discrimination based on longstanding gender roles leads to female disempowerment, which the Women's Movement and the National Organization for Women (founded in 1966) hoped to correct. Social media pundits are still arguing about women's rights, gender roles, and how much power women should yield, which provides a clear indication that the Women's Movement has not succeeded in dismantling the pernicious persistence of sexism and binarized gender roles in our culture. In other words, that Collins manipulates gender roles in The Hunger Games trilogy to complicate her characterizations does not, by itself, make the series feminist. I believe that feminist criticism is best understood as something akin to looking through a prism, so that we "see" feminism on a spectrum. In other words, feminism cannot fully be evaluated only as a binary between that which is "sexist" or "feminist," the false binary to which the internet so often falls prey. I thus encourage all educators, artists, fans, readers, and scholars to think about feminism in multi-variate—almost rainbow-hued—terms.

Many methodologies exist to help people understand that feminism exists along a spectrum or (easier to operationalize) as a Likert Scale. The tools for thinking critically about feminism's gradations are shaped by a historical trajectory that builds on each era preceding the one before it. To guide readers of this volume, I provide an overarching question that guides each section of this essay. I also provide related keywords in feminist theory that students can learn so they can begin to analyze feminism from various perspectives that have emerged during different eras. The keywords are also designed to serve as vocabulary words that help educators teach students how to analyze various developments, facets, and aspects of feminist criticism across a broad range of feminist possibilities. I follow up each section with additional questions designed to serve as thought-provoking exercises in the classroom.

Second and Third Wave Feminist Questions

How Do Female Characters Exercise Power in a Narrative?

The main question in this section will be to ask how female characters exercise power in any given narrative. Specifically, I focus on "empowerment," which is the social granting of rights and opportunities that are equal for everyone. In historical terms, the Suffragettes of the nineteenth and early twentieth century who advocated for women's right to vote constituted the "First Wave" of feminism. Empowerment, to them, was to come from having access to the ballot box. In the Second Wave of feminism in the 1960s–80s, feminism focused more on social empowerment: how were women empowered? How were they disempowered? Feminists began to ask these questions: What is "masculine"? What is "feminine"? When are women allowed to be "masculine," and when are men allowed to be "feminine"?

In terms of feminist empowerment, The Hunger Games trilogy's depiction of power and power-struggles is not fully feminist. Yes, Katniss is a strong female leader, as are President Coin, Johanna, Enobaria, and Commander Paylor from District 8. Indeed, in assessing the Girl on Fire in terms of gender role fluidity and empowerment, The Hunger Games series is far more feminist than the series it supplanted in the bestseller lists: the Twilight series. But how does Katniss gain power? How does she earn it, and when is she given it—and by whom? In this section, the keyword for students who are learning to critique whether a text reflects ideas associated with feminism is therefore *empowerment*. In the section that follows, I will describe how the original "Girl on Fire" deploys empowerment as a concept.

Katniss's first and most basic form of empowerment comes from her father, who taught her how to hunt and forage. Gale further hones her hunting skills. After she becomes a Tribute, Cinna empowers her, ironically enough, by transforming her into an object to be viewed by the Capitol's citizens. Later, Haymitch, Plutarch and Finnick in *Catching Fire* empower her by giving her different types of information, as do Boggs, Gale, Castor, Pollux, and Mesalla in *Mockingjay*. The female leader of District 13—President Coin— eventually finds Katniss to be threatening; only President Snow can provide Katniss with the information she needs to perceive Coin's corruption. In other words, Katniss gains power from very few women, and when she does so, it is largely within the scope of traditionally female roles, such as being caretakers or stylists. Among other examples, her mother and sister teach her about herbal cures and nursing. Katniss subsequently nurtures Rue, who is associated with music, agriculture, and gymnastic agility, and Rue in turn empowers Katniss by teaching her information and helping her stay safe. Although Johanna helps rescue Katniss from the Quarter Quell arena, Johanna expresses her petty resentment of Katniss more than once. Cressida produces the videos that transform Katniss's embodiment into the Mockingjay who leads the Revolution in a gesture that is perhaps the most gender-neutral of Katniss's empowerers. However, if we follow Foucault in believing that power is ubiquitous and comes from everywhere, and that individuals exist in "a perpetual relationship of force" (*History* 93; *Power* 92), then Katniss cannot legitimately be said to have been in a perpetual relationship of force in which women give her as much or more power than she receives from them—and she relies far more on men than on women to empower her.

Additional questions for educators and students to explore include one basic question and one more complex one:

1. What is the definition of empowerment?
2. How are female characters empowered or disempowered—and by whom?

What Qualities of Feminism Does the Narrative Demonstrate?

In this section, I focus on more specific terms of female empowerment, particularly those qualities that help position the narrative along a spectrum.

In 1988, at the beginning of the Third Wave of feminism, Lissa Paul taught children's literature scholars to analyze novels with female protagonists in terms of entrapment: specifically, physical, economic, and linguistic entrapment. Building on her work, nine years later, I defined a feminist book for youth as being one in which the "main character is empowered regardless of gender" (4). I have since asked my students to evaluate feminism along a spectrum using these tools: choice, voice, and community—particularly female community. The keywords for this section, therefore, are: (1) *entrapment*, (2) *voice*, (3) *choice (agency)* and (4) *community*.

Paul's emphasis on entrapment, particularly economic entrapment, is pertinent to a reading of The Hunger Games trilogy. Katniss is initially trapped by her relationship to economic capital because she is so impoverished. By the end of the series, she is trapped in the Victor's Village, in part, because of her relationship to her victor-gained wealth, so she remains economically entrapped. Throughout the series, Katniss has been limited in her choices—a factor which Paul's analysis of physical and linguistic entrapment taught me to consider in terms of the evaluative concepts of "choice" and "voice." Choice involves agency and having the power to act (which includes, but is more complex than, physical entrapment alone). In terms of agency, Katniss has several choices, including her first major choice: to volunteer as a Tribute in place of Prim. After that, her choices are almost always constrained by the Capitol. She is trapped in two arenas, and the choices she makes in the arenas of *The Hunger Games* and *Catching Fire* only need to be made because of the oppressive power of the Capitol and its (largely male) Gamemakers; the same applies to her work in the Revolution. She has been physically entrapped, too, in *Mockingjay* by President Coin in District 13 and again when she is confined within President Snow's mansion. In addition, in terms of voice and linguistic agency, Katniss is frequently silenced: in her village, in the arenas, during her medical recoveries, within the community of District 13—this despite its promises of freedom for rebels. This silencing is balanced by her serving as the voice of the Revolution in her role as the Mockingjay; nevertheless, that is still an instance of a vocalization necessitated as a reaction to a repressive patriarchal structure, as Katniss is very unwilling to serve as the Mockingjay.

If Katniss is limited in terms of voice and choice, she is even more constrained in her ability to maintain female community. As Ann M.M. Childs has demonstrated, Katniss is unable to sustain true companionship with females (187). The list of her female support system includes her mother, Prim, Rue, Madge, Johanna, and Greasy Sae. Only with the latter does Katniss maintain a long-term relationship with another woman, but Greasy Sae seems to be more of a servant than a peer or friend. In other words, my students typically perceive the series as partially feminist in terms of Third Wave feminism: Katniss has some choice, some voice, and little female community. She is allowed to experiment with gender roles and still exert empathy; she is temporarily empowered to lead a Revolution, although she ends the series emotionally broken and physically cloistered. As the thirteen-year-old I mentioned in my introductory anecdote anticipated: Katniss is married heteronormatively and has children because her husband has pressured her to do so. But she is isolated, trapped in a bunkered compound, and tortured by nightmares. This hardly seems like a triumph of feminism.

Additional questions educators might ask students thus include the following:

1. How is the character empowered (or disempowered) physically or in terms of language or economics?
2. When do the female characters, especially the female-identified protagonist, have voice, choice, or community in this story? When do they lack voice, choice, or community?
   a. Draw a number line and place an "x" along it for how much "voice" the protagonist has, a "y" for how much "choice" she has, and a "z" for how much female community she has.
   b. How does this data visualization help you argue about the strength (or weakness) of this narrative's feminism?
   c. How are the answers to your questions feminist? How are they not feminist?

Post–Third Wave Feminist Questions

In What Ways Does the Narrative Value or Devalue the Physical?

This section asks questions about the physical (or "material") world. Late in the twentieth century and in the early part of the twenty-first century, feminist scholars began to explore how problematic it is for people to think of the "mind" as separate from the "body"—which is called "the Cartesian split" of mind and body (because that notion is based on one interpretation of Rene *Descartes'* work). Feminist philosophers such as Elizabeth Grosz have argued that in too much Western philosophy and religion, the "Man" is equated with the mind while the "Woman" is equated to the body (5–6). Cognitive linguists who specialize in the relationship between how people think and how our culture works also insist that it is impossible for a body to exist without a mind; they refer instead to the "embodied mind" as an integrated biological unit (Lakoff and Johnson 37–38, 551). Thus, material feminists are those who emphasize the importance of the physical world, including the material body and its interactions with the physical world that define and situate the human body. The idea of the mind and body being separate is particularly offensive to material feminists, who ask questions such as the following: How can a body go through puberty without the brain's pituitary gland? How can menstruation exist without the existence of hormonal triggers from the brain, the endocrine system, and the nervous system? How can a pregnant body exist without a brain supporting the appropriate hormonal and neurological networks? Most important: how can people know themselves to be "female" unless they have a mind to guide them in understanding their own bodies? The keywords for reading as a material feminist are therefore: (1) the *material*, (2) the *embodied mind* and (3) the *objectification* of the human body—which is, simply put, the process of one's body being treated or perceived as a non-human and/or agentless object.

Material feminism also requires us to acknowledge the importance of the material and how material objects shift our physical perceptions—and shift meaning themselves as our embodied perceptions shift. Thus, according to material feminism, the material itself also has agency to change humans (Trites, *Twenty-First* 3–17). For example, when Katniss first sees the Mockingjay pin Madge gives her, she thinks about how many people it could feed, but when Madge pins it on her, it becomes a symbol of friendship (*Hunger* 12, 38). The pin's meaning shifts again in *Catching Fire*—and shifts Katniss's perception of herself, too—when she learns that it is the pin that Madge's aunt wore into the arena when that young woman was herself a Tribute (196–97). Katniss is again changed by that specific material object when her perception of it next shifts: she discovers that she herself *is* the Mockingjay (386). She must bear herself now—enact herself—as the embodied symbol of the inanimate object she once wore (Trites, *Twenty-First* 3).

Bread is another material object that shifts with characters' perceptions of it in the trilogy, and bread simultaneously changes those who perceive it to be both an object and a symbol of some important concept. Initially, bread is a sign of life: Katniss is saved from starvation by Peeta (whose name can be equated with pita bread, as my students frequently note). As a child, he intentionally burns some bread from his family's bakery to give to her, earning a beating to his own physical embodiment from his mother in the process. In that instance, he uses bread as his own Third Wave feminist indicator that he is respectfully willing to sacrifice his embodiment to save Katniss's life. In the first arena of *The Hunger Games*, bread again becomes a symbol of respectfulness when Rue's district, after her death, sends their specialized bread to thank Katniss for the sensitive way she has enshrouded Rue. In *Catching Fire*, bread becomes an actual instrument or substitute for language when the rebels use bread to communicate pivotal directions for the time and place the rebel Tributes can be evacuated from the arena. "The district where the bread originated indicated the day. Three. The number of rolls the hour. Twenty-four" (385). Indeed, the name for the country Panem itself is derived from the Latin accusative, the conjugation associated with demand: "Give us this day, our daily bread" is translated from this Latin imperative: *Panem nostrum quotidianum da nobis hodie.* In other words, the meaning of the name "Panem" is closer to "*give* us our bread [on] this day" than to the Latin nominative noun for bread, *panis.* Bread—as a material symbol for power—represents all that the rebels demand throughout the trilogy. When bread is ingested, it empowers the body, and so it is an agent. When bread becomes a symbol of freedom—as it did during the French Revolution and also in The Hunger Games trilogy—it becomes a different type of agent that empowers humans, but either way, bread is displaying agency.

Katniss herself catalogs the material objects whose significances have changed for her, even while her own ability to perceive these objects recursively changes her: "My mockingjay pin. Peeta's token, the gold locket with photos of my mother and Prim and Gale inside. A silver spile for tapping trees, and the pearl Peeta gave me" (*Mockingjay* 32). Many of these objects that she has collected by the time she arrives in District 13 help her to focus on her perception of the materiality involved in her own embodiment: The physicality and symbolism of her pin. The locket depicting the faces of those she loves, which she wears around her neck. The spile she has drunk from in the Quarter Quell to save not only her own embodiment but also the embodiment of her allies. And the pearl. She carries it in her pocket, caressing it at times, worrying it at others, but also considering it to be a token of Peeta's unconditional acceptance of her.

Moreover, The Hunger Games trilogy provides many opportunities for students to analyze not only how false the idea of the mind/body split is, but also ideas about how perception works within the mind. For example, throughout the series—and especially in the arena or in battle—Katniss witnesses parts of her own body as if they are objects, not as if they are an integral part of her very being. In the arena of *The Hunger Games*, after Katniss is burned by fire balls, she becomes—quite literally—"the girl on fire." She describes her own leg as if it is an object, removed from her body: "I roll the leg back and forth on the ground.... But then, *without thinking*, I rip away the fabric with my bare hands"—as if someone can move their hands without a brain motivating them to think (176, emphasis added; Trites, *Twenty-First* 89). She then hallucinates she is shaking ants from her hands, and "someone's screaming, a long high-pitched scream that never breaks for breath. I have a vague idea that it might be me" because she cannot perceive her own embodied voice (194). When she loses her hearing, she "paws" at her left ear "to compensate for the wall of nothingness" she is experiencing, as if she were an animal who cannot control her compulsive actions (228–29; Trites,

Twenty-First 89). In the second arena, Katniss wishes "my arms would stop jumping around" (*Catching* 300); she "cannot get my leg to cooperate. As I struggle to get up, it gives out"—as if her leg has agency of its own (301). She also perceives her own leg as an object: "a leg turned to wood" (302). In all of these examples, Katniss is objectifying her own body. In the climactic moment of *Catching Fire*, when she is electrified because she has fired a wired arrow into the arena's force field shell, disabling it, she is "thrown backward to the ground, body useless, paralyzed, eyes frozen," while she simultaneously fails to recognize how important her perceptual cognition is to the embodiment that the Capitol has objectified in one way and which she herself has objectified in another way (379). Just as she becomes a literal "girl on fire" in the first arena, in a climactic moment near the end of *Mockingjay*, she again becomes a literal girl on fire, but one who objectifies her own body again when she is the victim of District 13's firebombing of the Capitol: "I am Cinna's bird, ignited.... The feathers of flame ... grow from my body. Beating my wings only fans the blaze. I consume myself, but to no end" (348). In psychological terms, Katniss is experiencing disassociation. In material feminist terms, she has become—because of the wars of the patriarchy—unable to understand how fully integrated her body and mind is.

Students can learn to look for those metaphors when Katniss refers to human embodiment as if it is "like" an animal or a non-thinking material object, as she does when she compares how her lost hearing makes her feel like an animal in the first arena, or as she does when she thinks Haymitch is assessing her prowess and Peeta's as if they were "like animals" (58), or when she admits to feeling "like some trained dog" for the Capitol (*Hunger* 117). Katniss compares Rue to a bird for her ability to fly around the trees; later, Katniss understands why Peeta would want to die so that he doesn't feel "[l]ike the mutts. Like a rabid beast bent on ripping my throat out" (*Catching* 313). Peeta tells Katniss that he wants to be "more than just a piece in their Games" (*Hunger* 142). Katniss eventually accepts and repeats, multiple times, Peeta's understanding that she and the other Tributes are only objectified tools in someone else's game (e.g., *Hunger* 142, 236; *Catching* 242, 385; *Mockingjay* 59, 215, 297). The adults with power over Katniss—Presidents Snow and Coin, the Capitol itself—have trained Katniss to think of herself and others in objectified terms.

Material feminism encourages us to recognize our embodied being, lest we ignore our bodies, objectifying them and subsequently hating them, in a false belief that our brains are more important than our bodies—as if we could have bodies without brains or brains without bodies. While female objectification often involves viewing women solely in sexual terms, this type of objectification also robs women of their ability to think of themselves as agents who can enact power for themselves. Ultimately, reading as a material feminist enables us—and our students—to empower themselves and ourselves by valuing *all* aspects of our personhood.

Additional questions educators might ask students include the following:

> 1. What do the terms "material," the "embodied mind," and the "objectification" of the human body mean?
>
> 2. Can you find examples of the protagonist or other characters reporting that their bodies are acting "without" their minds or "without thinking"?
>
> 3. What are some of the problems with thinking about the mind as separate from the body?
>
> 4. Do characters experience objectification or objectify others? If so, who? Please provide examples.
>
> 5. How are the answers to your questions feminist? How are they not feminist?

When Does the Narrative Value Individualism or Money More Than a Community of People?

Another tool I teach my students to use when they evaluate feminism is to ask them to look at political economics: exactly when does the narrative place a greater value on individualism than the collective community? Does the narrative define corruption in terms of valuing profit-making over humanity? Anti-neoliberalist theory undergirds my thinking on this topic.

Many political theorists define *neoliberalism* as an economic theory that advocates for as much deregulation of the free market as possible. In *The Hunger Games*, neoliberalism manifests itself in the way the series values individual entrepreneurs, in how the human body is commodified (that is, viewed or used as a commodity), and in how the land itself is also commodified in terms that prove to be gendered. David Harvey (2005) argues that neoliberalism is "a theory of political economic practices that proposes that human well-being can best be advanced by liberating individual entrepreneurial freedoms and skills within an institutional framework characterized by strong private property rights, free markets, and free trade" (2). These issues are pertinent to feminism in the way that women are commodified in ways similar to the exploitation of the environment. The keywords for my argument in this section are thus (1) the "*entrepreneurial*," (2) the free market trading that leads to the *commodification* of the human body and (3) the "strong private property rights" that lead inevitably to the *exploitation of the land* (see Connors and Trites, "Neoliberalism's").

Neoliberalism advocates in favor of the individual entrepreneur rather than advocating for a regulated market economy that works to provide a collective social safety network for those in need. Teachers, students, and scholars who are interested in studying the phenomenon of the Girl on Fire will undoubtedly recognize that, as a literary trope, she is self-reliant and independent, able to sell her abilities in a marketplace where her services as a hero are valued, and she is entrepreneurial in her creativity and her ability to manipulate her own strengths so that she can transform the situation around her. Indeed, Pomerantz and Raby argue that neoliberalism has allowed YA literature to privilege the "smart supergirl" as a trope specifically because she has individually-defined talents that make her—more than others—a successful entrepreneur in the business of saving the world (291).

Katniss Everdeen was one of the earlier neoliberal "smart supergirls," which seems to be unsurprising, given that the novel hit the *New York Times* "Bestseller List" exactly three weeks after the market crashed in September of 2008. The book might have been released to relative obscurity had young readers not been eager to read about someone who could save a panicking country from the excesses of its financial leaders, from the aftermath of 9/11, and from the effects of the nation fighting wars in both Afghanistan and Iraq—the latter of which was surreptitiously waged in the name of access to cheap oil. Two points matter most to my argument: the super-smart hero of the post–2008 crisis needed to be young, since generations older than teen readers were the ones who had "messed things up." The corollary follows that the savior at that moment in time needed to be female, since the patriarchy was responsible for the financial crisis—an historical phenomenon reinforced after Hillary Clinton was defeated in the primaries by a male in August 2008. Ironically enough then, in September 2008, neoliberalism's focus on celebrating individual talent in the marketplace made it possible for a YA author like Collins to publish successfully on the topic of teen characters whose individual talents could save the world from its own male, neoliberal financial and political leaders.

Readers of The Hunger Games trilogy need look no farther than Panem's President Snow for an exemplar of the white, patriarchal individual talent corrupted by an overzealous interest in his own power and profit. Katniss is the young, female antidote to his neoliberal self-interestedness. She says of him: "I know him to be the consummate survivor. It seems hard to believe he didn't have a retreat somewhere, some bunker stocked with provisions where he could live out the rest of his snaky little life," even if the rest of the Capitol were to perish (*Mockingjay* 360). Snow believes that if the Capitol "released its grip on the districts for even a short time, the entire system would collapse" (*Catching* 21). In other words, as the leader of the Capitol, he casts himself as the superspecial savior of Panem. Snow, however, also knows that the entire economy of the Capitol is dependent on the resources the districts supply. As Katniss observes: "The Capitol's fragile because it depends on the districts for everything. Food, energy, even the Peacekeepers that police us" (169). Snow can only control Panem when he can control both its human and its material capital.

But Snow is little more than a pimp, albeit as successful and entrepreneurial as any pimp could possibly be. He commodifies young people, allowing twenty-three children's bodies to be slaughtered in the annual Hunger Games. Tributes are nothing to him but useful, exploitable, objectified bodies. As Snow tells Katniss: "We both know I'm not above killing children, but I'm not wasteful. I take life for very specific reasons" (356). Snow's "very specific reasons" for murder reduce children to use-values; that is, they are only valuable for how they can be used to give him power. And those who survive the arena as victors, Snow further commodifies. He sells victors' bodies to citizens of the Capitol who wish to exploit the young person sexually. As one of those victors, Finnick, says: "President Snow used to … sell me … my body that is…. I wasn't the only one. If a victor is considered desirable, the president gives them as a reward or allows people to buy them for an exorbitant amount of money. If you refuse, he kills someone you love. So you do it" (*Mockingjay* 170). Feminist theorists Martha Nussbaum (257) and Rae Langton (228–29) identify the exploitation of the human body as a feminist issue because exploited bodies are always already objectified: denied agency, silenced, and violated—a process that can happen to men, as Finnick demonstrates, but that has historically been perpetrated more often by males against the female body and/or the queer body. As a result of Snow exploiting him while he lives in the Capitol, Finnick himself becomes an entrepreneur of information. He trades on the gossip he learns in the bedroom to leverage power for himself, and he later reveals via a national videocast information about how Snow himself rose to power by poisoning his enemies. Together, Finnick and Haymitch are able to reveal to Katniss how Snow's economy works. It is simple, manipulative, and vicious: he maintains his dominance as the entrepreneur in chief by using children, selling victors' bodies, and selling out those victors' loved ones.

In 1975, Annette Kolodny traced the relationship between a patriarchy that exploits women in the same way that land is exploited:

> America's oldest and most cherished fantasy [is probably] a daily reality of harmony between man and nature based on an experience of the land as essentially feminine—that is, not simply the land as mother, but the land as woman, the total female principle of gratification—enclosing the individual in an environment of receptivity, repose, and painless and integral satisfaction [4].

Ynestra King argues that industrialism (like neoliberalism) "reinforces the subjugation of women" (19). Karen J. Warren is an ecofeminist who argues that the patriarchy rationalizes systems of oppression to justify "the domination of nonhuman nature (and/or animals) by humans" (57). Neoliberalism is often condemned by ecocritics, who argue that neoliberalism encourages business enterprises to expand economic production by moving into new territories, which necessarily creates environmental tensions (Pellizzoni and Ylönen 4). Ecofeminism has thus linked a strong connection between the exploitation of women's bodies and the exploitation of natural resources. Women and the land are not to be conflated as constructs; rather, the comparison lies in the similar way they are exploited.

Sean P. Connors notes this process at work in The Hunger Games trilogy: "Collins criticizes an oppressive patriarchal conceptual framework that treats marginalized groups of humans, including females, as raw materials it can remake for its own benefit.... [Katniss's] involvement in the Hunger Games can be construed as a metaphor for the violence that society inflicts on young women" (Connors 143). Katniss and her family depend on the land to nourish and nurture them; the Capitol, on the other hand, depends on the Districts to feed them, and the Capitol also depends on technology (muttations, video broadcasting, surgical alterations, and the arenas of the Hunger Games themselves) to control and dominate the people of Panem and their land (Connors 144–45). The Capitol "dehumanizes residents of the districts" (150)—in part by "conflating them with raw materials and goods they produce"—so Tributes from District 12 are costumed in the opening ceremonies in clothing that metonymically links them to either coal or the fire it produces, just as the citizens of the Capitol mine and exploit both the people and the land of District 12 (Connors 147; see also Baker 203).

As Roxanne Harde notes, "the bodies of those children figuratively *become* their home districts" (57, emphasis added). Harde defines how Katniss's body symbolizes the Appalachians: "Her body stands ... in for her homeland, an ecosystem repeatedly destroyed and rejuvenated" by constant mining and exploitation (57); her skin is "olive"; she is named for an "aquatic plant" that grows in the region, and she feels most grounded when she is ensconced within the Appalachians' verdant grounds (58). Moreover, Harde interprets the processes [Katniss's] body undergoes—preparatory processes, such as aesthetic interventions and training; medical processes to heal the trauma she suffers, such as bone fusion and skin grafts—as representative of the exploitive processes visited upon the Appalachian range ... with its actual history of underground, strip, and mount-top removal mining, and its fictional destruction at the hands of the Capitol (58).

Harde also notes that Katniss's body "reinforces the connection of her female body to the rolling contours of the Appalachians" (64). In other words, the neoliberal forces of the Capitol exploit the land and environment, the bodies of children from every district (who are equated with the land on which their district is situated), and the bodies of the victors who survive the carnage of the arena. In one grim way, the Capitol could be said to be egalitarian in exploiting males and females equally—but ecofeminism helps us understand that the exploitation of *anything* is a feminist failure (see also Connor and Trites).

Feminist critiques of neoliberalism and feminist theories of ecocriticism provide yet another dimension that demonstrates the range of possibilities for feminist expression in YA literature. Some YA novels may foreground ecofeminism, as Karen Hesse's verse novel about Dustbowl Oklahoma in the 1930s, *Out of the Dust* (1997), does. Others may offer a direct critique of neoliberalism, as in M.T. Anderson's dystopic critique of consumerism, *Feed* (2002). Neal Shusterman relies on feminist critiques about commodifying the adolescent body in his dystopic *Unwind* (2007). But the most complex feminist novels rely on ecofeminism to critique the commodification of the body and neoliberalism's emphasis on individual entrepreneurialism simultaneously, as occurs in Sherri L. Smith's novel about the future of New Orleans, *Orleans* (2013), and in Alaya Dawn Johnson's dystopia *The Summer Prince*, set in Brazil (2013). Both of these novels involve Girls on Fire saving others amidst the exploitation of teenaged bodies; the exploitation is driven by neoliberal forces that hierarchize society and exploit both nature and the local environs. And both of these Girls on Fire favor collective support over entrepreneurial competition.

Additional questions educators might ask students about the relationship between feminism and neoliberalism include the following:

1. What do the terms "neoliberalism," "entrepreneurial," "commodification," and "exploitation of the land" mean in a feminist context?

2. Does this story, or others that you know, feature a "smart supergirl"? Is she saving the world because no one else can? Are her special abilities believable? Is too much expected of her? Does the story explain why it must be a girl who "saves the world"?

3. When are bodies turned into "things" or valued only for being bodies (not people) in this story? Is someone else making a profit from those people-as-bodies or exploiting them?

4. How is nature or the land exploited in this novel? Is a patriarchal government rationalizing that exploitation of the land? If so, how?

5. Are women's bodies equated with the land? If so, are both women's bodies and the land being similarly exploited?

6. How are the answers to your questions feminist? How are they not feminist?

The goal of all of the questions I have posed in this essay are intended to be three-fold: (1) to help determine students' ability to use terminology correctly; (2) to identify students' ability to understand that feminism is a multi-variate method of critiquing literature and (3) to assess students' metacognitive ability to self-reflect about their own learning.

Conclusion

No singular rubric will satisfy our ability to analyze all Girls on Fire in terms of feminism. A Second Wave model that emphasizes power (i.e., gender roles, independence, strength, and empowerment) provides one way to place these narratives on a spectrum ranging from "sexist" to "feminist." A Third Wave tool is more relational (voice, choice, and community) and can be used to assess novels along a similar spectrum. Material feminism reminds us to read for the impact of the material on characters and also how to examine the body's agency, as when we look for instances of objectification (Trites, *Twenty-First Feminisms* 86–93). Anti-neoliberalist theory helps us read for an overvaluation of individual entrepreneurship and the commodification of both the body and the land. Girl on Fire narratives, however, are best assessed using all of these measures together. The ideas that I have identified are all established principles of feminism that can help teachers, readers, and students understand the complexity of the Girl on Fire's relationship to gender, embodiment, empowerment—and to feminism itself. Thinking in terms of gradations rather than binaries can helps students' critical thinking and critical reading as they learn to think of "a range of possibilities" rather than thinking in terms of black or white. Additionally, discerning readers will have observed that feminism does not involve male-bashing or depriving men of power, so these issues help students think about an important social movement in more complex terms. Feminism involves *equality*, especially in terms of rights under the law, opportunity, and access to social power, regardless of race, gender, ability, orientation, religion, or any other factor. The Girl on Fire at her best seeks justice for herself and for all others.

Ultimately, the Girl on Fire is a leader. As a leader, she must have vision, strength, integrity, and inspire others to follow her. But to be a feminist leader, she must also recognize the agency of those around her, support others, listen thoughtfully, be caring and aware of human embodiment and the consequences of trauma, and she must work for the greater good, rather than her own personal gain. She does not necessarily need to define "happily ever after" in terms of being heteronormatively married, as the eighth-grader in my opening anecdote had unconsciously internalized. Indeed, many fictional characters meet these qualifications. Wonder Woman comes to mind, as does Dumbledore, but they are not teenagers. If being a teenaged leader who meets all these criteria seems like a tall order, well then, that might just explain why

there are so few entirely feminist Girls on Fire depicted in YA literature—
yet. But me? I have faith in the future.

WORKS CITED

Anderson, M.T. *Feed*. Candlewick, 2002.
Baker, Carissa Ann. "Outside the Seam: The Construction of and Relationship to Panem's Nature." *Space and Place in the Hunger Games*. Eds. Deidre Anne Evans Garriott, Whitney Elaine Jones, and Julie Elizabeth Tyler, McFarland, 2014, pp. 198–219.
Childs, Ann M.M. "The Incompatibility of Female Friendships and Rebellion." *Female Rebellions in Young Adult Dystopian Fiction*, eds. Sara K. Day, Miranda G. Green-Barteet, and Amy L. Montz, Ashgate, 2014, pp. 187–201.
Collins, Suzanne. *Catching Fire*. Scholastic, 2009.
_____. *The Hunger Games*. Scholastic, 2008.
_____. *Mockingjay*. Scholastic, 2010.
Connors, Sean P. "'I Try to Remember Who I Am and Who I Am Not': The Subjugation of Nature and Women in *The Hunger Games*." *The Politics of Panem*, ed. Sean P. Connors, Sense, 2014, pp. 137–56.
_____, and Roberta Seelinger Trites. "Neoliberalism's Erasure of Race in Young Adult Fiction: Sherri L. Smith's *Orleans* as Counter-Example." *Raced Bodies, Erased Lives*, eds. Miranda Green-Barteet and Meghan Gilbert-Hickey, UP of Mississippi (forthcoming).
Foucault, Michel. *History of Sexuality, Volume I*. 1976, translator Alan Sheridan, Vintage, 1995.
_____. *Power/Knowledge: Selected Interviews and Other Writings, 1972–1977*. Ed. Colin Gordon, Pantheon, 1980.
Friedan, Betty. *The Feminist Mystique*. Norton, 1963.
Grosz, Elizabeth. *Volatile Bodies: Toward a Corporeal Feminism*. Indiana UP, 1994.
Harde, Roxanne. "'[I]t's My Skin That's Paid Most Dearly': Katniss Everdeen and the Appalachian Body." *The Embodied Child*, eds. Roxanne Harde and Lydia Kokkola, Taylor & Francis, 2017, pp. 57–69.
Harvey, David A. *A Brief History of Neoliberalism*. Oxford UP, 2005.
Hesse, Karen. *Out of the Dust*. Scholastic, 1997.
Johnson, Alaya Dawn. *The Summer Prince*. Levine, 2013.
King, Ynestra. "The Ecology of Feminism and the Feminism of Ecology." *Healing the Wounds: The Promise of Ecofeminism*, ed. Judith Plant, New Society, 1989, pp. 18–28.
Kolodny, Annette. *The Lay of the Land: Metaphor as Experience and History in American Life and Letters*. U of North Carolina P, 1975.
Lakoff, George, and Mark M. Johnson. *Philosophy in the Flesh: The Embodied Mind and Its Challenge to Western Thought*. Basic, 1999.
Langton, Rae. *Sexual Solipsism: Philosophical Essays on Pornography and Objectification*. Oxford UP, 2009.
Lisa. "The Hunger Games Is Not a Feminist Masterpiece." *The Fandomentals*, October 11, 2017, https://www.thefandomentals.com/hunger-games-not-feminist-masterpiece/. Accessed 22 February 2019.
Nussbaum, Martha. "Objectification." *Philosophy and Public Affairs*, vol. 24, no. 4, 249–91.
Paul, Lissa. "Enigma Variations: What Feminist Theory Knows About Children's Literature." *Signal*, Sept. 1987, pp. 186–201.
Pellizzoni, Luigi, and Marja Ylönen. *Neoliberalism and Technoscience*. Ashgate, 2012.
Pomerantz, Shauna, and Rebecca Raby. "Reading Smart Girls: Post-Nerds in Post-Feminist Popular Culture." *Girls, Texts, Cultures*, eds. Clare Bradford and Mavis Reimer, Wilfred Laurier UP, 2015, pp. 287–311.
Sarkeesian, Anita. "The Hunger Games Novel and Katniss Everdeen." *Feminist Frequency*, 10 April 2012. https://feministfrequency.com/video/the-hunger-games-katniss-part-1-the-novel/. Accessed 13 March 2019.
Shusterman, Neal. *Unwind*. Simon & Schuster, 2007.
Smith, Sherri L. *Orleans*. Penguin, 2013.

Stark, Rachel. "Why Katniss Is a Feminist Character (And It's Not Because She Wields a Bow and Beats Boys Up)." TOR.COM, 21 March 2012. https://www.tor.com/2012/03/21/why-katniss-is-a-feminist-character-and-its-not-because-she-wields-a-bow-and-beats-boys-up/. Accessed 13 March 2019.

Thaller, Sarah. "A Feminist Bait-and-Switch: The Hunger Games and the Illusion of Empowerment." *Parlor: A Journal of Literary Criticism and Analysis*, 21 September 2016. https://www.ohio.edu/parlour/news-story.cfm?newsItem=04A7BBE4-5056-A874-1D563D477E575CA0. Accessed 1 March 2019.

Tilton, James. "The Hunger Games and Feminism." Prezi.com, 11 October 2017. Accessed 17 March 2019.

Trikha, Ritika. "The Awesome Career Lessons in *The Hunger Games*." *Business Insider*. 10 March 2012. https://www.businessinsider.com.au/career-lessons-from-hunger-games-2012-3. Accessed 22 February 2019.

Trites, Roberta Seelinger. *Twenty-First-Century Feminisms in Children's and Adolescent Literature*. UP of Mississippi, 2018.

_____. *Waking Sleeping Beauty: Feminist Voices in Children's Novels*. U of Iowa P, 1997.

Warren, Karen J. *Ecofeminist Philosophy: A Western Perspective on What It Is and Why It Matters*. Rowman and Littlefield, 2000.

Williams, Kyndall. "The Gender-Neutral Games." *Of Foxes and Hedgehogs*. 28 March 2012. https://offoxesandhedgehogs.wordpress.com/2012/03/28/the-gender-neutral-games/. Accessed 22 February 2019.

ADDITIONAL RESOURCES ON FEMINISM AND THE HUNGER GAMES TRILOGY

Day, Sara K., Miranda A. Green-Barteet, and Amy L. Montz, eds. *Female Rebellion in Young Adult Dystopian Fiction*. Routledge, 2014.

Dunn, George A., and Nicolas Michaud, eds. *The Hunger Games and Philosophy: A Critique of Pure Treason*. Wiley, 2012.

Garriott, Deidre Anne Evans, Whitney Elaine Jones, and Julie Elizabeth Tyler, eds. *Space and Place in the Hunger Games*. McFarland, 2014.

Guanio-Uluru, Lykke. "Female Focalizers and Masculine Ideals: Gender as Performance in Twilight and the Hunger Games." *Children's Literature in Education*, vol. 47, no. 3, 2016, 209–24.

Hansen, Kathryn Strong. "The Metamorphosis of Katniss Everdeen: The Hunger Games, Myth, and Femininity." *Children's Literature Association Quarterly*, vol. 40, no. 2, 2015, 161–78.

Manter, Lisa, Lauren Francis. "Katniss's Oppositional Romance: Survival Queer and Sororal Desire in Suzanne Collins's the Hunger Game S Trilogy." *Children's Literature Association Quarterly* vol. 42, no. 3, 2017, pp. 285–307.

Meeusen, Meghann. "Hungering for Middle Ground." *The Politics of Panem*, ed. Sean P. Connors, Sense, 2014, pp. 45–61.

Pharr, Mary F., Leisa A. Clark, Donald E. Palumbo. *Of Bread, Blood, and the Hunger Games: Critical Essays on the Suzanne Collins Trilogy*. McFarland, 2012.

Ruthven, Andrea. "The Contemporary Postfeminist Dystopia: Disruptions and Hopeful Gestures in Suzanne Collins' *The Hunger Games*." *Feminist Review*, vol. 116, no. 1, pp. 47–62.

PART TWO

#MeToo: Sexual Realities, Activism and Empowerment

Young Adult Literature and Girls on Fire as Fuel for Teaching the #MeToo Movement

ARIANNA BANACK, CAITLIN METHENY
and AMANDA RIGELL

In October 2017, a tweet by Alyssa Milano asking sexual assault survivors to reply "me too" sparked a cultural firestorm (@Alyssa_Milano). As of September 2018—after nearly a year of trending—the phrase #MeToo had been used on Twitter over 19 million times, representing the magnitude of sexual assault and harassment (Pew Research Center). The Girl on Fire has emerged as a strong, intersectional character and role model in young adult literature (YAL) and real life in response to the pivotal cultural movement of #MeToo. Because the Girl on Fire spirit can represent degrees of inner strength, advocacy, bravery, and resilience, pairing her character with women in the #MeToo movement illustrates how individuals can come to exhibit these characteristics gradually over time, moving through their trauma to develop inner strength and serve as a role model for others. As this reckoning takes hold, educators need to be equipped with the tools to discuss these important topics with their students (Colantonio-Yurko, Miller, and Cheveallier 2; Cleveland and Durand). The #MeToo movement is not an issue limited to Hollywood or the pages of a YA novel; it is an issue relevant to students and teachers in schools today. With that in mind, this essay offers implications of the Girl on Fire and the #MeToo movement for educators to explore in their classrooms alongside engaging activities for students.

For decades, Laurie Halse Anderson's novel *Speak* has encouraged young women to tell their stories of sexual assault (Cleveland and Durand), and the recent republication of *Speak* in graphic novel form suggests that it has sustained relevance for the nearly twenty years since its release. Following the example of Anderson's seminal text, contemporary YAL authors continue to tackle the #MeToo movement, providing insight and criticism of modern rape culture (Gamerman). While more YA novels are addressing #MeToo, educators and researchers also recognize the importance of discussing rape culture and the #MeToo movement with young people; for example, adolescents who read *Speak* were shown to have "significantly lower levels of rape myth acceptance in both boys and girls" (Malo-Juvera 420). By using YAL as a vehicle to discuss the Girls on Fire in #MeToo, "it is possible to engage young teens in meaningful discussions, resulting in change" (Malo-Juvera 420) surrounding topics of sexual violence and speaking up.

This essay explores the relationship between the Girl on Fire represented in YAL and women in society who embody her spirit. From the 150-plus USA Gymnastics team members who testified about sexual assault by their physician to Dr. Christine Blasey Ford's testimony before the Senate Judiciary Committee, Girls on Fire have begun to fight for a space to tell their stories, both in the public eye and on the pages of YAL. The different ways female protagonists embody the spirit of the Girl on Fire will be examined in four young adult realistic fiction novels—*Shout, Speak, Moxie,* and *The Nowhere Girls.* Additionally, these literary representations of sexual assault are used to draw comparisons to current activists in the #MeToo movement with the intent of inspiring student readers to action through service learning opportunities.

Due to the ELA Common Core State Standards's ("English Language Arts Standards") emphasis on thematic analysis, character development, and close reading skills, we believe a secondary or post-secondary English classroom is the best setting to implement these ideas. However, because sexual violence may be covered in health sciences courses, and social movements addressed in social studies, we encourage teachers to use our suggested activities as an opportunity for interdisciplinary lessons and discussion. Making space to discuss #MeToo and Girls on Fire in a curriculum is important as "students should understand the issue of sexual violence as a traumatic and real part of the lived human experience, especially because young adults are heavily represented in sexual violence statistics ... 42.2% of rape victims first experience rape before the age of 18" (Colantonio-Yurko, Miller, and Cheveallier 2). For implementation options, teachers could choose one of the YA novels as a whole class read and suggest the others as supplemental reading, use all four texts in a literature circle model, or pair one of the YA novels with a canonical text.

We acknowledge that teachers' curricula are tightly constructed and at times prescriptive, but we believe that teaching novels that feature the Girl on

Fire in the context of #MeToo is both timely and necessary. The #MeToo movement is an important cultural movement prevalent in the media and should not be ignored in our classroom curricula. Bringing this conversation into our classrooms allows teachers to correct misconceptions about sexual violence and can "offer students an opportunity to participate in the national discussion around this topic" (Colantonio-Yurko, Miller, and Cheveallier 9–10).

Sparking the Fire: Pre-Reading Activities

As educators prepare to discuss Girls on Fire linked to the #MeToo movement in the classroom, we suggest beginning the unit by asking students to reflect on their own definitions of Girl on Fire and #MeToo. Using a journal prompt, teachers might ask students to reflect on the following questions: *What does it mean to be a Girl on Fire? Who are examples of Girls on Fire in literature or real life? What is the #MeToo movement? How are Girls on Fire represented in #MeToo?* To scaffold an understanding of identifying features of the Girl on Fire for students who aren't familiar with the trope, teachers can start a whole class list on the board before asking students to journal independently. Some characteristics educators may list are: demonstrates bravery, an advocate for self and others, possesses inner strength, and is resilient. Educators can also play the song, "Girl on Fire" (Keys), as a way to inspire student thinking about Girls on Fire. Students can look at the song lyrics and music video to help determine characteristics of a Girl on Fire before they begin journaling. After students have had time to brainstorm in their journals, the class should return to the whole class list, discuss their responses and come to a consensus on the defining features of a Girl on Fire and begin contextualizing Girls on Fire within #MeToo.

To provide background information about #MeToo, educators can use the website metoomvmnt.org to share information about #MeToo's founder, Tarana Burke, and the historical context of #MeToo's roots. Educators might choose to create a PowerPoint with guided notes or ask students to explore the website on their own and report out their findings. Educators can also ask students to create a timeline, including influential figures, on the #MeToo movement. This timeline should then be displayed in the classroom and referenced throughout the unit.

Before reading, students can also complete an opinionnaire or anticipation guide by circling *strongly agree, agree, disagree,* and *strongly disagree* in response to statements like:

- If a girl is dressed a certain way she is asking for attention.
- Sexual violence most often occurs between strangers.

- If someone doesn't say "no," it doesn't count as rape.
- Males don't experience sexual violence.
- If a girl doesn't fight back it doesn't count as rape.
- Rape doesn't happen between two people in a committed relationship.
- If someone doesn't report a rape for years it's usually a lie.

Educators can continue to generate their own statements or they can use the 22-item Illinois Rape Myth Acceptance Scale (IRMA) to gauge students' acceptance or rejection of rape myths (U.S. Department of Health and Human Services). After debriefing, educators can build on this by ensuring that students understand key terms such as *rape* and *sexual assault* (Colantonio-Yurko, Miller, and Cheveallier 4; Malo-Juvera 410). Using easily accessible definitions from the Rape, Abuse, Incest & Neglect Network (RAINN) like "sexual penetration without consent" for *rape*, "sexual contact or behavior that occurs without explicit consent of the victim" for *sexual assault*, and "an agreement between participants to engage in sexual activity" for *consent* can help give students a foundation to build their learning upon. These definitions can be drawn upon throughout the entirety of the unit for students to reference when thinking about the types of sexual violence portrayed in a YAL text. Additionally, educators are encouraged to share statistics about sexual violence with students to help ground the #MeToo movement in facts (for example, every 92 seconds another person experiences sexual assault [RAINN]). By providing students with background information about #MeToo, important Girls on Fire, and sexual violence statistics, we believe that students will be better prepared to have conversations around these issues in a YA novel.

Stoking the Fire: #MeToo and YAL

The pressure on women to not report a sexual assault out of shame and fear of not being believed are central themes in much YAL published today as a direct reflection of current society. As women's voices are silenced in real life, so too are the characters in YAL. For example, in the YA novel *Saints and Misfits*, the protagonist, Janna, reflects on her sexual assault and says, "the truth is no one can know" (Ali 2). In this section we will explore fictional Girls on Fire within four YA novels, paired with real life activists who light the path for others to break their silence. In doing so, we will also suggest discussion topics and activities teachers can explore with their students.

Shout

Shout by Laurie Halse Anderson is a poetic memoir and call to action that weaves together personal stories from Anderson's life while simultaneously pointing out the failures of society's rape culture; through short vignette poems, Anderson explores her own experience with rape and also highlights struggles faced by other victims of sexual assault. Anderson's Girl on Fire attitude is prevalent throughout the memoir and encourages readers to stand up and speak their truth. Anderson recognizes the worry sexual assault survivors experience when deciding whether or not they should report a rape for fear of being taken seriously. Her poem in *Shout*, titled "ignore stupid advice," addresses this issue and states:

> Don't get raped
> cuz the jackasses and the idiots will say
> that's your fault too [232].

Students can juxtapose Anderson's prose with reality: in September 2018, Dr. Christine Blasey Ford came forward to share her account of sexual assault by Brett Kavanaugh after more than three decades. News and social media provided a medium for the onslaught of countless questions concerning the validity of Ford's narrative, including why she chose to stay silent for so long. Ford's public testimony and choice to stay silent are comparable to Laurie Halse Anderson's struggle to find "[her] courage to speak up twenty-five years after [she] was raped" (*Shout* 1). While recounting her experience of sexual assault throughout *Shout*, Anderson continuously reiterates her reasons for staying silent, noting that the people in her life "definitely didn't talk about rape" (67). Educators can ask their students to discuss the theme of silence prevalent throughout *Shout*, then compare the theme to Dr. Ford's experience. Teachers should implore students to discuss how Anderson and Ford were Girls on Fire, both throughout their periods of silence *and* after they broke their silence. For example, they might note how Dr. Ford showed great inner strength as she maintained her composure throughout her public testimony; she also demonstrated great bravery in publicly sharing her experience of sexual assault in front of a national audience. Teachers can discuss how Anderson demonstrates the Girl on Fire spirit of advocacy by educating students about sexual assault when she visits schools to speak and through encouraging her readers to speak up through her prose in *Shout*.

By establishing a connection between YAL, the current #MeToo movement, and actual Girls on Fire like Anderson and Ford, it becomes apparent that the issue of sexual violence does not exist in the confines of a classroom or on the pages of a YA novel, but reaches far beyond those limitations and into our current world. Anderson explicitly links YAL and reality when she addresses the #MeToo movement in *Shout* through a poem titled "#Metoo." She writes,

> As we support
> report
> reveal the violence
> they desperately want
> us
> to conceal [200].

Anderson refuses to be silenced and encourages survivors of sexual assault and allies of survivors to shout about the #MeToo movement. Educators can ask students how Ford and Anderson represent the spirit of a Girl on Fire through speaking about sexual assault. Students can examine video footage of the Ford trial (see Figure 4.1 for links) and analyze excerpts from *Shout* with the goal of identifying moments when Ford and Anderson act as a Girl on Fire. If students need scaffolding before diving into discussion, educators can provide examples of when Ford and Anderson embody the Girl on Fire. For example, Anderson exemplifies the Girl on Fire spirit when she discusses visiting schools to talk about her novel *Speak* and

> owns the microphone
> preaches facts about power
> and bodies and sex and violence
> speaks up, on fire [*Shout* 185].

After comparing Ford and Anderson as Girls on Fire, students might write their own poetry about Girls on Fire as a culminating project. Educators can use the following prompt for the project: *Using our reading of* Shout, *our examination of the #MeToo movement, and our learning about influential Girls on Fire, create a portfolio of poems around Girls on Fire and #MeToo. Your poems can be fictional or based on people/characters we've read about.* Students can share their poems in class with their peers or publish their work online using the website Underlined ("Create").

Speak

Told from the perspective of ninth grade Melinda, *Speak* by Laurie Halse Anderson examines the frightening reality of sexual assault and the ensuing emotional turmoil. The novel opens with the first day of high school, where Melinda is seen as an outcast by her peers because they believe she purposefully ruined a summer party by calling the cops; her peers do not know, however, that she was raped at the same party. Isolated and struggling with two conflicting emotions—ignoring the problem, hoping it will go away, and wanting to talk about it at the same time—Melinda withdraws more and more into herself, skipping class, ignoring school assignments, and rarely talking. It is Melinda's art teacher, Mr. Freeman, who helps her to cope with the emotions that she has tried to repress and find her voice to finally speak about and against her rapist.

When using *Speak* in the classroom, it is important for teachers to recognize and discuss with students that not all Girls on Fire are vocal revolutionaries on the front lines of large-scale social change. Like Melinda, some Girls on Fire are alone, silently struggling; yet, they demonstrate seemingly minute moments of courage, strength, and resistance. In addition to the pre-reading activities already outlined, teachers can ask students three questions that tie specifically to Melinda's experiences in *Speak*: *how does Melinda embody the Girl on Fire spirit?*; *what does it mean to be courageous or brave?*; and *what are different ways someone can "speak up" or resist assault and violence?* We recommend teachers revisit these three questions frequently while reading the novel to engage students with close reading of Melinda's thoughts, choices, and struggles. For instance, teachers can ask students to analyze Melinda's inner monologue and choices in several scenes involving Rachel. First, when Melinda toys with warning her about Andy, she says, "I stall. Rachel will hate me. (She already hates me.) She won't listen. (I have to try.) I groan and rip out a piece of notebook paper. I write her a note, a left-handed note, so she won't know it's from me" (*Speak* 152). Then again, when Melinda decides to write: "I didn't call the cops to break up the party. I called them because some guy raped me. Under the trees. I didn't know what to do" (*Speak* 183). The note-writing scene is also an important moment for teachers to discuss the fear of believability that victims often face when they choose to speak up because we see Rachel's negative reaction to Melinda naming Andy as her rapist.

Similarly, students should analyze and discuss several scenes significant to Melinda's character arc that demonstrate her Girl on Fire spirit and the eventual reclaiming of her voice. First, they can examine the scene in which Melinda asks herself "Was I raped?" (164) after refusing to name her trauma for the first two-thirds of the novel; next, students can discuss when she adds "Guys to Stay Away From: Andy Evans" (175) to the bathroom wall graffiti and sees the reactions from her peers and feels "like [she] can fly" (*Speak* 186). Finally, students should analyze the significance of the scene when she faces a second attack from Andy and yells "NNNOOO!!!" (194), and the entire last vignette of the novel where she acknowledges that despite her trauma, she can heal and grow (*Speak* 196–98). Furthermore, it would behoove all teachers to explicitly address the tree symbolism prevalent throughout the novel and to ask students to analyze how Melinda's art mirrors her mental health and Girl on Fire spirit. Early in the novel, when Melinda closes herself off from her friends and family in denial of her trauma, she struggles to even create a tree in art class; yet, as she begins to acknowledge what happened to her, she is able to draw trees in stages from death to regrowth. The development of the tree's health is a direct reflection of Melinda's mindset and the slow process to reclaim her voice. This is significant in connection to the real women of the #MeToo movement because it illustrates to students that not every Girl on Fire exhibits initial outward bravery and resiliency; however, as time passes they are able to claim and outwardly express the spirit of the Girl on Fire.

Following the pre-reading and during-reading discussion, *Speak* can serve as a powerful tool to help students consider the difficult decision that Girls on Fire, like Melinda, make to speak out against sexual assault. Melinda's experience highlights the struggle between wanting to wish away the trauma, while also feeling the need to talk about it, but simultaneously fearing no one will believe her. After reading this novel, we recommend that teachers draw students' attention to the real women who have found the voice to speak out against sexual assault many years after the trauma took place, such as the 150-plus U.S. women's gymnastics team members who testified against Larry Nassar, the 80-plus actresses who fueled the fire against Harvey Weinstein, and—as a possible extension of students' discussion with *Shout*—Dr. Blasey Ford's testimony against Brett Kavanaugh.

To introduce students to the many women who possess the Girl on Fire spirit through their decision to speak out against sexual assault, we recommend using rotational stations—so all students touch each artifact (i.e., a video, an article, etc.) for a short time—or a jigsaw activity—so small group "experts" can teach their peers about Girls on Fire in today's society. Figure 4.1 below outlines several options teachers may use to address other Girls on Fire in the stations or jigsaw activity. Furthermore, if teachers choose to use stations instead of a jigsaw, we recommend including a rotation dedicated to drawing and/or analyzing art as a reflection of the Girl on Fire spirit because art serves as a catalyst for Melinda's healing in *Speak*. For example, teachers may consider incorporating copies of paintings from various stages of van Gogh's life—as well as short contextual notations about him if students do not have prior knowledge—and ask students to analyze how the art reflects his well-being throughout his life. Alternatively, teachers may also consider pulling images of different mediums of art (i.e., paintings, graffiti, photography, sculpture, etc.) that express various tones, moods, and events and ask students to associate human emotions or experiences to the art.

When asking students to examine these sources in small groups, teachers should remind them to analyze how the women involved in these different sexual abuse scandals embody the Girl on Fire spirit. While we selected three timely and oft-referenced sexual abuse scandals for small groups to consider, teachers should not feel bound to these three examples and are encouraged to incorporate other Girls on Fire if they so choose. Additionally, teachers should ask students to brainstorm reasons why these victims kept quiet about the abuse for numerous years and what may have inspired them to finally speak out. Finally, teachers should ask students to analyze Melinda's thoughts, struggles, growth, and action in relation to how each of these Girls on Fire in American society spoke out.

Figure 4.1: Today's Girls on Fire

Teachers can assign as few or as many of the following sources for stations or a jigsaw activity asking students to analyze Girls on Fire in American society and compare their experiences to the struggles that Melinda faces in *Speak*.

Girl(s) on Fire	News Articles	Videos
Dr. Christine Blasey Ford	"How Christine Blasey Ford's Testimony Changed America," from *Time*	Watch Christine Blasey Ford's opening statement on CNN
U.S. Gymnastics Team	"'This Is Bigger Than Myself': How the Women of the U.S. Gymnastics Team Found Their Voice," from *Vanity Fair*	Olympian Aly Raisman's court address at Larry Nassar's sentencing on YouTube. Olympian Simone Biles's interview with Megyn Kelly from TODAY on YouTube
Actresses from Hollywood	"Harvey Weinstein Timeline: How the Scandal Unfolded," from the *BBC* "Harvey Weinstein Paid Off Sexual Harassment Accusers for Decades," from the *New York Times* Rose McGowan: The Interview, *Nightline* on ABC	

Moxie

Moxie, set in an east Texas football town, examines a schoolwide culture of toxic masculinity. Football players are celebrated as gladiators in a boys-will-be-boys tradition. They wear sexually explicit shirts, verbally taunt girls in class, rank them in an NCAA March Madness–style bracket, and initiate "bump-and-grab" assaults on girls in the hallways at school. When Vivian, the protagonist, sees a new student, Lucy Hernandez, endure such treatment, she feels compelled to fight back. After launching an anonymous *zine* (magazine) inspired by her mother's Riot Grrrl past, she finds like-minded classmates who join her in subverting the male-dominated school culture. While she orchestrates a resistance movement behind the scenes, she also navigates her first romantic relationship with one of the "good guys," who, despite his support of her activism, struggles to empathize with her experiences. The novel provides insight for adolescent readers into everyday Girls on Fire, intersectional feminism, male allies, perpetuation of power structures, and the power of print and social media in advocacy.

Vivian, the novel's protagonist, makes intentional choices about identifying herself as a feminist, reflecting her Girl on Fire spirit:

> it occurs to me that this is what it means to be a feminist. Not a humanist or an equalist or whatever. But a feminist. It's not a bad word. After today it might be my favorite word. Because really all it is is girls supporting each other and wanting to be treated like human beings in a world that's always finding ways to tell them they're not [Mathieu 269].

As teachers and students investigate *Moxie*'s implications for adolescent feminists, a close reading of the novel's language around the intersection of gender, race, and sexual identity can spark important classroom conversations. To facilitate a small-group or whole-class discussion, teachers might consider a "Quotes and Notes" activity, a double-entry journal activity to inspire student reflection about how *Moxie* mirrors tensions or gender-based conflicts in their own schools.

Figure 4.2: Quotes and Notes:
Intersectional Girls on Fire in *Moxie*

Teachers can use the excerpts and questions below to spark small group discussions or facilitate Socratic seminars to follow up on *Moxie*'s introduction of intersectional feminism.

Quotes	*Notes*
"I guess I was wondering," [Kiera] starts, "if this club is ... like ... open to new members?" "She means is it just white girls," Amaya says, finishing her lemon bar (167).	What are some of the barriers to talking openly about race?
"What's awkward is how this place is as fucked up when it comes to race as it is about anything else," she tells me ... "I mean, look at this cafeteria" (168).	How do you see gender, sexuality, race, or class impacting the groups and cliques at our school? When do you notice?
East Rockport High isn't just white girls, for sure. I glance over to	What does *representation* mean? How can clubs, groups, teams, or schools

Quotes	*Notes*
where Kiera and Amaya are sitting. I think about how in this one way, maybe Moxie could be even better than the Riot Grrrls. Even stronger (169).	practice fair representation of all students?
"And what's also gross is it's always a white girl who wins [March Madness], anyway. And all the girls who aren't white get pissed about it and it's like, wait, isn't it screwed up that anyone wins this bullshit in the first place?" I frown. "I never thought about it like that. That a white girl always wins." "Well, no offense," says Kiera, eyeing me, "but you're white, so you wouldn't have." But then she offers a wry smile, so I think it's okay. I smile back (244).	How do gender, race, sexual iden tity, and class affect the following characters: Vivian, Lucy, Kiera, Marisela, Emma, Claudia, and Seth? How are gender, race, sexual identity, and class represented in the novel?

As students embrace their own Girl on Fire identities, their teachers might consider encouraging them to write poems that represent their perspectives on feminism. Students can create "found poems" or blackout poems from the pages of *Moxie,* create an acrostic poem using words like *feminist, feminism, Girl on Fire,* or read excerpts from *Shout* as exemplars of free style prose. Students can journal in concentric circles about their identities (girl, student, athlete, daughter, friend, person of color, sister, person of faith, etc.) and choose which lens they want to use to express their views on gender equality. Ana Castillo's poem "We Would Like You to Know" (81), which talks back to stereotypes about Mexican immigrants, provides an excellent mentor text for girls and women to use to speak their truths about growing up as a Girl on Fire as they talk back to stereotypical portrayals of women. These activities give students autonomy to express their learning in a creative and personal format.

Beyond the novel's utility as a text to open a dialogue on how to be a Girl on Fire and feminist, *Moxie* also examines the significance and potential of male allyship. Seth, Vivian's boyfriend, is kind and supportive, and as their relationship evolves, Vivian helps him aspire to listen actively to women. As the book ends, he says, "But I promise that from now on I'm going to try to listen better about the stuff I can't totally understand because I'm a guy" (Mathieu 316). This character's emergent understanding is the beginning of an awareness that can be further fostered in the classroom through examination of texts like *Moxie*.

Moxie opens the door for conversations about educating male allies, a critical part of ending rape culture and toxic masculinity, and teaching boys that the spirit of the Girl on Fire isn't just for girls. In an essay for *Time*, Laurie Halse Anderson writes:

> Teenage boys are hungry for practical conversations about sex. They want to know the rules. They want to be the good guy, the stand-up, honorable dude. Their intentions might be good, but their ignorance is dangerous. Our society has begun talking a bit more openly about these issues, but that doesn't mean teenage boys suddenly have all the information they need.

In order to support male students who seek to become allies, teachers might consider highlighting stories of male survivors of harassment and assault, men who have been outspoken in their support of women, and information that will help boys and men understand the #MeToo movement with greater empathy. Some editorials, profiles, essays, and articles that might facilitate discussions of male allyship include:

- *Vanity Fair*'s profile of male survivors who have chosen to speak out: "'I Was Terrified, and I Was Humiliated': #MeToo's Male Accusers, One Year Later."
- *The Washington Post*'s profile of female students who chose a restorative justice approach to educate male peers who rated their attractiveness: "Teen boys rated their female classmates based on looks. The girls fought back."
- George Yancy's op-ed for the *New York Times* admitting and decrying his own sexism: "#IAmSexist."
- Laurie Halse Anderson's essay for *Time* about speaking to teenage boys about sexual harassment and violence: "I've Talked with Teenage Boys About Sexual Assault for 20 Years. This Is What They Still Don't Know"
- Jason Reynolds' afterword for the 20th Anniversary edition of *Speak* (Anderson, 2019), an open letter to boys about their relationships with women.

Students of all genders can begin examining and questioning power structures like the ones portrayed in *Moxie*. For example, the principal's son, Mitchell, is the primary sexual offender in the book. The principal denies all allegations against his son. He funnels money to the school's average football team, of which Mitchell is the captain, while the nearly-state-champion girls' soccer team wears uniforms from the 1990s. Building on this discussion, teachers might ask students to explore power imbalances in their immediate communities. This analysis might take place at a micro-level, asking questions like: *Who has the highest discipline rates in the school? Who earns the most positive recognition at school? Are there disparities between how different athletic teams are treated? What about clubs vs. athletics? Who is called on more in classes? What about in STEM classes? How are sex education classes structured at our school?* Or the approach might be a macro one: *What are some of the wage imbalances (like gender lines) in our community? How does the national sports culture shape local sports culture? How is masculinity portrayed in mainstream media? How is femininity portrayed on social media? What restrictions does social media place on women's bodies? What are some gender disparities across careers?*

For adolescent students who aren't yet enfranchised, facing down power structures may feel intimidating or overwhelming. In our ELA classrooms, we can begin with literary magazines, class blogs, or online discussions, and encourage students to embrace the Girl on Fire spirit and share their work publicly through publication when they are ready. One publication resource for adolescent readers is NewPages Young Writers Guide ("Writers Resources").

Teachers of adolescent readers could consider mini-research projects for students, tracing a history of feminist movements, historic Girls on Fire, and the three waves of feminism. Opportunities for comparison-contrast studies abound as students discuss how early feminists disseminated information and organized their movements, then reflect on the impact of social media in today's Women's March, #MeToo, #BelieveWomen, #WhyISpokeUp, and #TimesUp moments and their significance in organizing for action. Students will be able to see how Girls on Fire have evolved throughout history to become important leaders and catalysts for change in our current society.

Finally, the publication at the center of *Moxie*, Vivian's handmade zine, is also an important catalyst for discussion in a YAL-centered classroom. Vivian's Girl on Fire spirit through grassroots activism, within her own sphere of influence, and Lucy's choice to share the student walkout during the book's climax on social media, can spark conversation about the roles of print and digital media and the influence of Girls on Fire in the #MeToo movement. Teachers might consider establishing a makerspace for print or digital zine creation as part of their novel study of *Moxie*. Vivian's growing understanding of Third Wave Feminism provides a lens for students to begin exploring the movement themselves. Barnard College presents helpful resources for zine creation, including video tutorials, through their Zine Library ("Teaching with Zines").

The Nowhere Girls

The Nowhere Girls by Amy Reed is a realistic fiction novel brimming with Girls on Fire—from the three protagonists, Grace, Rosina, and Erin, to the secondary characters. Educators will find many role models in this text who demonstrate to students that there are various ways to embody the Girl on Fire spirit. *The Nowhere Girls* begins with Grace, the new girl at school, who learns about a former student named Lucy who was run out of town after accusing a group of popular boys of gang raping her. Many students in the school believed Lucy, but didn't speak up for her and ultimately, the boys were not charged and Lucy left the town. As Grace makes friends with Rosina and Erin, she discovers more about Lucy's story and the rape culture that is perpetuated in the community and school. To fight back against the injustices women in their town endure, the three girls decide to form an advocacy group called "The Nowhere Girls."

If educators choose to use the anticipation guide outlined in the earlier pre-reading section, they can add statements about student advocacy to further reflect *The Nowhere Girls*. Statements could include:

- Adolescents are not capable of enacting social change.
- Social change only occurs with radical action.
- A good leader must be loud and outgoing.
- Nobody will take an adolescent advocacy group seriously.

During reading, educators should highlight the moment Grace, Rosina, and Erin begin to embrace their inner Girl on Fire. They anonymously e-mail a call to action to the girls in their school: "Are you tired of being silent? … We will meet Thursday after school in the basement conference room of the Prescott Public Library…. Are you ready to do something? Are you ready to take matters into your own hands? Join us. Together, we are stronger than they are. We will not be silent any longer" (Reed 114–15). This is their first step towards creating their advocacy group and, ultimately, changing the rape culture in their community. Throughout the novel, the girls continue sending emails, holding meetings, posting flyers in their school, and advocating for the truth to be told. As the group of "Nowhere Girls" demand justice for Lucy and accountability for the men who live in Prescott they find they are stronger together. When the group arrives at the local police station demanding for their stories to be heard, Grace says, "The sound is deafening…. It is all the girls, all their voices, calling out as loud as they can. They burn down the darkness. They brand the night" (Reed 399).

The variety of characters in *The Nowhere Girls* gives educators a chance to ask students to analyze the different ways a person can be a Girl on Fire. The students can discuss the differences between Cheyenne, a girl who reports another rape by a popular boy in school, Margot, who takes control of the in-person "Nowhere Girl" meetings, Grace, Erin, and Rosina, who organize "The Nowhere Girls" behind the scenes without asking for recognition, and many other characters who seize the opportunity to speak up. As students read, they can create a character chart where they compare the different characters that act as Girls on Fire, and contrast the ways in which they do so.

Figure 4.3: The Nowhere Girls Character Chart

Students can use this chart to compare all the Girls on Fire featured in *The Nowhere Girls.*

Character Name	Girl on Fire Characteristics	Girl on Fire Moments	Textual Evidence
Grace	Courage	Starting the Nowhere Girls and holding the first meeting	"There has to be a way we can reach all the girls of the school and bring them together" (Reed 110).
Margot	Leadership	Leading the second Nowhere Girls meeting	"I want you to know that this is the kind of grassroots organizing that leads to real and lasting change" (Reed 142).

It is important to recognize that Girls on Fire do not need to take on the world alone, and students can analyze the many small, but significant moments in *The Nowhere Girls* when the characters work together to affect change. Through their character chart, journal prompts, and class discussion, students can identify the little acts of bravery in the novel where the characters embody the Girl on Fire spirit; for example, Erin gathering all the student's email addresses, the three girls sending the first email, and driving one student to the police station to report a sexual assault. Small acts of bravery and advocacy can lead to bigger change, which is an overarching theme *The Nowhere Girls* demonstrates to students.

While *The Nowhere Girls* is a fictional text, there are current advocacy groups that students can learn about during this unit. The Redbrigade Lucknow group, for instance, is an organization based in India dedicated to stopping sexual assault. Their website states:

> In 2011, I along with a group of 15 girls, most of them the victim of one or other form of sexual assault decided to fight back. Ours is a group of Survivors. We started an awareness campaign regarding women issues through street plays and workshops under the name Red Brigade; dressed in red and black, red denoting danger and black denoting protest. Learnt self-defense techniques and started training/equipping other girls with the self-defense techniques ["About Us"].

It is important for educators to point out that the founders of Redbrigade Lucknow are adolescents, similar to the characters in the book and the students who may be reading the novel. This fact may be empowering for adolescents who are reading the text by helping them to understand that there are successful teen advocacy groups in the world. Students can explore the Redbrigade Lucknow website and take notes on their mission, vision, and specific outreach efforts. As a culminating project, students can create a website (either online using Wordpress or using a paper template) for *The Nowhere Girls* group using the Redbrigade Lucknow's website as a model. They can rewrite the "manifesto" found on pages 149–51 in *The Nowhere Girls*, create mission and vision statements, a slogan, a symbol, and develop outreach programs they believe The Nowhere Girls would want to implement. If educators used the anticipation guide during pre-reading activities, they can implement it again at the end of the novel. We suggest instructors hold onto the pre-reading worksheets and ask students to compare their post-reading answers; it may be beneficial to assess if any answers change after reading *The Nowhere Girls,* discussing Girls on Fire, and learning about international advocacy groups.

Spreading the Fire: Inspiring Student Action

With the wide array of harassment, hate, and divisiveness in the world today, it is important to instill characteristics of a caring society in our future leaders. Madeline Kunin, former deputy secretary for the Department of Education, furthered this realization when she stated, "Service-learning resurrects idealism, compassion, and altruism … we cannot survive as a nation unless we hold onto these qualities and teach them to our children" (National Commission on Service-Learning 38). It is for this reason that we recommend teachers include a service-learning activity as the culminating project to conclude the Girls on Fire unit plan; more specifically, we encourage teachers to consider implementing a *Community Action* project using the activism from the YA novels as inspiration for students to elicit change within their communities.

Terry and Bohnenberger outline a service-learning typology on three tiers of student engagement with service-learning. Tier I, *Community Service,* involves volunteering and increasing awareness of the community (25). Tier II, *Community Exploration,* moves beyond general awareness as students begin to explore and engage with the community (26). Tier III, *Community Action,* involves students applying their gained knowledge through the awareness, exploration, and engagement phases to have a real impact on their community (26).

We believe *Community Action* is an appropriate medium for students to engage with the themes of empowerment from sexual assault and the Girl on Fire spirit because of the widespread and lasting effects of service-learning implementation. Four overarching themes highlight how service-learning positively impacts students' academic learning, civic responsibility, personal and social development, and career exploration (National Commission on Service-Learning 25–28). Perhaps most significantly, in tracing the arc of a Girl on Fire, students involved in service-learning increase their knowledge of community issues, develop a greater understanding of politics and ethics, and feel an increased desire to make a difference as active members of society. They develop a stronger sense of self, feel more confident in their own social competency, become better communicators, acquire problem-solving skills, show empathy towards others, embrace diversity, and exhibit fewer problem behaviors (Conrad and Hedin 65–67; National Commission on Service-Learning 26).

A Catalyst for Change: YAL-Inspired Service Learning

As a culmination to the Girl on Fire unit using the aforementioned novels, we suggest several options for students to engage in community action projects. One idea for service learning may be for students to create an anti-harassment campaign aimed at their schools or immediate community. Students can research current campaigns, like Time's Up, and create their own anti-harassment action plan to share with the community (idea adapted from "The Reckoning"). They can share their campaign through organizing community meetings, posting flyers, sending e-mails, promoting it on social media, and partnering with local community organizations. Students might also create a series of YouTube videos to share as a part of their campaign. As a mentor text, students should watch late night talk show hosts like: "Samantha Bee, Stephen Colbert, Trevor Noah and Jimmy Fallon [who] have [weighed] in on the #MeToo movement with passion and humor. Let students watch one or more of the excerpts from the shows above…. Just as late night hosts do, they should use specific evidence … other resources and their own experiences to defend their position" (Proulx, Pepper, and Schulten). By publicly sharing their knowledge, students can embody the Girl on Fire spirit through service learning and activism in their local community.

To further expand and extend the poetry portfolio assignment we've outlined with *Shout*, educators can add an advocacy extension by asking students to present their poems, paired with facts about the #MeToo movement, to the staff and students in their school. Students can read their poems and share information about #MeToo in the school auditorium during a school- or grade-wide assembly. Students might also present resources for people who experience sexual assault and offer suggestions for how other students can represent the spirit of a Girl on Fire in their daily lives. The scope of this project can be widened by including the community; a similar event might be held at a local parks and recreation site or community center where students are able to share their work in a public forum.

Throughout *Speak*, Melinda's art projects reflect her mental health. As an extension to the stations rotation and/or the jigsaw activity we've described, students could embark on a community art installment to empower Girls on Fire. For example, students may create artistic representations detailing their understanding of the experiences of Dr. Blasey Ford, Olympian Aly Raisman, actress Rose McGowan, etc. Alternatively, students may create their own representations of the #MeToo movement: their opinions, their reactions, their goals, their struggles. An option to incorporate "fire" imagery to further reflect the Girl on Fire spirit could be given to students as well. This project can be accomplished on a small scale within the classroom or grade level—displayed on the walls within the room or down a common hallway—or it can be broadened to reach a larger audience. With school permission and assistance from the art staff, an empowering and inspirational mural may be created on the school grounds. With support from the community, this project may extend to a public space as well, or the public could be invited into the school for a community viewing session. While Melinda's chosen medium for expression is illustration, students should not be limited to paper and pencil for their artistic representation of the Girl on Fire spirit. Teachers should encourage students to create web-based art, write and perform music, produce a video, paint, write, and act out a theatrical performance, etc.

To extend *The Nowhere Girls* website project into an advocacy project, students can create a class blog where they post resources about sexual assault, compose blog posts that share personal stories (anonymously and/or with permission), and highlight influential Girls on Fire in the #MeToo movement. Students may also wish to interview and feature advocates within the school building or community itself. The blog can serve as a safe space for students to share experiences and resources, as well as inspire change. Students can ask that their blog be added to the school website, shared on social media, and e-mailed to the school listserv. As students maintain the blog, a natural extension may be to form an in-person club to discuss the blog content and highlight other issues in the community they wish to advocate for.

In *Moxie*, Lucy Hernandez tells Vivian about a club at her former school in Houston called GRIT: Girls Respecting and Inspiring Themselves:

> We even had a couple of guy members. We did fund-raisers for the local women's shelter and talked about stuff that we were concerned about. I was hoping there would be a club like that here. So I could meet other feminists, you know? [Mathieu 77].

In the toxic culture of their school, the Moxie movement Vivian launches relies on anonymity to maintain the security of individual girls, rather than being recognized as a school club. Their need for anonymity is a cautionary tale for K–12 teachers who may be overlooking oppressive sexual climates in their own schools. When the students in *Moxie* walk out of school, Vivian notes that "It's the most engaged I've seen [the teachers] all year" (Mathieu 298).

A natural extension of *Moxie* into an advocacy project is teacher-student collaboration to create recognized communities of action within their schools. Extracurricular clubs like Lucy's GRIT would give students forums for voicing their experiences and concerns around gender-based harassment or assault, and could provide school administrators an opportunity to honor student voices while establishing student and staff conduct policies. Clubs that focus on allyship might look to Gay-Straight Alliance models. Clubs focusing on raising awareness of sexual equality issues might consider establishing cultural-relevance-minded book clubs modeled after ProjectLIT to foster discussion and exploration of other young adults taking on advocacy roles. Students looking to create a chapter of a national organization can find a list of current student and youth organizations on Speak Out's website ("Links to Student and Youth Organization"). By encouraging students to form an advocacy-based group grounded in issues they are passionate about, teachers can create spaces and opportunities for students to take action within their community.

Through service learning activities such as these, students will have the chance to put the Girl on Fire spirit into action. While we as teachers can give students opportunities and tools, ultimately they must blaze their own path to inspire change within their sphere of influence. Our hope is that through the reading of these novels and inclusion of service-learning projects, students will feel inspired to apply and extend their learning about #MeToo and Girls on Fire outside the confines of the classroom.

Blazing Forward: Implications for Educators

Girls on Fire exist in our classrooms, the YA novels we love, and throughout our world today. The Girl on Fire has transcended her association with Katniss and the pages of YA dystopian novels to become synonymous with the characteristics of courage and advocacy. As #MeToo has become an international movement, Girls on Fire can be found speaking out in the media and in YA novels that educators may wish to feature in their classrooms. In this essay we have outlined several examples of how teachers might help students embody the Girl on Fire spirit, both through reading YAL and examining the experiences of Girls on Fire in today's society. For additional education about furthering the important work of advocacy, teachers should visit Everyday Advocacy's website ("Become an Everyday Advocate") for tips to facilitate and encourage students to embody the Girl on Fire spirit and develop an action plan for change in light of the #MeToo movement.

WORKS CITED

"About Us." *Red Brigade Lucknow.* 2017, Retrieved from www.redbrigade-lucknow.org/about-us/ourmission.html, Accessed 29 Mar 2019.

Ali, S.K. *Saints and Misfits.* Simon & Schuster, 2017.

@Alyssa_Milano."If you've been sexually harassed or assaulted write 'me too' as a reply to this tweet." *Twitter,* 25 Oct. 2017, 4:21 p.m., Retrieved from www.twitter.com/Alyssa_Milano/status/919659438700670976?ref_src=twsrc%5Etfw%7Ctwcamp%5Etweetembed%7Ctwterm%5E919659438700670976&ref_url=https%3A%2F%2Fwww.theguardian.com%2Fculture%2F2017%2Fdec%2F01%2Falyssa-milano-mee-too-sexual-harassment-abuse.

Anderson, Laurie Halse. "I've Talked with Teenage Boys About Sexual Assault for 20 Years. This Is What They Still Don't Know." *Time,* 15 Jan. 2019, http://time.com/5503804/ive-talked-with-teenage-boys-about-sexual-assault-for-20-years-this-is-what-they-still-dont-know/. Accessed 27 March 2019.

_____. *Shout.* Viking, 2019.

_____. *Speak.* SPEAK, 1999.

_____. *Speak.* Square Fish, 2019.

Barnard Zine Library. "Teaching with Zines." Retrieved from https://zines.barnard.edu/teaching withzines. Accessed 8 May 2019.

BBC News. "Harvey Weinstein Timeline: How the Scandal Unfolded." *BBC,* updated 10 Jan. 2019, https://www.bbc.com/news/entertainment-arts-41594672. Accessed 17 Dec. 2018.

"Become an Everyday Advocate." *Everyday Advocacy.* Retrieved from www.everydayadvocacy.org/become-an-everyday-advocate. Accessed 8 May 2019.

Bradley, Laura. "'I Was Terrified, and I Was Humiliated': #MeToo's Male Accusers, One Year Later." 4 Oct. 2018, *Vanity Fair,* vanityfair.com/hollywood/2018/10/metoo-male-accusers-terry-crews-alex-winter-michael-gaston-interview. Accessed 31 March 2019.

Castillo, Ana. "We Would Like You to Know." *My Father Was a Toltec: And Selected Poems.* Anchor Books, 2004, pp. 81.

Cleveland, Erika, and Sybil Durand. "Critical Representations of Sexual Assault in Young Adult Literature." *The Looking Glass: New Perspectives on Children's Literature,* vol. 17, no. 3, 2014.

Colantonio-Yurko, Kathleen C., Henry Miller, and Jennifer Cheveallier. "'But She Didn't Scream': Teaching About Sexual Assault in Young Adult Literature." *Journal of Language and Literacy Education,* vol. 14, no. 1, 2018, pp. 1–17.

Conrad, Daniel, and Diane Hedin. "The Impact of Experiential Education on Adolescent Development." *Child and Youth Services,* vol. 4, no. 3/4, 1982, pp. 57–76.

"Create." *Underlined.* 2019, Retrieved from www.getunderlined.com/create. Accessed 8 May 2019.

Edwards, Haley Sweetland. "How Christine Blasey Ford's Testimony Changed America." *Time,* 4 Oct. 2018, http://time.com/5415027/christine-blasey-ford-testimony/. Accessed 17 Dec. 2018.

"English Language Arts Standards." Retrieved from www.corestandards.org/ELA-Literacy. Accessed 8 May 2019.

Gamerman, Ellen. "#MeToo, Coming to a Bookstore Near You." *Wall Street Journal,* 31 Jan. 2018. Retrieved from www.wsj.com/articles/metoo-coming-to-a-bookstore-near-you-1517408548. Accessed 29 Mar 2019.

Grigoriadis, Vanessa. "'This Is Bigger Than Myself': How the Women of the U.S. Gymnastics

Team Found Their Voice." *Vanity Fair Hive*, 29 May 2018, https://www.vanityfair.com/news/2018/05/how-the-women-of-the-us-gymnastics-team-found-their-voice. Accessed 17 Dec. 2018.

Kantor, Jodi, and Megan Twohey. "Harvey Weinstein Paid Off Sexual Harassment Accusers for Decades." *The New York Times*, 5 Oct. 2017, https://www.nytimes.com/2017/10/05/us/harvey-weinstein-harassment-allegations.html. Accessed 17 Dec. 2018.

Keys, Alicia. *YouTube*, YouTube, 19 Oct. 2012, www.youtube.com/watch?v=J91ti_MpdHA.

"Links to Student and Youth Organization." *Speak Out*. www.speakoutnow.org/resource/links-youth-and-student-organizations. Accessed 8 May 2019.

Malo-Juvera, Victor. "Speak: The Effect of Literary Instruction on Adolescents' Rape Myth Acceptance." *Research in the Teaching of English*, vol. 48, no. 4, 2014, pp. 407–427.

Mathieu, Jennifer. *Moxie*. Roaring Brook Press, 2017.

Me Too Movement. https://metoomvmt.org/. Accessed 29 Mar 2019.

National Commission on Service-Learning. *Learning in Deed: The Power of Service-Learning for American Schools*. 2002, Retrieved from www.ed253jcu.pbworks.com/f/Learning DeedServiceLearning_American+Schools.PDF. Accessed 27 Mar 2019.

"Olympian Simone Biles: Larry Nassar 'Took a Part of Me That I Can't Get Back.'" *YouTube*, uploaded by Megyn Kelly TODAY, 31 Jan. 2018, https://www.youtube.com/watch?v=9d-Z7V5kZvQ.

Pew Research Center. *Number of Twitter Posts Mentioning the #MeToo Hashtag, Oct. 15, 2017-Sept. 30, 2018*. 2018, Retrieved from www.pewresearch.org/fact-tank/2018/10/11/how-social-media-users-have-discussed-sexual-harassment-since-metoo-went-viral/ft_18-10-11_metooanniversary_hashtag-used-19m_times/. Accessed 29 Mar 2019.

Proulx, Natalie, Christopher Pepper, and Katherine Schulten. "The Reckoning." *The New York Times*. 25 Jan. 2018. Retrieved from www.nytimes.com/2018/01/25/learning/lesson-plans/the-reckoning-teaching-about-the-metoo-moment-and-sexual-harassment-with-resources-from-the-new-york-times.html. Accessed 29 Mar 2019.

Rape, Abuse, and Incest National Network. "About Sexual Assault." Retrieved from https://www.rainn.org/about-sexual-assault. Accessed 29 Mar 2019.

Reed, Amy. *The Nowhere Girls*. Simon Pulse, 2017.

"Rose McGowan: The Interview." *Nightline*. ABC, 31 Jan. 2018, https://abc.go.com/shows/nightline/episode-guide/2018-01/31-013118-rose-mcgowan-the-interview. Accessed 17 Dec. 2018.

Schmidt, Samantha. "Teen Boys Rated Their Female Classmates Based on Looks. The Girls Fought Back." 26 Mar. 2019, *The Washington Post*, washingtonpost.com/lifestyle/2019/03/26/teen-boys-rated-their-female-classmates-based-looks-girls-fought-back/?utm_term=.2be518b46855. Accessed 31 March 2019.

Terry, Alice W., and Jann E. Bohnenberger. "Service Learning: Fostering a Cycle of Caring in Our Gifted Youth." *Journal of Secondary Gifted Education*, vol. 15, no. 1, 2003, pp. 23–32.

U.S. Department of Health and Human Services. *Updated Illinois Rape Myth Acceptance Scale (IRMA)*, 2010. Retrieved from https://www.hhs.gov/ash/oah/sites/default/files/ash/oah/oah-initiatives/paf/508-assets/conf-2011-herman-irma.pdf. Accessed 29 Mar 2019.

"Watch Aly Raisman Confront Larry Nassar in Court." *YouTube*, uploaded by CNN, 19 Jan. 2018, https://www.youtube.com/watch?v=HWWFB6RZwgg.

"Watch Christine Blasey Ford's Opening Statement." *CNN*, 27 Sept. 2018, https://www.cnn.com/videos/politics/2018/09/27/christine-blasey-ford-full-testimony-senate-hearing-vpx.cnn.

Yancy, George. "#IAmSexist." 24 Oct. 2018, *The New York Times*, nytimes.com/2018/10/24/opinion/men-sexi.-me-too.html?module=inline. Accessed 30 March 2019.

Say Something, Do Something

Creating Allies and Agents
Through The Nowhere Girls *on Fire*

KATIE SLUITER *and* GRETCHEN RUMOHR

One of the most heartbreaking moments of Katie's sixteen years of teaching came the day a senior B.A. student tearfully admitted to Katie that she had been sexually assaulted as a freshman and had never said anything to anyone about it. Resulting from the loneliness and shame that followed the assault, her grades in school plummeted, her behavior became erratic, and she engaged in numerous acts of self-harm. At the peak of her despair, she attempted suicide and was placed in a mental health facility. After bearing witness to that student's testimony, Katie began to wonder how many others were walking the halls of school burying painful memories of violation. According to the National Sexual Violence Resource Center, "one in five women will be raped at some point in their lives" and "91% of victims of sexual assault and rape are female." Additionally, "one in four girls will be sexually abused before they turn 18." These statistics suggest that a quarter of our female students will endure some sort of sexual assault before graduation.

As an intervention in this culture of sexual violence, Tarana Burke founded the #MeToo Movement in 2006, giving advocacy and resources to the myriad survivors of sexual assault. Describing the movement's mission, she stated on the organization's website, "Our vision from the beginning was to address both the dearth in resources for survivors of sexual violence and to build a community of advocates, *driven by survivors*, who will be at the forefront of creating solutions to interrupt sexual violence in their communities" (emphasis added). In 2017, women in the entertainment business began to meet and the Time's Up Movement "was born out of the need to turn pain into action" ("Time's Up Now"). Hollywood stars, directors, producers, and others in the industry pushed the movement to the public by wearing "Time's Up" pins at award shows and other events to denounce sexual harassment, abuse, and discrimination in the workplace. Both the #MeToo and #TimesUp movements reach out to an entire population of women.

In addition to tools like those created by Burke and others, as English educators, we believe that the bridge to empowering students from helplessness to advocacy lies in teaching well-crafted literature for teens paired with authentic opportunities for writing. In her book *Teaching for Joy and Justice*, Linda Christensen explains, "I want students to understand that change doesn't just happen: People work for change, whether ending slavery, fighting for the rights of women, stocking grocery shelves with produce from local farms, or creating schools where all students, regardless of their ethnicity or their parents' income, receive a rigorous, engaging curriculum" (85). It is our job as teachers to help our students explore where change is needed, so they can become "on fire" for change, working constantly, working consistently, in their efforts to transform others' lives. Christensen begins teaching about writing for justice by helping her students define key terms (ally, target, perpetrator, and bystander) that will aid them in identifying injustices (85). Using quality young adult literature such as Amy Reed's *The Nowhere Girls*, teachers can guide students into grasping the roles that people take when an injustice occurs, specifically sexual assault and harassment.

Reed's novel also models what it means to be "on fire" for change. The "Girl on Fire" character that Sarah Hentges conceptualizes is one who is an injustice-fighting leader. She not only coordinates and advocates for justice, but she also inspires hope that a bigger change can take hold. *The Nowhere Girls* features not just one "Girl on Fire" character, but many, and is a text that can serve as the entrance students need to become engaged in discussing and writing for real change in their local communities.

In this essay we begin by unpacking the novel *The Nowhere Girls* by Amy Reed in order to show how the Girl on Fire is represented in the text and why it is an appropriate model for leading students to write for justice. We will outline before, during, and after reading activities that will guide students through understanding the magnitude of sexual assault and harassment as an epidemic in society, as well as provide opportunities for students to reflect on the roles of target, perpetrator, bystander, and ally. The objective then is that students will embody the spirit of the Girl on Fire and move from being a target, a bystander, or a perpetrator to an ally and, in some cases, an agent of change.

How The Nowhere Girls *Demonstrates Girls on Fire*

Reed's novel portrays not just a Girl on Fire, but also *Girls* on Fire. The book's three main characters—Grace, Rosina, and Erin—differ wholly in their histories, hobbies, families, and sexual orientation, yet unite toward a common goal. When Grace finds "Kill me now. I'm already dead" carved on her bedroom windowsill, she investigates and discovers that the carvings came from Lucy Moynihan, the former resident of the room, who was gang raped then left town after naming her assailants the year before (3). Horrified and angry, Grace teams with Rosina, a queer, punk Latina, and Erin, a science geek with autism, to lead a successful, Lysistrata-inspired grassroots revolt. Together, they convince their fellow female classmates to withhold all sex from all partners as they seek justice for Lucy, protest the misogynist culture at their high school, and advocate for sexual assault victims.

Aside from its engaging plot, there are other reasons why *The Nowhere Girls* is a worthwhile choice in a secondary English classroom. Reed portrays Girls on Fire through the characters' discussions about teenage sex and consent, considering how morality, authority, and religion—especially Christianity—dictate norms. In addition, Reed's use of "Us" as sporadic chapters—the point of view of several anonymous girls throughout the community—broadens each character's perspective to the archetypal experience of everywoman, lending voice to a variety of females at Prescott High. The "Us" chapters serve as a way for the reader to hear the voices of all female-identifying students in the novel, even those that may disagree with the main character's methods of overthrowing the misogynistic culture of their community. Overall, the text encourages readers to witness how nearly every woman learns to believe, and support, other women.

Preparing Students to Read

Considering the content of *The Nowhere Girls* and its description of sexual assault, it is imperative that students be provided multiple spaces where they can process and communicate any complicated feelings, experiences, or ideas that surface when reading the text. Overall, incorporating regular methods such as journaling, exit slips (responses students turn in as they leave class), and pair/share responses (student-to-student talk focusing on content and connections) can keep the lines of communication open and make it more likely that students will get the help they need if they encounter any triggering content. One obvious caveat regarding such communication is that teachers are mandated to report sexual assault if a student reports it, so they should be clear with students about that statute.

A variety of pre-reading activities such as a poll and opinionnaire can help students to better understand the severity of sexual assault against women in the United States, including national and local statistics, as well as to sort out their own beliefs and biases. Such activities can also help students to think ahead about the trauma that will be introduced in the novel and aid in student understanding of the roles played by the ally, target, perpetrator, and bystander in incidents of sexual assault.

Teachers can start with an anonymous poll of what students already know or have experienced in regard to sexual assault and/or harassment. This can be done via digital tools such as Padlet, Nearpod, or Pear Deck, which allow for student names to be hidden, but their answers made public. Students can engage in a digital version of the classic KWL (what do you Know, what do you Want to know, what did you Learn) chart, answering such background questions as: What percentage of women do you think have experienced sexual assault? Do you personally know anyone who has experienced sexual assault? Do you know what to do if you experience sexual assault? Would you tell anyone if you were assaulted? From there, students will move into a "Data Dig" activity where students do individual research to find answers to questions they still have (the what do I Want to know portion of the KWL) in order to familiarize themselves with national statistics about sexual assault. Tools such as Nearpod allow teachers to guide students through this activity collectively or individually, moving back and forth through tasks. The initial survey questions paired with students' data discoveries can lead students to write responses about what they learned, what surprised them, and any connections they can make (the "What did I Learn" portion of the KWL). These responses can then springboard small and whole group discussions about how rampant the problem of sexual assault is and where power—both negative and positive—resides when considering sexual assault, aiding students in identifying targets, bystanders, perpetrators, and allies.

An opinionnaire can also help students consider a focus question for the novel: Do I believe in lone wolf allyship and working for change, or is there power in numbers? Jeffrey Wilhelm's (2007) opinionnaire activity (see Figure 5.1) can support valuable pre-reading discussion, as having students sort themselves according to their answers and then dialogue about responses can build interest and frontload the importance of advocacy.

Once students have worked through their own prior knowledge, armed themselves with more background information, and clarified the roles of the ally, the bystander, the perpetrator, and the target, they will be prepared to begin reading *The Nowhere Girls*.

Supporting Students While Reading

Given the high-interest nature of *The Nowhere Girls*, students will likely read the novel quickly. As they read, we don't wish to hold them back, but rather help them consider textual themes about the need to stand up against sexual harassment and violence, the importance and power in female alliances, and the plausibility of teenagers effecting real change in their communities by being "on fire" for justice. Using articles from *Newsela* such as "They Spoke Out Before #MeToo About Sexual Assault," "In an Internet World, Teens See That Past Mistakes Live On," and "In These #MeToo Times," students can participate in a Jigsaw activity ("The Jigsaw Method"). To complete this activity, the teacher puts students into groups of three, giving one article to each student in the group. After taking time to read and annotate, students break off into "expert" groups—comprised of students who have all read the same article—to discuss what they read more deeply. The goal is to clear up any misunderstandings and collaborate on a clean, clear way to present the article. Students then move back to their original group and teach each other their articles. In a true jigsaw activity, students are assessed on all three articles, either in quiz format or, more appropriate for this subject, a writing prompt in which they need to reference all of the sources for their answer.

In using Jigsaw Methods, the wisdom of Kylene Beers and Robert E. Probst can help students to engage and comprehend the issue further as they re-read dense passages and consider contrasts, contradictions, and extreme language in each article. Students can also be asked: What do you suppose this particular *Newsela* article author would say about power in numbers? How is this belief similar to, or different from, your opinion about the lone wolf or the powerful pack? What would this *Newsela* article author say about question #3 (or others) in the opinionnaire? Finally, who are the targets, perpetrators, bystanders, and allies in these articles and how do they compare to the ones identified in *The Nowhere Girls*?

In addition to reading nonfiction articles to connect themes in *The Nowhere Girls* with real world application, students should read other creative and informative texts to see how others have treated the themes of sexual assault advocacy. Integrating complex texts into whole class novel study is a way to enhance the reading of the novel under study as well as teach Common Core State Standards (CCSS) that call for students to "read and comprehend literature, including stories, dramas, and poems" as well as "read and comprehend literary nonfiction in the [grade level] complexity band proficiently, with scaffolding as needed at the high end of the range." The CCSS also require students across secondary grades to compare works with similar themes and topics to texts in other mediums and genres. With this in mind, a powerful intertextual activity for *The Nowhere Girls* is a silent discussion.

For an effective silent discussion, the teacher will choose 4–6 short texts (depending on class size) that share themes that are relevant to *The Nowhere Girls*—specifically, the need to stand up against sexual harassment and violence, the importance and power of female alliances, and the plausibility of teenagers effecting real change in their communities. The texts should differ in point of view, genre, or medium. Possible pairings with *The Nowhere Girls* include: the Langston Hughes poem, "Theme for English B"; the Laurie Halse Anderson poem, "Shame Turned Inside Out" (Anderson 226); a sexual assault awareness infographic from the YWCA; a "living display" photo from the Ellsworth Air Force Base; one of the chapters in *The Nowhere Girls* titled "The Real Men of Prescott"; and an excerpt from page 297 of *The Nowhere Girls* (starting with "A girl looks around" and ending at the break). These texts are printed and put on large chart paper and situated around the classroom. The instructor then informs students that the first discussion of the class period will be done in silence. Students are grouped (three to five students) and given one of the pieces of chart paper to read. A visual timer is set for eight minutes as students silently read and then, with a pencil, write "I notice/I wonder" statements in the blank area of the chart paper around the printed text. If a member of the group wants to respond to another member's statement, they must do so in writing. When time is up, they will get up and move to the next piece of chart paper and spend eight minutes with that one. Again, students are encouraged to respond to comments and add their own. When each group has rotated through all six texts, students are given eight additional minutes to do a gallery walk and examine what their peers have written. At the end, students debrief with their group for two minutes before a full class reflection happens. Before the class period ends, students respond in their notebooks about how each text relates to what they know about targets, perpetrators, bystanders, and allies, making connections between the short texts and the characters in the novel.

Supplemental texts—both articles and other genres—will help students to visualize scenarios other than those illustrated in the novel so that they can begin to consider what it takes to become a Girl on Fire. In *The Nowhere Girls*, it takes the elements of Grace feeling unseen and unheard in her own family coupled with questions about the former denizen of her bedroom who appeared to feel the same way. The fire then is sparked when she realizes why Lucy felt "already dead." Rosina and Erin are more reluctant Girls on Fire, while some of the other female identifying students barely even flicker, even during the stir of excitement the group causes with its sex strike. So what sets students ablaze for justice? We are not convinced it is the teacher's job to provide this answer; rather, students should delve into this query themselves through student talk.

Well-designed discussion questions can also guide students toward

Figure 5.1: Pre-Reading Opinionnaire
The Nowhere Girls Pre-Reading Opinionnaire

Read each statement carefully. Circle whether you strongly agree, agree, disagree, or strongly disagree with the statement. Be prepared to defend your position.

1. It is possible to be powerful even if you are alone.
   Strongly Agree   Agree   Disagree   Strongly Disagree
2. Treating others with respect depends on how we respect ourselves.
   Strongly Agree   Agree   Disagree   Strongly Disagree
3. There is power in difference.
   Strongly Agree   Agree   Disagree   Strongly Disagree
4. Men and women are both responsible for the way women are treated.
   Strongly Agree   Agree   Disagree   Strongly Disagree
5. Sex can be used as a weapon.
   Strongly Agree   Agree   Disagree   Strongly Disagree

textual analysis and engagement. Such questions can be used in large and small group contexts as well as for the purposes of journal prompts, exit slips, and "turn and talk" options. Overall, students should be asked how power works to create justice in the novel, and whether there can be justice for Lucy without power. In addition, students should be asked how the novel encourages each of us to advocate for change, and how they wish to act for change after reading the novel. These questions can be asked during and after reading. Beyond general questions, Brian White's "authentic questions," which utilize prediction, author's generalization, and structural generalization, extend the work already put in motion by the data dig, Wilhelm's pre-reading opinionnaire, and the jigsaw discussion strategy. Throughout this questioning, students are encouraged to draw upon their own reactions as well as textual evidence as they respond. Such questions also engage CCSS-based concepts such as characterization, narrative structure, and detail. Examples of authentic questions include:

Prediction

- (After Erin sends out the email to all females at the school, page 122) So far, where do you see power residing in Prescott and its residents? In your opinion, how do you think power will be challenged after what Erin has chosen to do?
- (After reading "The Real Men of Prescott," page 104) Considering the blog's message, how do you think that gender will determine the men's power in this novel? (After reading about the Nowhere Girls' second meeting, page 151) How do you think gender will determine the women's power after this important meeting and manifesto?

How does this determination align with/differ from what you see in real life?

- (At end of novel) We learn that Eric Jordan now sees the Nowhere Girls in a different light—"a group, solid and formidable, and so much bigger than him … these girls are going to define his life as much as he has already defined theirs" (399). Do you think that Eric will become more aware of, and right, his wrongs? What about Eric's characterization leads you to this conclusion?

Author's Generalization

- (After the Nowhere Girls discuss ending the sex strike, pages 246–64) What do you suppose Reed is trying to communicate about the power of sex through the girls' discussion of the strike?
- (Throughout the novel) What do you think Reed is trying to communicate about power through depicting the differences in personality between Grace, Rosina, and Erin?
- (After Grace talks to her mother, page 270) What do you think Reed is trying to communicate about support as she describes the parent/child relationships of Grace, Erin, and Rosina?
- (Throughout the novel) Why do you think Reed included Amber in this story? What would you tell/do for Amber if given the opportunity?

Structural Generalization

- How do you suppose this novel would have differed if Rosina had discovered Lucy's words? In your opinion, would this have had power-related implications?
- Why do you suppose Reed told this story from the perspectives of Grace, Erin, Rosina, and "Us"? What might have been lost by focusing on only one perspective?
- The novel ends on a rather positive note, implying that the Nowhere Girls have come together and that crimes will be punished. How might this novel have differed if it had ended with Cheyenne refusing to report her assault? With the authorities discrediting Cheyenne?

Grounding each of these questions is the goal for students to recognize the various ways that power functions in the novel and, in turn, understand how power can function in their own life as they work for change.

Finally, there are a variety of sources that can be used to help students make text-to-self, text-to-film, and intertextual connections. *The Hunting Ground,* a documentary focusing on rape on college campuses, can be used prior to reading to help students understand the prevalence of sexual assault; it can also be used for post-reading reflection, helping students consider how they might advocate for safety and justice at their future college campuses. Prout's *I Have the Right To* is an advocacy book by a sexual assault survivor and is accompanied by a well-developed advocacy website; students could consider textual events in *The Nowhere Girls* and suggest how characters' rights were violated or upheld in light of textual information. For teachers wishing to do literature circles on the topic of sexual assault, there are several choices. *Exit, Pursued by a Bear* (Johnston) is one of the few young adult novels that, from beginning to end, demonstrates the ways that sexual assault victims *should* be treated (with respect and care). Students who read this text will find themselves encouraged and ready to help survivors. *Blood Water Paint* (McCullough), a historical young adult novel, explores how a sexual assault victim heals through art. And *Tradition* (Kiely) uses a multi-perspective approach to explore sexual assault on a boarding school campus. Kiely's discussion of what constitutes rape is especially valuable, and can fuel further class discussions about how to combat misconceptions about sexual assault. As students respond to each of the above resources, teachers can draw upon the Rape, Abuse, and Incest National Network, RAINN, (rainn.org), which provides a wealth of information, support, advice, and referrals for advocates and survivors alike.

Post-Reading Engagement and Beyond

Given that *The Nowhere Girls* describes our current culture of misogyny so compellingly, as students will discover through the supplemental texts provided, there are multiple opportunities to further examine the novel and apply what one learns personally. Thus, students can be encouraged to think beyond the text through intertextuality, community supports, writing, and digital advocacy. Through these modes, students will be able to take the role of ally to the next level and become an agent of change.

One text connected to *The Nowhere Girls* is Aristophanes' ancient Greek comedy, *Lysistrata*. In this play, the female residents of the Greek city-states are tired of their husbands warring with each other. One female resident, Lysistrata, manages to convince her fellow females to embark on a sex strike until their husbands agree to stop fighting. While this is an effective strategy, it is not without controversy, as their husbands beg for sex. *Lysistrata* is thoroughly entertaining as well as applicable to *The Nowhere Girls*. It is also rather short, and excerpts could even be utilized in an effort to have students do a side-by-side textual analysis: students could compare The Nowhere Girls' manifesto with Lysistrata's declaration—both of which happen rather early in both texts.

Aside from reading the play, students can further consider the power of sex throughout the centuries by watching the documentary, "Operation Lysistrata," which describes how two women originally desired to perform the play in order to protest the war in Iraq, but then used worldwide performances of this ancient play—ranging from England to Havana to Japan to Northern Greece to Iceland—to employ "grassroots activism, conflict resolution, community building and the role of art in a functioning democracy" in order to bring about world peace ("Culture Unplugged Studios").

There are also opportunities for students to become more aware of community resources in their efforts to reach out for help as well as support those working for justice. The "Find Your YWCA" button on the national ywca.org site can lead teachers to the organization's "Prevention and Empowerment" services, which strive to "[empower] young women to see themselves as leaders in creating change." Teachers can share these resources with students or, better yet, invite YWCA volunteers to the classroom to discuss matters relating to power, sexual assault advocacy, and specific ways students can get involved.

Creative writing offers another opportunity for students to examine the role of allyship. In her book *Teaching for Joy and Justice,* Christensen recognizes the value of "turning pain into power" through the use of poetry (16). In one chapter, she uses the poem "Knock Knock" by Daniel Beaty as a mentor text for writing a story about pain, and then describes how she asks students to write a letter poem giving themselves advice they need to hear. This assignment would work with *The Nowhere Girls,* too. After reading the novel, teachers could present Beaty's poem to students and guide them to write a letter poem both to themselves and to a character in the novel. Since a guiding principle throughout the novel study is that there is power in numbers, writing poetry is a way to put that idea into practice. As Christensen states, "sharing these stories helps lay our burdens down and makes us feel less lonely" (16). The letter format might also be a less intimidating form of writing for students than asking them to compose an original poem.

Beyond poetry, teachers can utilize the genres employed in *The Nowhere Girls* to help students write in similar ways. After reading the Nowhere Girls' manifesto (149–51), students could consider their own activist causes, and what they are willing to leverage to address them. The goal could be taking a stand against sexual assault; however, there could be students that wish to advocate for other causes, such as the environment, human trafficking, or gun violence in schools. Once the cause and the mode of advocacy has been identified, students can think of a possible audience for this message, and how best to reach that audience. They might even create several different versions of their message, shaped to each audience. Perhaps their audience is fellow classmates, with the result that an appropriate genre would be the school newspaper's editorial section, the newspaper's social media page, or their own social media account with judiciously-crafted hashtags in order to garner attention. Once this rhetorical triangle has been explored, students can read resources such as *The Atlantic's* "Manifestos: A Manifesto" and Megan Morgan's "How to Write a Manifesto." Students can consider whether adding photos or other images can enhance their message. Each of these steps can scaffold students' writing of their own manifestos, which can be published in impactful ways.

From Reading, to Writing, to Action

Each of the above goals and activities work as kindling for a fire, helping students to familiarize themselves with sexual assault, connect with literary characters who've experienced it and advocated for change, consider real-world research and applications, and write for change within the context of these new discoveries and experiences. The final step—taking action—can be on a collective or individual level: organizing a fundraiser to benefit a local women's shelter or YWCA; participating in a relevant charity walk or run; volunteering at a food or clothing bank that serves victims of domestic violence; and advocating for literacy programs that benefit women who are vulnerable to poverty and violence. Regardless of the action they take, the texts teachers choose, and the ways that students engage, it is important that teachers treat literature as a way to affirm, develop, strengthen, and maintain the value of empowering and life-changing curricular spaces for all people affected by sexual assault. Asking students to reflect upon the action that they organize and participate in can add yet another level of introspective engagement.

Managing Possible Objections

We are aware that this particular text—and the overall topic of sexual assault—is not free of controversy: it contains profanities, using a vernacular with which most youth would be familiar; it acknowledges sex as a pleasurable act, which could make some adults uncomfortable; and it discusses masturbation, which is rare in YA literature and adult literature as well. Such content could make the book a target for censorship; however, as shown with most banned books, the content would in reality make the text more high-interest. Considering some of these challenges, teachers could forgo teaching the book as a whole-class text, choosing instead to include it in their classroom library. They could also use it as part of a literature circle unit or identify and share excerpts that demonstrate characterization, description, or persuasion. Regardless of concerns, though, we note that *The Nowhere Girls* does not rely on the "pornification" of sex, as Reed writes about sensitive matters relevantly, honestly, and without drama. Of course, the manner in which an author treats sensitive subject matter may do little to assuage push back from parents. However, teaching our students about the real world—to engage this world and not just survive it—is of utmost importance for creating a better future, individually and collectively. We strongly believe that *The Nowhere Girls* exemplifies Christensen's roles of the target, the perpetrator, the bystander, and the ally, and represents the Girl on Fire trope as an exemplar for students who wish to move to allyship and advocacy.

For educators, this is the kind of book that could require a deep breath prior to teaching it. As teachers, we may need to channel our own inner "fire," though doing so could inspire other educators to do the same. After all, NCTE's Right to Read (2012) resolution tells teachers not to "[emphasize] their own safety rather than their students' needs," instead directing teachers to give "spirited defense" to brave books like *The Nowhere Girls*—books that "do not lie to the young about the perilous but wondrous times we live in, books which talk of the fears, hopes, joys, and frustrations people experience, books about people not only as they are but as they can be" (para. 17).

Works Cited

Anderson, Laurie Halse. *Shout: A Poetry Memoir*. Viking, 2019.

Beers, Kylene, and Robert E. Probst. *Reading Nonfiction: Notice & Note Stances, Signposts, and Strategies*. Heinemann, 2015.

Christensen, Linda. *Teaching for Joy and Justice: Re-imagining the Language Arts Classroom*. Rethinking Schools Publication, 2009.

Common Core State Standards Initiative, www.corestandards.org/.

Hanna, Julian. "Manifestos: A Manifesto: The 10 Things All Great Manifestos Need." *The Atlantic*, Atlantic Media Company, 24 June 2014, www.theatlantic.com/entertainment/archive/2014/06/manifestos-a-manifesto-the-10-things-all-manifestos-need/372135/.

The Hunting Ground. Directed by Kirby Dick. Chain Camera Pictures, 2015.

"In an Internet World, Teens See That Past Mistakes Can Live On." *Newsela*, 1 Oct. 2018, newsela.com/read/staying-power-of-mistakes/id/46414/.

"In These #MeToo Times, You Might Hear Your Music or See Art Differently." *Newsela*, 6 Feb. 2019, newsela.com/read/me-too-art-artists/id/49066/.

"INFOGRAPHIC: Sexual Assault Awareness Month." *YWCA Walla Walla*, www.ywcaww.org/saam-infographic/.

The Jigsaw Classroom. www.jigsaw.org/.

Johnston, E.K. *Exit, Pursued by a Bear*. Turtleback Books, 2017.

Kelly, Michael. *Operation Lysistrata*, 2008, www.cultureunplugged.com/documentary/watch-online/play/51971/Operation-Lysistrata.

Kiely, Brendan. *Tradition*. Margaret K. McElderry Books, 2018.

McCullough, Joy. *Blood Water Paint*. Penguin Group USA, 2019.

"Me Too. Movement." *Me Too Movement*, metoomvmt.org/.

Morgan, Megan. "How to Write a Manifesto." *WikiHow*, 29 Mar. 2019, www.wikihow.com/Write-a-Manifesto.

"National Sexual Violence Resource Center (NSVRC)." *National Sexual Violence Resource Center*, www.nsvrc.org/.

"Need to Talk? We're Here for You." *RAINN*, www.rainn.org/.

Prout, Chessy, and Jenn Abelson. *I Have the Right To: A High School Survivor's Story of Sexual Assault, Justice, and Hope*. Margaret K. McElderry Books, 2019.

Reed, Amy Lynn. *The Nowhere Girls*. Simon Pulse, 2017.

"Sexual Assault Awareness and Prevention Month Kicks Off with Living Di." *Ellsworth Air Force Base*, 11 Apr. 2016, www.ellsworth.af.mil/News/Article-Display/Article/807213/sexual-assault-awareness-and-prevention-month-kicks-off-with-living-display/.

"They Spoke Out Before #MeToo About Sexual Assault; Have Advice for Others." *Newsela*, 15 Feb. 2018, newsela.com/read/survivors-before-metoo/id/40377/.

"TIME'S UP Now." *TIME'S UP Now*, www.timesupnow.com/.

"Welcome." *YWCA West Central Michigan*, www.ywcawcmi.org/welcome/.

White, Brian. "Pulling Students Toward Meaning or Making Meaning with Students: Asking Authentic Questions in the Literature Classroom." *Language Arts Journal of Michigan*, vol. 9, no. 1, 1993, pp. 11–40.

Wilhelm, Jeffrey D. *You Gotta BE the Book: Teaching Engaged and Reflective Reading with Adolescents*. Teachers College Press, 2016.

Troubling Girls on Fire
in Young Adult Literature

*A Critical Examination of Systemic Violence
and Sexual Trauma in* Asking for It

KATE LECHTENBERG, JENNA SPIERING,
AMANDA HAERTLING THEIN
and NICOLE ANN AMATO

"I really wanted it to end differently though, to provide us with the message that there is hope for victims of rape and that they can win the fight against all the hate, shame, and pain they experience. I get the idea about truthfulness, but I just wanted to see a development of Emma's character into a stronger, determined person."

"I also had a real issue with the ending. Nothing was resolved which kind of made me feel like reading this book was a waste of my time."

"I wanted Emma to fight for justice, but that did not happen."

The quotations that frame this essay come from students in our young adult literature (YAL) courses in response to Louise O'Neill's novel, *Asking for It*. O'Neill's novel depicts 18-year-old Emma O'Donovan's experiences with a devastating sexual assault followed by persistent shame and humiliation from those in her family, school, church, and community who are invested in a patriarchal ideology wherein young men are "good boys" and girls like Emma are "asking for it." Although Emma and her family initially press charges against the young men involved in her assault, Emma ultimately concludes that she cannot survive the years of degradation she would have to endure in order to bring her case to trial.

Many of our students struggled to empathize with Emma, who is depicted as a prototypical unlikeable and narcissistic "mean girl" in the first half of the novel. And while students expressed greater empathy toward Emma after her sexual assault, the second half of the novel was nonetheless disappointing for many of our students who felt let down when Emma decided to drop the criminal charges against the boys who had raped her. As instructors, we were left wondering how we could encourage our students to more carefully consider not only the trauma Emma faced as a victim of rape, but also the systems and institutions that work against women and girls who decide to speak up about sexual violence.

Giving students a framework for considering individual and structural aspects of sexual violence is especially important since Emma's experiences in a patriarchal society call to mind current events. When United States Supreme Court nominee Brett Kavanaugh was accused by multiple women of sexual misconduct, we watched along with many women across the United States as one of Kavanaugh's accusers, Christine Blasey Ford, became a feminist hero of sorts when she publicly testified against Kavanaugh in a congressional hearing. Ford's direct and fearless testimony in an effort to disrupt institutional complicity in patriarchy, sexism, and sexual violence resembles feminist heroines within the YAL trope of Girls on Fire.

As described by Sarah Hentges, Girls on Fire—feminist protagonists who speak to the power of activism and resistance in leading to social transformation—are numerous in today's dystopian YAL. Katniss Everdeen, the protagonist who leads a social uprising in Suzanne Collins's *The Hunger Games*, is nearly synonymous with the Girl on Fire trope, which offers young readers examples of characters who, in the face of injustice, exploitation, and oppression, know what is right and are willing stand up and fight for themselves and others. What makes these characters especially compelling is that they feel real and aspirational. Hentges explains, "The Girl on Fire is rarely a perfect, infallible hero; she is most often a real girl struggling to find herself and keep her friends or family safe against impossible odds" (6). Hentges also notes that the stories of these brave, yet vulnerable girls typically end happily, or at least with peaceful resolution.

While this message of agency and empowerment is critical, in this essay we consider its limitations—especially with regard to victims experiencing the trauma of sexual violence. Readers may recall, for example, that as quickly as Christine Blasey Ford rose to prominence, she was brought down by a system that refuses to believe women who voice their experiences of sexual violence to enact change. Kavanaugh was confirmed and today sits on the United States Supreme Court. What did Ford accomplish as a Girl on Fire? While she wasn't successful in toppling the patriarchy in United States government, might she have accomplished something different? For other women? For herself?

In this essay we consider several key questions about what it means to be a Girl on Fire in the face of sexual trauma and the systemic complicity and violence that allow for such trauma. What does the trope of the Girl on Fire suggest about girls who don't "catch fire" when they experience sexual violence? What happens when the fire burns out and things don't end happily? In this essay, we explore these questions through an analysis of *Asking for It*, and we frame our essay with two key conceptual ideas that help us trouble the Girl on Fire trope in YAL depicting sexual violence in general and in *Asking for It* in particular: first, the blurring of reality and dystopia, and second, trauma as a sociocultural—rather than individual—event. We argue that O'Neill's novel offers an important counterstory to the Girl on Fire trope in dystopian YAL by providing a real and honest depiction of the paralyzing anxiety and depression that are often a response not only to the trauma of sexual assault, but also to systems, institutions, and ideologies that fail to believe girls and women.

Dystopian Fiction and the Blurring of Reality

In the closing scenes of *Mockingjay*, Katniss considers her relationship to reality, asking herself, "Real or not real? I am on fire" (Collins 348). After experiencing physical and emotional violence at the hands of the government, the loss of her sister, and the destruction of every close relationship that has sustained her, Katniss questions everything about herself, her relationship to her body, and her relationships with others. This conflict between what is real and what is not real is central to the Girl on Fire trope, which is rooted in dystopian fiction. Dystopian fiction as a literary genre is "not real" on multiple levels, both as fiction and as dystopian imagining of the possible consequences of today's injustices. At the same time, Hentges addresses the frequent blurring of the line between dystopian fantasy and Trump's United States in today's media, politics, and popular culture. She explains, "Dystopia imagines what the future will inevitably be … without intervention in the present" (Hentges 23). Comparisons between lived experiences in the United States today and Atwood's *The Handmaid's Tale* or Orwell's *1984*, for instance, bring the "real" of contemporary life into ever closer relation to the "not real" of dystopian fears that once seemed distant.

While Hentges's definition of dystopia provides a link between dystopia and reality, Emma's traumatic experiences with sexual violence in *Asking for It* offer a real/not real contrast that is nearly incomprehensible to many readers: we don't want it to be real, given contemporary mythologies of feminist progress and judicial fairness. The graphic violence of Emma's gang rape by a group of young men is difficult to comprehend on its own. However, the ways in which Emma is shamed by her peers, her parents, her church, social media, and the criminal justice system seems impossible to many readers, including students in our courses. In this sense, *Asking for It* requires us to confront the reality of patriarchal stances toward sexual assault and the objectification of women that seems nearly dystopic in its extreme vision of one community's response to sexual assault and one young woman's repeated shaming and devastation. Yet, O'Neill has reported that *Asking for It* is inspired by real events, namely the brutal sexual assault of one young woman and the subsequent community-wide defense of her perpetrators in Steubenville, Ohio (Sproull). What happens to Emma, then, is very real. In short, while *Asking for It* may not be a traditionally dystopian novel, we argue that the physical, emotional, relational, and institutional violence that Emma experiences at the hands of her rapists, family, community, and justice system invite us to consider dystopian questions about whether and how the boundary between reality and dystopia has been dangerously eroded.

Trauma as More Than a Singular Event

In troubling the Girl on Fire trope—especially with regard to sexual violence against women—we draw on Critical Trauma Studies to argue that Emma's assault is not a singular event that she can stand up against, but is instead a piece of a larger, more nuanced, and more persistent violence located in the fabric of her patriarchal social and cultural context that is enacted against her before and after the assault itself.

Derived from the Greek word for *wound*, trauma is defined as a violent, distressing, or disturbing event. Scholars of Critical Trauma Studies (Casper and Wertheimer), however, trouble event-based models of trauma, calling for a definition of trauma that considers the everyday effects of systems of oppression such as racism, classism, and sexism. In other words, how do we understand the effects of sexism and patriarchy if we only consider these effects in light of acts of extreme sexual violence? Defining trauma in relation to a singular event, in this case Emma's rape, fails to acknowledge the misogynistic and patriarchal social context in which Emma's rape occurred. Emma's rape then becomes exceptional rather than a result of systematic forces in her hometown and its larger social, cultural, historical, and political contexts. Emma's trauma and subsequent struggles become her responsibility to work through, and, when she doesn't work through them, she is seen as a failure.

A limited definition of trauma coupled with expectations of the Girls on Fire trope may allow readers like our students to struggle to understand Emma and the conclusion of her story. Our students' responses illuminate the consequences of viewing Emma's trauma as the result of a single event.

This view of trauma absolves Emma's community of responsibility and allows Emma to be seen as a "failure" for not standing up against her trauma with the sort of fearlessness, persistence, and righteous indignation expected of Girls on Fire.

In this essay, then, we argue that *Asking for It* depicts the persistent, systemic violence Emma experiences as a young woman in a patriarchal society. Through that depiction, her trauma is tethered not to a singular event that she might stand up against in the manner that readers have come to expect of a Girl of Fire, but is instead one element of a much more deeply ingrained violence that she must respond to through more nuanced and less overt forms of agency.

In the sections that follow, we first discuss some of the ways that Emma's experiences of systemic violence and trauma as a young woman in a patriarchal society impede her from responding as a traditional Girl on Fire. Then, we focus on Emma's responses to the violence and trauma she experiences, reconceptualizing what agency and being "on fire" might look like for girls and women who have similar experiences.

Systematic Violence and Persistent Trauma

Violence is an element found in much dystopian literature featuring Girls on Fire. Hentges writes, "In Girls on Fire novels, state violence is prevalent, individual violence is self-defense and survival, and collective violence is rebellion—a means toward change" (126). In other words, in Girl on Fire novels, experiences of violence are many and are met with agency, activism, and defiance. Given the prevalence of Girls on Fire in today's YAL, it is perhaps not surprising that readers like our students often want and expect Emma to fight back in the face of sexual violence, and are disappointed when Emma is rendered despondent and broken. However, Emma's devastation and lack of overt activism is a response not only to the acute sexual violence that she endures, but also to the many layers of systemic violence and injustice that create the conditions in which sexual violence is perpetrated and tolerated. As we detail below, Emma lives in a society that holds normative expectations for female physical beauty, "slut-shames" (e.g., Sweeney 1579) women as a means of controlling female sexuality, and is complicit in sexual violence against women by refusing to believe women or take action when sexual assault occurs. Each of these layers of violence and oppression contribute to Emma's responses to sexual violence and are important when considering why Emma does not—and cannot—become the sort of Girl on Fire readers have come to expect.

Expectations for beauty and sexuality. Throughout the first half of

Asking for It, Emma is depicted as constantly vigilant about her physical appearance. She is particularly concerned with how her appearance is perceived by the boys and men around her. Emma is depicted as preoccupied with appearing desirable to boys and she is resentful of anyone who she perceives to be more attractive. For instance, in reflecting on how she feels during sexual experiences, Emma explains, "During sex I'm thinking about what I look like, trying to make sure the other person is having a better time with me than they did with the last girl" (O'Neill 81). However, it is difficult to read Emma's thoughts on this topic as individual pathology. Rather, O'Neill depicts Emma's near-obsessive monitoring of her appearance as the "slow violence" (Hentges 126) of a community and a society that insists girls look and act in certain ways and punishes them when they do not conform.

Moreover, Emma is depicted as constantly judging her peers' appearances, in addition to her own. Each time the reader is introduced to a new character, Emma shares her inner-dialogue about the character's physical appearance. For instance, when she is greeted by a classmate before school, Emma thinks to herself, "It's Chloe Hegarty, her hair standing up in a halo of frizz at her hairline, breakouts all over her jaw and chin, one patch of acne crusted-over with yellow pus. I wish she would go to the dermatologist. I turn away, pretending I need to get something from my bag" (O'Neill 13). The reader is introduced to Ali, one of Emma's close friends, with the following observation: "She's wearing too much eyeliner, black goop crusting in the corners of her eyes" (9). Finally, prior to hearing that a new girl, described as pretty, has moved into her neighborhood, Emma thought, "I had been worried when I heard that until I saw Maggie and realized that, yes, she was pretty. But she wasn't prettier than me" (16–17).

It may be tempting for readers to see Emma's preoccupation with her own beauty and that of her peers as indicators of a shallow and narcissistic personality. But, at the same time, the reader witnesses the way that Emma's physical appearance is both celebrated and policed by everyone around her, allowing for a more complex consideration of why Emma behaves as she does. In the opening scene, Emma's mother comes into her bedroom, questions her choice of top, reminds her to take her vitamins and to watch her posture, and tells her she looks a little bloated, wondering, "Do you have your period?" (5). Later, Emma attends a soccer match where her dad calls her a "princess" before introducing her to another adult man who looks her up and down, saying, "You have a heartbreaker on your hands there, Denis. I'd say you must be beating them off with a stick" (47). Finally, Emma monitors her own gendered dispositions, for instance noting that "by the time the final bell rings, I am exhausted. I have to smile and be nice and look like I care about other people's problems or else I'll get called a bitch" (12). The gendered and sexualized manner in which Emma's physical appearance and feminine demeanor are policed in the first half of the novel reflect a culture that is systematically constraining—and violent—for women and girls.

Controlling female sexuality. At the same time that Emma is constantly encouraged to adhere to ideals of feminine beauty and sexuality, she is also cognizant of the expectation that she not appear *too* interested in her appearance—a fine line is drawn between being attractive and desirable and being too mature or self-involved. And, that line moves as Emma moves across social contexts in her world.

The novel illustrates a persistent culture of "slut-shaming"—one in which women and girls are punished for being perceived as sexually promiscuous in a society that rejects them if they are not sexually promiscuous enough. Emma feels compelled to consent to sexual experiences with boys because she wants to be well-liked by them and knows she is expected to be sexual, as she does in this memory from a recent party: "Kevin's hands on my shoulders, pushing me down, saying *Go on, come on Emma*. It seemed easiest to go along with it. Everyone is always saying how cute he is anyway" (27). At the same time, she knows that her sexuality is not acceptable to her family, her church, or the rest of her society. She explains, "Even before they come, I'm wondering how I'm going to make them keep their mouth shut about what we did or didn't do" (81).

Even before Emma's assault, it is clear that she has internalized the idea that sexual assault is the fault of girls and women, not boys and men. For instance, when Emma's friend Jamie is sexually assaulted, Emma tells her, "It's happened to loads of people. It happens all the time. You wake up the next morning and you regret it or you don't remember what happened exactly, but it's better not to make a fuss" (84). Further, boys in Emma's community repeat similar ideas, for instance, "'Girls are all the same,' Dylan says, rolling his eyes. 'Get wasted, get a bit slutty, then in the morning try to pretend it never happened because you regret it'" (27). While this is an overt example of slut-shaming, there are more subtle examples as well. For example, after Emma comments on the way an adult man had ogled her as she watched a soccer match, Jamie, referring to Emma's low-cut top, says, "'Well, what do you expect, princess? You're about to take someone's eye out'" (47), demonstrating the degree to which the girls themselves have internalized the slut-shaming rhetoric of the culture they live in.

These instances of internal and external policing and controlling of female sexuality illustrate the persistently objectifying and sexually violent culture that Emma is already a part of when her assault occurs.

Complicity in sexual violence. Emma's sexual assault marks the midpoint of the novel and from this point forward the reader is witness to a host of instances that illustrate the complicity and silence of Emma's community in response to her assault. For Emma, a key moment of recognition of this complicity comes when she remembers that, in the midst of her assault, her friend, Eli, had come into the room to take the keys of one of the boys so he would not drink and drive. Emma reflects that "drunk driving is bad, we had always been told. Drunk driving is dangerous. Drunk driving kills people, it ruins lives. There are other ways to ruin lives. We were never warned about those" (198). In this moment, Emma realizes that while teenagers in her community are lectured in schools and by their parents about the perils of drugs and drunk driving, sexual assault is approached with silence despite the similarly devastating consequences. Educational, religious, and familial systems therefore failed not only Emma and other girls who were assaulted, but the perpetrators of this violence as well by ignoring and thus condoning objectification of, and violence toward, women.

As Emma begins to talk about her assault, her character is called into question and her actions challenged by law enforcement. Emma's friends not only fail to believe her, but they post terrible comments about her on social media. The only vocal position anyone in Emma's community takes is to advocate for the boys who harmed her. Emma is not supported in church by her priest, Father Michael, who eventually becomes the character witness for the boys who raped Emma and gives a sermon about assuming innocence until proven guilty. Emma's parents may be the most egregious example of inaction; they are clearly embarrassed by her assault and worry primarily about the damage it has done to their reputation in the community. As she describes her father who is unable to look at her after she is raped, Emma thinks, "His eyes, rat-black, when he looks at me now, gleam for a second, full of *your fault, why were you there? What were you wearing? They say you slept around, did you? Did you? Did you?* And I know that I'm not his princess anymore and I never will be again" (287, emphasis in original). At one point her mother says, "They're good boys really. This all just got out of hand" (301).

While readers may hope for Emma to be a traditional Girl on Fire—rising up from the rubble to fight against evil—the ongoing violence and trauma that she experiences in the aftermath of her assault, from people in nearly every facet of her life, make clear that such an uprising would likely be both devastating and futile. In the section that follows we consider other, more nuanced and less conventional ways in which Emma finds feminine agency, and what such agency might look like for other girls who experience sexual trauma and cannot "catch fire." Later, we will consider how educators might invite readers to consider the systemic violence inflicted on Emma and other women in literature, and how these readings might transform our understandings of agency for women and girls in trauma.

Reconceptualizing Feminine Agency

Children's literature scholar Roberta Seelinger Trites focuses on agency and voice as defining qualities of feminist protagonists. She argues, "While in prefeminist novels the protagonist tends to become Sleeping Beauty, in a movement from active to passive, from vocal to silent, the feminine protagonist remains active and celebrates her agency and her voice" (8). In fact, in the first part of the novel, Emma might be read as "celebrating" her agency and voice, although she uses her strengths as defined by her patriarchal society to disempower other women, including her friends; to leverage her beauty to please men and gain social status; and to encourage her friend Jamie to ignore the rape that she experienced before the events of the novel. While the early Emma does not meet Trites's definition of a feminist protagonist given that her actions adhere to patriarchal and objectifying expectations for women, she does certainly embody the active and the vocal aspects of a "strong" female character.

However, considering the trauma of "violence that slowly works its victims to the bone" (Hentges 126), we can also read Emma's less celebratory, active, and vocal choices following her assault as a necessarily different manifestation of agency within the context of trauma and institutional violence. This agency differs from Trites's original focus on celebration since Emma, like Katniss in *The Hunger Games*, must contend with the effects of trauma that have taken root within herself. As Katniss explains, "the evil thing is inside, not out" (Collins 383). Therefore, after her rape, Emma's agency takes shape in stark contrast to the confident, beauty-focused, socially-dominant choices she made earlier in the novel. After her rape, Emma's voice and actions fail to meet traditional expectations for both what makes a female strong and how a rape survivor "should" react. Moreover, her choices are heavily informed by the misguided guilt she feels about her assault, and by the lack of concern she receives from the people she loves. Rather than viewing her choices and silence as weak, wrong, or anti-feminist, we might instead read her choices as valid and necessary parts of her solo survival mission in her new dystopian reality.

A survivor's internal voice. Traditionally, a Girl on Fire uses her voice in a public way, and while there is a public dimension to the legal complaint Emma files against her perpetrators, the focus in the second half of the book is on her inner voice, bringing readers "closer to the character's reality" (Hentges 113). Shortly after Emma learns about the Facebook page documenting her rape, the book moves forward one year to the last month of her final year of high school. And, Emma's reality has shifted dramatically. The second section, "This Year," begins with Emma waking up:

I am awake. And then I remember.
I am awake and I instantly wish that I was not.
(Life ruiner.)
(I have ruined their lives).
Guilt paints itself onto my skin. I am tarred in it and feathered [O'Neill 169].

O'Neill intersperses present-tense narration of the everyday events of Emma's daily survival with parenthetical self-recriminating thoughts and memories about the rape that took place almost a year ago. Refusing to attend school, Emma spends her time sleeping, reading online articles about her case, remembering the images posted on Facebook (e.g., 'Pink flesh. Legs spread apart. [I thought you were a good girl, Emma]')" (185), and going to therapy. Repeating these thought patterns within her daily life—guilt, painful images, and the belief that she has ruined lives—may appear to be a far cry from the Girl on Fire who uses her voice publicly to inspire social change, but Emma's voice is purposeful: she is remembering her abuse and processing her trauma. Emma tells us about the lies she tells her therapist and her family (that she will go to school, do yoga, etc.), but for the reader, Emma's voice communicates the honest pain of survival.

The "right" kind of agency. In addition to using her voice differently than traditional female characters with agency, Emma's choices and actions in the second part of the book reflect a departure from the expectations for strong women. Immediately after her rape, Emma refuses to have a sexual assault medical examination because she "didn't want to be in a waiting room with other girls who had been … *that word*" (210). Although avoiding the reality of what has just happened to her is a commonly reported and completely valid response to experiencing sexual trauma, Emma is repeatedly criticized for her survival response. Her lawyer eventually faults her decision, saying, "There would normally be forensics, of course, but since Emma refused to go for tests in the Sexual Assault Treatment Unit…" (210). Similarly, days after the perpetrators are first questioned, she tweets about watching *SpongeBob* with her brother, and her actions are turned against her by friends on social media. One classmate retorts, "*You say you were 'raped' and then you tweet happy shit? #IDontGetIt #DumbBitch*" (179). Emma internalizes these critiques and adds her own continuous line of questioning, constantly putting herself on trial: "(Maybe I had been asking for it)" (254), and, "*Does that sound like the behavior of someone who was violated in the most horrific way?*" (286). The choices Emma makes are judged to be inappropriate by her family, friends, and community, with little regard for the emotions and experiences that have led to these choices.

In addition, Emma struggles with or rejects most of her therapist's recommended actions, and she makes other choices that her therapist directly advises against. Her therapist recommends journaling, "as a way of remembering. They all want me to remember. (I don't want to remember)" (276). Emma rejects this action, choosing instead actions her therapist would label as "a bad idea" (183), like bookmarking a list of online editorials about her case for repeated readings. Though Emma doesn't tell her therapist, she also watches violent films and pornography labeled "*Reluctance*" and "*Non-consent.*" Emma explains, "I watch for clues. Is that what happened to me? Is that what I look like? (Pink flesh.) (Pink flesh.) (Splayed legs.) I want to see these girls cry, too. They are something to hold on to, something to ground me, to make sure I don't float away" (263). Emma's visceral pain is evident in these actions as she continues to make choices alone in the only way she knows how.

Beyond the media choices that would not be endorsed by her therapist, in the first months after her rape, Emma goes to parties, even one hosted by one of her perpetrators. She explains, "I try to reclaim that night. I try to make new memories to replace the ones that were stolen from me. I try to make it my choice, my decision" (286). She also tries to initiate a sexual encounter with Conor, her childhood best friend and one of the few people who stick by her after the rape, as a way to erase what was done to her by replacing it with Conor's genuine care for her. She rationalizes this action, explaining, "I know that if he's inside me, he can make me forget, he can make me clean" (164). And ultimately, Emma attempts suicide twice, saying, "I am going to make it end" (242).

None of these choices is easy to understand, obviously therapeutic, or traditionally empowering. And indeed, many of them—most obviously, her suicide attempts—are destructive. Yet these choices and actions are Emma's marks of survival in the immediate and short-term aftermath of her rape. The clarity of Emma's voice brings readers directly into her experience and begs us to reconceive of what we assume to be right, strong, and appropriate responses to trauma. Emma is actively engaged in the work of surviving sexual trauma, and her vivid and painful voice and choices require us to look beyond the strong/weak and right/wrong binaries imposed by the individuals and systems that have failed to support her in the first place.

"I have to be brave for the other victims": Acting for self or others?
Hentges notes that "many Girls on Fire choose the well-being of others over their own" (130), and Emma exemplifies this survivor quality. She even makes her initial choice to bring a legal complaint because she thinks it would be easier for her brother, Bryan. She says, "I thought it would be better for him to think of me as the victim (helpless, blameless, stupid) rather than a dirty slut (*slut, liar, skank, bitch whore*), like everyone else" (O'Neill 222). Later, when she withdraws the complaint, Bryan views it as a failure, stating, "After all this, you're just going to give up?" (299). Emma's focus is constantly on how her actions impact her family and her perpetrators, calling herself a life

ruiner, wondering if her family wishes that she were dead, and repeatedly saying that it was all "my fault."

While putting others' well-being before her own might, in other situations, be viewed as noble, given the violence done to Emma, we must reconsider whether these choices are actually agentic choices and actions. Traditionally, "choice is a feminist principle toward self-actualization as well as self-determination" (130), but when Emma makes choices based in the misogyny and patriarchy that she has internalized, as well as the lack of support shown her, we cannot view her choices as true indications of her desires. On one hand, she feels pressured by her concern for other people's well-being, and on the other hand, she feels pressured to be a feminist symbol, explaining, "I have to stand up and be counted. I have to set a good example. I have to be brave for other victims…. I don't want to be their champion. I don't want to be brave. I don't want to be a hero" (284).

Her final choice, the choice to withdraw the complaint, is the perfect example of a choice that reflects a *lack* of agency. When she tells her family that she has decided to withdraw the complaint because the success rate is so low, in her narration she also confesses her concern for her family's ease and comfort: "My voice goes up at the end of the sentence like I'm asking a question. And maybe I'm asking a question, maybe I'm asking them if this is what they want from me, if this will make it all better" (296). Her father is "almost glistening with hope" (297) at the prospect of Emma's withdrawal of her complaint, and her double-voiced acquiescence and internal monologue represent her lack of choices, even while she appears to make a decisive choice. She narrates, "I hesitate, waiting, *waiting* for my mother or my father to rush in and tell me not to be silly, that of course I'll win, that I have to win, because I'm innocent in this, because I am the victim, because this wasn't my fault. But no one speaks… 'I am serious,' I say. *Please tell me not to, Daddy. Please tell me I should go ahead with this, please, please, please.* 'I just want to get on with my life'" (297–98). Emma's mother celebrates her choice by baking her scones, and her father looks her in the eye for the first time in months and tells her that he is proud of her, that she made the right choice, and they can all move on. Meanwhile, Emma concludes that "it's important that I look normal now. It's important that I look like a good girl" (317).

Clearly, it is important to other people—her family, her friends, her perpetrators—that she return to normality because it allows them to return to the comfortable but erroneous assumption that sexual trauma is an individual event in which they bear no responsibility. This choice does not empower her; instead it represents a move toward survival in the only way she knows how, given the lack of support she had from individuals and institutions. Clearly, not every choice is evidence of agency. Emma chooses to stop fighting, yes, but she chooses to do so because she doesn't have the support to make the choices and pursue the action she actually desires. Confronting the possibility of two more years until trial, she knows that without support, she cannot be a traditional Girl on Fire, a feminist symbol for others. Without support, Emma is doing the best she can to survive. There is no inspirational or contagious fire. For Emma, at this time in her life, it is enough that she is able to survive alone.

Teaching Implications

Reconceptualizing feminine agency in light of Emma's experiences of systemic violence, traumatic sexual assault, and her lack of family, community, and institutional support also has implications for teaching *Asking for It*, as well as other novels that feature protagonists who have survived sexual assault and trauma. First, we offer a set of potential discussion questions that align with our analytical insights about the agency and the institutions and cultural patterns that inform our understanding of Emma's character and choices (see Table 6.1). We frame these questions broadly so that they can be applied to any novel that involves sexual trauma, and many of the questions can be adapted to enrich feminist readings even more generally, beyond instances of sexual trauma.

Our analysis of sexual trauma and proposed discussion questions can enrich the study of common canonical texts in the curriculum as well. Consider, for example, a discussion of *To Kill a Mockingbird*'s Mayella Ewell in which teachers ask students to consider whether Mayella's choices reflect agency for herself or others, or how she positions herself in relation to discourses of evidence and guilt. Discussing these layers within a canonical text, alongside a contemporary novel like *Asking for It*, and/or in conjunction with recent news articles about rape and sexual assault survivors might give more depth to the discussion of Mayella Ewell's relatively flat characterization and her social context. While secondary teachers already frequently discuss gender expectations in texts, these questions have the potential to add important layers to the analysis of characters, settings, and cultures rather than dismissing them as a product of their time, distant from contemporary readers' current realities.

Moreover, these questions can be useful in comparative analysis of characters' experiences of gender expectations, policing of sexuality, and sexual violence in a realistic novel like *Asking for It* and in dystopian novels. Comparing the persistent violence and trauma or the expectations for beauty and sexuality in the dystopian setting of *Brave New World*, for example, may invite readers to re-see the everyday violence of contemporary gender expectations and institutional patterns of support (or lack of support) within realistic

Table 6.1: Understanding Emma:
Agency and Institutions

Analytical Themes	Potential Questions for Literature Discussion
Systemic violence and persistent trauma	What evidence of violence and persistent trauma exists before sexual trauma occurs? That is, how have the conditions been set?
Expectations for beauty and sexuality	How do characters navigate conflicting expectations for gender, beauty, and sex?
Systemic and institutional response to systematic violence	How do families, religious institutions, criminal justice systems and other aspects of communities respond to sexual violence? How do people close to trauma survivors respond to the changing emotions and actions related to a survivor's sexual trauma?
The internal voice of survivors of sexual violence	What do we learn about survivors' experiences, agency, and sense of self from their internal thoughts?
Judgments about "correct" choices	What implicit and explicit messages do survivors receive about how they "should" act after being raped?
How do survivors position themselves (and how are they positioned) in relation to discourses of responsibility, guilt, and evidence?	Who or what informs a survivor's choice to pursue or not pursue legal justice? Does a decision to pursue justice necessarily reflect an agentic choice?
Making choices for self or others	What are the costs and benefits of pursuing justice for sexual trauma?

novels like *Asking for It* or within contemporary news texts. Ultimately, pairing a dystopian novel's power for social critique with Emma's dystopian reality in *Asking for It* can raise the question of whether we have, in fact, arrived at one version of a dystopian culture in responding to sexual trauma.

Posing questions that ask students to reconsider the systemic violence and trauma of sexual assault may allow teachers and students to consider more complex gender critiques, beyond a basic "traditional" versus "feminist" reading approach. Deborah Appleman's (2015) work on introducing literary theory to secondary students is commonly cited in English education scholarship, and her approach to a "feminist/gender lens" focuses on introducing the precepts of a feminist critique and teaching students to write "traditional" versus "feminist" analyses of a given character, scene, or text. The student quotations that frame our essay, and which criticize Emma's lack of strength and justice-oriented actions, are in line with Appleman's "traditional" readings of the text that do not account for the patriarchal and misogynistic constraints that inform Emma's characterization, choices, and actions. As Appleman might have predicted, these students viewed Emma as weak and the ending as unsatisfying.

Following Appleman's approach, teachers would then ask students to engage in a feminist critique considering "how the portrayal of female characters reinforces or undermines sexual stereotypes" or how the reader or author's gender informs the text and related interpretations (193). However, the student examples of "feminist" critiques Appleman includes are often brief statements focused on evaluating how female characters are repressed, objectified, or manipulated by male characters or patriarchal systems. While these critiques are certainly relevant to Emma in *Asking for It*—indeed, many of our students commented that Emma was a victim of her culture's expectations for young women—our analysis suggests that the simple binary of "traditional" and "feminist" readings that Appleman introduces may encourage a neat good/bad or strong/weak dichotomy that ignores the subtleties of how Emma is trying to use her voice and her choices to survive within a complex system of violence and trauma that informs and constrains her. The questions we suggest build on Appleman's now-established activities that introduce a gender lens by surpassing the "traditional" versus "feminist" reading to consider more nuanced questions about systems, relationships, trauma, and agency.

Moving Forward

Reading and teaching *Asking for It* or any book involving sexual trauma requires literacy educators to acknowledge that no single Girl on Fire can repair historically entrenched systems of patriarchy and misogyny, and that protagonists who are survivors of sexual assault exhibit forms of voice and agency that defy traditional expectations for strong female characters. This approach to reading trauma adds nuance to our understanding of Girls on Fire who have experienced trauma—in dystopian fiction, realistic fiction, within our current realities, and within our own classrooms.

We introduced this book to our students amidst the #MeToo movement, and during the Fall 2018 semester, some of our students read *Asking for It* during the same week as the Brett Kavanaugh Congressional hearings. Unfortunately, there is little reason to believe that the isolation and vilification that Emma endures will disappear from our culture's approach to survivors of sexual violence any time soon. We believe, then, that this reading of *Asking for It* and other complex portrayals of Girls on Fire experiencing trauma plays an essential role in the "intervention" that Hentges argues is necessary to prevent the present from becoming a complete dystopia.

Works Cited

Appleman, Deborah. *Critical Encounters in Secondary English: Teaching Literary Theory to Adolescents*. 3rd ed., Teachers College Press, 2015.

Casper, Monica J., and Eric Wertheimer. *Critical Trauma Studies: Understanding Violence, Conflict and Memory in Everyday Life*. NYU Press, 2016.

Collins, Suzanne. *Mockingjay*. Scholastic Inc., 2010.

Hentges, Sarah. *Girls on Fire: Transformative Heroines in Young Adult Dystopian Literature*. McFarland, 2018.

O'Neill, Louise. *Asking for It*. Quercus, 2016.

Sproull, Patrick. "Louise O'Neill: 'I Think This Book Will Infuriate a Lot of People Because It's Going to Push Those Buttons.'" *The Guardian*, 2 Sept. 2015, www.theguardian.com/childrens-books-site/2015/sep/02/louise-oneill-asking-for-it-interview.

Sweeney, Brian N. "Slut Shaming." *The SAGE Encyclopedia of Psychology and Gender*. Ed. Kevin L. Nadal. SAGE Publications, Inc., 2017. 1579–1580. *SAGE Knowledge*. Web. 28 May. 2019, doi: 10.4135/9781483384269.n530.

Trites, Roberta S. *Waking Sleeping Beauty: Feminist Voices in Children's Novels*. University of Iowa Press, 1997.

PART THREE

The Girl on Fire
in the University Classroom

On Teaching Girls
Who Want to Burn

The Problems and Possibilities
of Feminist Education

TESSA PYLES

As a girl, no one taught me that I could burn. Quite the opposite, I learned that I should suppress everything about myself that did not meet acceptable notions of girl- and womanhood—sweetness, submission, nurturing, and the sexual desirability of men. In other words, I learned to quell *my* questions, *my* passions, *my* anger, *my* voice—*my fire*. It was not until I took my first Women's Studies course that I began to recognize the extent of the damage that the smothering of my flame had done, not only to me but also to countless other girls and women. Damage that we falsely learn is due to our own personal weaknesses or failures. Further, that classroom is where I began to understand the complexity of identity and experience within girlhood and womanhood. Importantly, it is where I began to learn about the intersecting impacts of racism, classism, sexism, homophobia, and ableism in the lives of girls and women. What I learned in that class, and in the many that followed, both challenged and liberated me. It set the world I thought I knew ablaze. I willingly stepped into the midst of the flames and caught fire. I tell the girls that I now teach that they have a right to burn. I show them that I burn with them.

This essay offers a critical reflection and analysis of some of my observations, experiences, and the lessons I am learning through teaching girl- and women-centered courses. Throughout, I provide accounts of classroom conversations and I cite excerpts of my students' writing. While I allude to a general course in some of the examples I give, in an effort to protect the

123

anonymity of my students, I do not use names and I avoid discussing when and at which specific institution I taught these courses. The university level courses I have developed and taught that focus on the experiences of girls and women include the following: "Girls on Fire: Gender in Literature and Culture" and "Girlhood in American Culture," as well as "Introduction to Women's, Gender, and Sexuality Studies." Though the disciplines and subject matter are varied, within each of these courses, I assign a range of texts that include foundational feminist theory and women's history, girls' studies scholarship, popular young adult (YA) fiction, and girl-written personal narratives, short stories, and poetry, as well as popular music and film. Every text my students engage in these courses reflects an aspect of girlhood or womanhood as it is impacted by oppressive and intersecting systems of power— sexism/misogyny, racism, homophobia, transphobia, ableism, classism, and xenophobia. Within many of these texts, girls and women not only convey how these systems affect their lives; they take action against them. They are "Girls on Fire." Yet, so many of the girls I have had the privilege to teach are navigating a gulf that is flooded with mechanisms that work to quench their fire, or even prevent its ignition.

This gulf is primarily shaped by the disconnect between mainstream messages of "Girl Power" twenty-first century girls are *told* they have and the experiences of disempowerment so many of my students share in our class-room and in their writing. This schism, or more to the point, the contradictions and fallacies within it, leaves many girls feeling frustrated. Worse yet, they often feel shame, and many feel broken by the actions others have taken against their minds and bodies. The schism leaves them feeling small and conveys the notion that they should make themselves even smaller. They internalize the fault of both their victimhood and their inability to rise above it as their own, and the consequences are often dire.

While these students are getting a university education, a pursuit that should empower them, they often struggle to reconcile why they still feel completely powerless. For many of my students, the inability to find empowerment in education is due to many academic institutions and disciplines' continued insistence that lived experience has no bearing on education and vice versa. bell hooks writes in *Teaching Community: A Pedagogy of Hope*:

> In modern schooling the messages students receive is that everything that they learn in the classroom is mere raw material for something they will produce later in life. This displacement of meaning into the future makes it impossible for students to fully immerse themselves in the art of learning and to experience that immersion as a complete, satisfying moment of fulfillment [166].

Essentially, in many classrooms, students internalize the notion that the experiences they bring to the classroom do not matter. In my classrooms, I emphasize the importance of personal experience, not only as a tool to access texts, but also for understanding the commonality of experience and a way to begin to build community, to heal, and, if desired, to burn. My students find themselves in my courses for any variety of reasons. These reasons often include fulfilling a requirement, or taking what they believe is an "easy" course. Some want to hone their own feminism, while others want to know if they are feminists at all, still others are searching for something they cannot quite articulate.

No matter their reasons for entering my classroom, I want my students to know that who they are and what they have experienced matters, and that they are powerful despite what the world has told them, and in ways they might not have yet imagined. In *Girls on Fire: Transformative Heroines in Young Adult Dystopian Literature*, Sarah Hentges defines "Girl on Fire" in the following way: "rarely a perfect, infallible hero; she is most often a real girl struggling to find herself.... She wants to discover the truth that has been kept from her, and from the populace more generally. She wants to cut the ties that bind and bring freedom to oppressed peoples. She is an outcast, a rebel" (6–7). In myriad ways, this describes my students. They think that their imperfect fallibility is another flaw to be fixed in the endless list of imperfections that has already been written for them to correct—their size, shape, skin color, hair texture/color, blemishes, sexuality, bodily functions, and more. As they discover the truth that has been kept from them, they begin to voice their anger and, in different ways, they begin to express their desire to burn. Teaching Girls on Fire and other girl- and women-centered courses has left me contemplating ways to help my students—girls who want to burn—find answers to the question they are asking with increased frequency and passion: How do we do it?

Fire Needs Air to Burn

In *Future Girl* (2004), Anita Harris interrogates "the idea that in a time of dramatic social, cultural, and political transition, young women are being constructed as a vanguard of new subjectivity" (1). Central to the mainstream positioning of girls as subjects is the notion that feminism has "enabled the current generation of young women to see themselves, and to be seen, as enjoying new freedoms and opportunities. They are far more at liberty to make choices and pursue lifestyles independently of their families, the state, and men in general. Young women have been encouraged to believe that 'girls can do anything' and 'girls are powerful'" (8). Like the girls Harris discusses, many of my students are aware of what they are capable of doing and achieving. However, not only are they coping with external pressures to gratefully revel in all the possibilities that have been laid at the feet of their generation, they are also dealing with the pressure to be "perfect" in mind, body, and action. Sexism, racism, classism, etc., as well as the impacts of these institutionalized systems of oppression, they have been told, are issues their mothers and grandmothers overcame, thus any shortcomings or failures to achieve can be chalked up to a lack of "personal responsibility."

As a result, girls are drowning in assaults on their minds, bodies, and characters, and internalizing the fault as their own. Not only are girls told they are empowered, they are also told that feminism, the movement that provided that power, is no longer needed. Worse still, the propaganda of feminism as a club for ugly, man-hating, non-shaving, miserable women still has a stronghold in the popular imagination. Whether or not they agree, those are just some of the adjectives my students use when I ask them to describe what they hear about feminists. In addition to these long-standing and blatant mischaracterizations of feminists and thus feminism, as I discuss in more detail below, my students come into my classroom believing that if they are to be feminists, then they must be perfect practitioners of the title/identity. They often express sadness and frustration that they cannot meet those standards, and therefore cannot be feminists. Additionally, even within some feminist discourse itself, we place too much expectation on girls.

For example, Michelle S. Bae and Olga Ivashkevich discuss the growing scholarship in girls' studies in "Reimagining Girls' Resistance," the introduction of their anthology, *Girls, Cultural Productions, and Resistance* (2012). They refer to this scholarship as a "vibrant expansion ... marked by a desire to situate girls as active agents and producers of culture and meaning and to understand their subject positions: a view that is distinctly different from a previously popular (and largely objectivist) construction of girls as victims of the dominant patriarchal discourses and representations" (1). While they acknowledge situating girls as active agents "as important and necessary," they also discuss it "as problematic and contested" (1). As they explain, the victim/active agent dichotomy, among others, "can lead us to simplistic assumptions that in order to see a girl as a subject, we have to reposition her as an 'active' maker of meaning who can intentionally resist the dominant constructions of gender and ultimately liberate herself from them" (1). In other words, we are attempting to empower girls simply by telling them that they are empowered, and we expect them to know what that means and what they are supposed to do with it. The pressure is too much.

It is no wonder that my students grasp onto and commonly cite and repeat Roxanne Gay's *Bad Feminist* when she writes, "In truth, feminism is flawed because it is a movement powered by people and people are inherently flawed" (x). As one of my students wrote in response to Gay's assertion, "This was something I was somewhat shocked to read, mostly because the main feminists I hear from try to make it sound like such a perfect and simple system, when in fact it is complex and multi-layered. I was honestly very happy to read her words that were calling feminism as it is and not sugar coating anything." Gay's one sentence is like a rush of fresh air, one that allows many of my students to breathe. Once they catch their breath, they begin to see more clearly the obstacles in their way, and they can begin to navigate a path to dry land.

Lessons I Continue to Learn

For many of my students my classrooms are often the first space where, on a very personal level, they begin to analyze, make sense of, and challenge the people and structures that have shaped their experiences. It is also a space where they dissect contradictory messages, and where, perhaps for the first time, they talk and write about what they have learned is private or personal within broader cultural, social, and political contexts. What they divulge to me is often raw and heartbreaking—sexual assault, intimate partner violence, body image issues, depression, extreme anxiety, suicidal ideation, and eating disorders, to name a few. Sometimes they mention these in passing as if it is just another thing they have experienced. Sometimes they will literally say or write that they are "pissed off," that what they and other girls and women endure is "bullshit," and sometimes they are confused about what they are thinking and feeling. In those moments, they provide caveats to protect or defend the person or people, and even institutions, that negatively affect their lives. In truth, teaching girl- and women-centered courses has challenged me in ways for which I was not prepared. One of the biggest challenges is learning to make a space for student engagement that is accessible and meaningful for them. This means that I have to check my own feminist hopes for my students at the classroom door.

Simply put, I have to step aside and let them determine what they need, including feminism. In myriad ways, I continue to learn to act as a support for my students and to employ strategies, communication, and expectations that prioritize their individual and community learning. Bae and Ivashkevich contend, "hegemonic feminist desire to see girls as 'conscious feminists' places girls' idealized identity prior to the girls' actual lived performances, which silences actual (and diverse) girls' voices from claiming who they are on their own" (2). They explain further that this "predetermined identity ... often undermines and renders invisible actual girls' lived experiences that are contradictory, complex, fluid, and multiple as well as discursive" (2–3). Therefore, I strive to employ a feminist pedagogy that meets students where they are, listens, customizes (as no one strategy can effectively serve every student), and holds a space for engagement in more personally and academically meaningful ways. For students who are grappling with issues and experiences that incite silence, fear, anger, and shame, creating a classroom space where they are able to speak or write those experiences without expectation of fealty to any "predetermined identity" or ideology is, I believe, one of the most feminist acts I can model.

Throughout the remainder of this essay, I provide examples for and discuss aspects of the two most prominent issues and topics that have led me to reevaluate how I am learning to challenge my assumptions and expectations, and to renegotiate my own feminist pedagogy. These issues and topics are silences in the classroom, and the bodily and embodied trauma so many of my female students experience. Of course, it is important to note that classroom silences and embodied trauma are often interrelated. As a result, I have learned that I must listen to what the silences are saying. Other times, I need to let go of the expectation that my students frame their contributions within that day's particular text(s) or theory, and instead I need to allow them to tell their stories on their own terms and in their own words. Similar to Bae and Ivashkevich's point, Judith Simmer-Brown posits, "As educators, one of the best things that we can do for our students is to not force them into holding theories and solid concepts but rather to actually encourage the process, the inquiry involved, and the times of not knowing—with all of the uncertainties that go along with that. This is really what supports going deep. This is openness" (105). Further, as Hentges explains, the Girl on Fire "is sometimes successful, and sometimes not. Sometimes brave, sometimes vulnerable.... Most often she endures and lives on her own terms, sometimes she just survives" (7). I continue to learn that my students learn more and find ways to "claim who they are on their own" when I treat them as Girls on Fire. This means I must work with them to create a classroom that encourages openness and that embraces success and failure, bravery and fear, thriving and surviving, and thus complexity, nuance, uncertainties, and yes, even silence.

Listening to Silence

Sometimes, as we embark on the activities of learning, I am met with silence. These silences can be frustrating. Admittedly, it is easy to make assumptions about my students and the reasons for their silence, including not reading and general lack of preparedness, shyness, or lack of interest, dislike of me and/or the course, even disrespect. However, as I remind my students, as well as myself, silences can be moments of contemplation, as well as time that students are building the courage to speak. Other times, silences are a learned behavior. For example, in the first Girls on Fire course

I taught, an English topics course which was also a Women's, Gender, and Sexuality studies elective, the silence of the girls in class was deafening. The course was comprised of twenty-four students, twenty of whom identified as women, four as men. Yet, at first, the men dominated the conversations. This was disconcerting for a few reasons, not the least of which is that it was a girl-centered course. At first, I was apprehensive to address the issue. I did not want to shame those not talking, and I did not want to shut down those who were. Yet, at about the third week of class, nothing had changed, and I decided that saying nothing was doing more harm than good. On the day I confronted this issue, I began by explaining that while I value every contribution to class discussion, we had to address the proverbial elephant in the room. I said, "In this Girls on Fire course, where every text is about girls and women or written by girls and women, that is comprised primarily of women, and is taught by a woman, we need to address the fact that it is mostly men who are talking." When I made this statement, I was simultaneously relieved that I addressed the issue, but also frustrated that I had not done it sooner, as I could actually hear a collective sigh of relief from many of the girls. I did not ask anyone individually to explain why they were not speaking. Instead, I asked that we discuss the issue within the existing framework of our course.

After I spoke, we sat in awkward silence. When one of the young men tried to break the silence, I asked him to wait to speak. Eventually, one young woman said, "I think maybe it is because we are afraid of being thought of as one of 'those girls' like we've been talking about." When I asked if she could expand on her point, she alluded to the fact that many of our course texts addressed the ways girls learn to silence themselves in order to be liked, accepted, and not thought of as loud, unladylike, etc. After this, another young woman joined in and said that while she did not disagree with her classmate's point, she believed that it is also a common occurrence in elementary and high school classrooms that boys speak over girls, unchecked and unchallenged by teachers. When one of the men in class decided to contradict this point by referring to his one experience of one female high school classmate speaking over him, others of the young women in the classroom broke their silences. They shared their own stories about the ways they are routinely silenced—at home, at school, and at work.

I too know what it is to be silenced in every capacity of my life. Because of my own experiences, I should have been attuned to the silences of my female students. However, the way this discussion unfolded was a powerful teaching moment—for them and for me. Perhaps for the first time, my female students saw their teacher intentionally make space for women. I did not ask the men in class not to speak, but I did have to ask the one to wait and make space for his classmates. This too was a new classroom experience for my students. Further, by asking my students to address this issue within a larger curricular, societal/structural framework, the pressure and focus was removed from them as individuals, and they could make connections to silences as shaped by systems of power that have long relegated women's voices to the margins. The conversation was uncomfortable at times, but also rigorous and engaging, as my students were challenging each other for the first time. That was also the last time silence from three-fourths of this class, or any class, was an issue. However, I have also come to learn that classroom silence is far too often an embodied response to the social, cultural, political, mental and physical violence far too many of the girls I teach experience in nearly every aspect of their lives. As such, girl- and women-centered classrooms can be, and I believe should be, places where, if they choose, students feel safe to break their silence and tell their stories.

Girls, Embodied Experience and the Power of Story Telling

The topics I cover in my girl- and women-centered courses—"Beauty," "Sex and Shame," "Fitness and Health," "Gender Identity/Expression, Sexuality and Sexual Desire," "Rape Culture," "Romance and Love," "Marriage and Partnership," to name a few—are not abstract to my students. I am literally teaching them about the stories of their lives. The longer I teach, the more I realize that they and their stories are the central texts; the required readings are supplementary and supportive tools. Thus, from day one, I convey to my students that I am prepared to hear their stories, to validate them, to provide, social, cultural, and political context, and to help them understand that they are not alone. In her own assessment of the power of storytelling, specifically within the context of girl-centered YA dystopian novels, Hentges explains, "Adhesion, integration, application, transformation—stories are bigger than just words on a page (or a screen)… We create stories where there are no stories; we become engaged with ideas and subjects we might not otherwise pursue if there's a good story to relay the information or persuade us to think a certain way about something. We tell stories about ourselves" (16). What Hentges writes is reflective of what my students say the impact of hearing and telling stories in the classroom has on them personally and academically.

For example, in a final weekly reflection, one student wrote, "I think sometimes as women we feel like the things we go through are just us but in reality other women feel the same ways we do. That makes me feel better to not feel alone but it also makes me upset that we all are forced to feel the ways we do." During one class discussion, this same student spoke about the ways hearing other students' stories affected her. She spoke about being "pissed off," but she said that even that was good because it meant that she was more aware. She also spoke about how the stories they all shared helped her learn and led to her feeling a greater sense of community and support. Another student wrote in her final weekly reflection, "Coming to an end in this class, I have lately found myself reflecting on all of the topics and material covered throughout the semester, as well as how it has affected my life personally. I have been able to make connections between the course material and my own life every week … and it has been some sort of an emotional release for me, if that makes any sense." I told her it makes perfect sense. I no longer view my work as teaching my students something they did not know; rather, it is to help them make sense of what they have experienced, to help guide them toward "adhesion, integration, application, and transformation" (Hentges 16). I convey the fact that, though still unique and important on their own, their stories are also common, and that commonality is a space from where connections toward greater understanding can be made, and from which power—both individual and collective—can grow. In short, it is a space in which sparks can be nurtured. However, this work is often very difficult, for them and for me.

In every course I have taught for the past seven years, three to five students per semester (all but one female identified) have told me they are victims of sexual assault or of some form of domestic or intimate partner violence. Sadly, this statistic is not shocking. However, it is heartbreaking and sobering to hear my students' individual accounts of their assaults, and maddening to hear how often silence is the prescription these girls are given, or that they understand silence as the best course of action. At the root of this silence is what girls have long been enculturated to believe. That is, if someone violates their bodies or minds, they were "asking for it" in some way. Even if they reject such a notion, they know that society as a whole does not. It is one of my students' responses to what should be a well-established fact that led me to understand in a way I had not previously realized that my classrooms, specifically those that center the experiences of girls and women, must be spaces where they feel safe to be silent and to speak their stories.

In the first Girls on Fire course I taught, I assigned a coming of age novel, *Rainy Royal* by Dylan Landis (2014), wherein the title character is raped. This was not the only account of rape that my students read about or discussed in my class, but it was the first. While Rainy Royal's sexual assault was not the focus of the book, I warned my students about the content, and provided an alternate reading and assignment, as well as permission to be absent for that class meeting. Before we began discussing and analyzing the book, I told my students that we could not shy away from the sexual violence, but that we needed to be sensitive and begin from the premise that "rape is NEVER the fault of the victim." After class, one of my students stayed behind, clearly waiting for the others to leave. She apologized to me for not speaking in class, and then explained that she did not know if she could speak without getting emotional. She then divulged to me that a few years prior, while still in high school, she had been raped. She quickly added that she had supportive friends and family who had made sure to get her into therapy. Then she said, "But no one ever said what you did today. No one ever blamed me, but no one ever told me that 'Rape is NEVER the fault of the victim.' I can't tell you how much I needed to hear that." As I mention above, that was not the first time, nor the last, that a student has told me that they had been raped. However, it was the first time I specifically addressed sexual violence in a class I was teaching.

In nearly equal numbers, young women talk or write about the eating disorder(s) they have, as well as the causes and impacts of those diseases. The readings that I assign, which include excerpts from Hanne Blank's *The Unapologetic Fat Girl's Guide to Exercise and Other Incendiary Acts*, Abra Chernik's "The Body Politic," and Michael Hobbes' "Everything You Know about Obesity is Wrong," often offer personal accounts of a range of body image issues, and the authors frame these issues within social, cultural, and political terrains. These textual connections are vitally important, as they allow my students to understand the impacts of these systems upon their own bodies. However, by the trajectory of their in-class discussions, students continue to show me that it is not enough to read and discuss someone else's account. Instead, if I am going to ask them to read about and discuss issues of which they have embodied experience, then they need to know that it is not only safe, but also academically acceptable, to talk about those experiences within our classroom, even if not always framed within theoretical concepts. A feminist pedagogy makes space for these personal/political connections in ways that other disciplines often do not. I always stress to my students that it is important to pull their personal experiences back to the texts at hand, because making those personal/political connections is vital for understanding many of the root causes for the systems and structures that have influenced their personal lives. Yet, holding space for these personal stories and connections must not be omitted.

In my experience, I have found that girls want and need to talk about their complicated relationships with their parents, their siblings, their boyfriends and girlfriends. They want to talk about feeling powerless to ask for more money when they know they are paid less than their male colleagues, and they want to talk about occasions when they spoke up, demanded equal pay, and got it. They need to talk about the shame they feel about the size and shape of their bodies, about their battles with anxiety, depression, and suicide attempts. They need to talk about eating disorders. They want to talk about how they are looked at and seen, how they are spoken to, as well as how they are spoken about. They want to talk about how they are touched, and how they are violated. They even want to talk about the functions of their bodies. For example, sometimes they want and need to talk about their periods.

As an example, after a class where my students read about "reproductive justice" as "the complete physical, mental, spiritual, political, social, and economic well-being of women and girls, based on the full achievement and protection of women's human rights" (Ross 4), my students (a class made up entirely of women) drifted into sharing stories about their periods. At first, I was tempted to become frustrated at what I perceived as my student's lack of engagement with the crux of Ross's text, one that centers the experiences of women of color. However, my students read a few texts on this subject, all of which focused on issues connected with reproductive justice. These included access to affordable healthcare, access to affordable birth control, abortion rights, as well as the right to bear and raise children in social, political, and economic safety. My students recognized the importance of these topics, but the majority of these issues are outside the scope of their lived experiences to date. However, they have almost all had to deal with the silences, stigma, and shame, as well as the medical issues and treatments, that encompass menstruation.

As such, they talked about their frustrations with society's attitudes about women's bodies generally, and menstruation specifically. They told stories about having birth control prescribed because of a range of medical issues. They also told stories about dealing with fears and assumptions from parents, family, and even some friends, about being on the pill and what that might mean for them in regard to their sexual freedom. They talked about the "tampon tax," and they made connections to the myriad other ways they have been penalized for having a female body. For these students, and for many students after them, telling their stories without concern that I will shut them down, or that I will ask them to already understand a larger theoretical concept, or even understand something they have yet to experience, gives them the opportunity to find their own way into the texts. It is important here that I acknowledge that while there is usually at least one female-identified student who is unashamed to discuss her body and bodily function in front of men, there is usually more reticence for many of the female students when men are present. Thus, this all female class approached such subjects without fear. However, even in classes that are not all female, on day one I tell students that bodies, bodily functions, sex, and many of the terms associated with all of these will be used. I acknowledge the potential for awkwardness and discomfort, but stress the importance of us all getting comfortable with being uncomfortable, not just where subjects of the body are concerned, but in regard to many of the issues we address that are not commonplace in daily conversations, such as racism, classism, etc. Students, I have found, respond well to my openness and my day-one disclosures of all that we will read and talk about throughout the semester. Sharing experiences of their own bodies, especially with others of their own age, helps them recognize the commonality of the issues they face, and helps them understand, in the ways second wave feminist "consciousness raising" groups did, that "The personal is political." These conversations also help some young women to acknowledge personal privileges they had not previously recognized.

What I consider a powerful example of this recognition of privilege transpired during a conversation about beauty as it is associated with body size. One student shared her experience about buying a prom dress. She explained that even at a size 10, she had difficulty finding a prom dress that did not cover up her body in ways smaller sizes did not. She talked about how the common experience of shopping for a prom dress, something that she always envisioned as a fun and exciting event, left her feeling terrible about herself and ashamed about the size of her body. This led to many of her classmates telling similar stories. Eventually, one young woman spoke up and said that the readings, as well as the conversation with her peers, helped her to understand the term "skinny privilege." She said that she had heard it before, but did not really understand what it was and did not know if she believed such a privilege existed. She then referenced a previous class conversation where we had discussed the ways privilege works to benefit people and behaviors that society has deemed "normal," and how one "normal" or "good" behavior for girls and women is to be thin. Then she nervously said, "I understand now that because I am white, thin, and able-bodied, I can walk into any store and, unless an item is out of stock, can buy almost anything. I am seen as being 'good' and 'normal,' and because of that, even though I did not ask for it, I have privilege."

While this revelation might seem elementary, for this student, and perhaps for the class as a whole, it was a stepping-stone. What she shared allowed the class as a whole to begin to put the pieces of their individual and collective stories together. Specifically, this student's recognition that it was not just her thinness, but also her whiteness and able-bodiedness, that marked her as "good" and "normal" exposed interlocking systems of oppression that serve to disparage and oppress girls and women in different ways dependent upon their intersectional identities. It led to other students discussing the prom and prom dresses within the context of cost and economic class, and others within the context of expectations of gender performance, specifically as it relates to sexuality. Perhaps my students would have come to these recognitions and deeper discussions without hearing each other share their prom dress shopping experiences. However, sharing their stories allowed them all to come to these recognitions in a space of safety and comradery, and without fear of getting something "wrong." While this is just one example, these types of situations become more common the more I make room for students to engage the texts and each other in ways that are accessible and meaningful for them. In other words, to follow their lead, and support them as they find ways to share their often-painful embodied experiences, as well as expose and challenge the people and systems that created the circumstances of their lives and tell them that the burden is theirs to bear. While these conversations do not always allow us to dig into deeper textual analysis and might gloss over difference of race and ethnicity, they are important beginning points that can lead to more nuanced understandings and analysis.

One topic that directly affects girls and young women (and even not so young women)—and often in the most physically and mentally damaging ways—is beauty. Every time this topic comes up, the young women in my classrooms have endless stories to share, in class or in their writing, about how this one word and all the meanings and expectations it encompasses have influenced their lives. When they read Jessica Valenti's *Full Frontal Feminism* (2007), specifically her chapter, "Beauty Cult," where she writes, "Ugly is powerful. Nothing has quite the same sting. Especially for the ladies. None of us want to be ugly; in fact, we all would really like to be beautiful—and it's killing us. Literally" (204), they respond with gratitude and a deeply embodied recognition of how true Valenti's words are. What follows are just a couple of examples of the ways my students have written about beauty, or more specifically, the fear of being ugly and its effects on their lives:

> From the time I was in the 5th grade, I was bullied for things I cannot control. I was too fat, too muscular, too weird, and just too much. I felt as though I took up too much space and wanted to disappear. I did not go out of my way to lose weight, but the real hit was to my mental health. I hated myself. I didn't want to exist anymore if my whole purpose was to be an example for other girls of what not to be. This struggle has been ongoing, hard, and flat out exhausting.
>
> Many people grow up by being told what beauty is by their parents or family members. For instance, growing up my mom wouldn't let me wear my hair a little higher up on my head or wear something different. She would look at me and say, "I hope you're planning on going and changing, you look like a bitch when wearing that." I was in elementary school when she told me this…. Growing up, the majority of Americans were taught that beauty also depends on weight, including me. Growing up my mom would not allow me to have seconds because she said I would grow up fat. I learned how society views beauty at a very young age, but I learned it a difficult way.

As I stated at the outset of this essay, the majority of young women who enter my classrooms are navigating a flood of unrealistic and contradictory expectations. They are fighting to stay afloat, and they are exhausted. They might want to ignite and even burn brightly, but if we, as their teachers, want to help them find the tools to start their fire, we have to make sure that is what they want. In other words, we have to meet them where they are. A step we can take is to provide them with the opportunity to put some of what they learn into action in a way that is meaningful for them, but which also shows them they have the potential and the power to effect personal and political change, in their own lives as well as in the lives of others.

Praxis Project: An Assignment of Empowerment

In my "Introduction to Women's Studies" class, instead of assigning a term paper, I assign a Praxis Project. This assignment is similar to the "action project" Hentges assigns in her Girls on Fire classes, which she details in her book. She explains, "Through their academic work for Girls on Fire, students can be empowered in myriad ways and can make an impact outside of the classroom" (209). In order for students to feel excited and invested in the assignment, I provide a list of options for these Praxis Projects. These options are: (1) hold a fundraiser for a local women's shelter or another non-profit group that is working for the safety and social justice of a minoritized and marginalized group; (2) hold a Women's, Gender, and Sexuality Studies lunch, coffee/tea, or dinner and organize a discussion with friends about one of our course topics; (3) hold a film screening and discussion framed by one or more of our course topics/themes; (4) create a piece of art that expresses how they experience a certain issue(s); (5) complete a self-care project. Students are also encouraged to mix and match these options or propose something new. In ways that are meaningful for them, this project allows students to bring together theory and practice (praxis).

Many of the topics covered throughout the semester inspire my students' projects. For instance, a student sat inside the Student Union and on a white board wrote, "What do you know about feminism?" Passers-by approached her and held conversations about what they understood about feminism and she was able to share what she had learned and help dispel myths. Other students have done body positivity projects where they ask passers-by to write what they love about themselves on a sticky note and post it on a board. These students report that participants have cried and thanked them for doing such a project. Another student held a talk with close friends about "Sex and Shame," wherein she and her participants spoke openly about their experiences with sex, including being dissatisfied but also being afraid to discuss such topics with their partners. These are just three examples of the ways students have used this assignment to reach out to their friends and community to raise awareness about issues that have personal meaning.

Sometimes, students decide that they need to practice self-care and allow themselves to be the focus of their projects.

Many self-care projects build from one reading that resonated with the students. As I mention above, one of the readings I assign students on the topic of "Fitness and Health" is Abra Fortune Chernik's "The Body Politic." Within this short narrative, Chernik writes about how she became anorexic and bulimic, as well as what aided her recovery. She writes, "I began reading feminist literature to further understand the disempowerment of women in our culture. I digested the connection between a nation of starving, self-obsessed women and the continued success of the patriarchy. I also cultivated an awareness of alternative models of womanhood" (80). Chernik encourages women, young and old, to embrace their bodies as they are and to take up space instead of trying to hide and shrink away. She implores, "Fat, thin, soft, hard, puckered, smooth, our bodies are our homes. By nourishing our bodies, we care for and love ourselves on the most basic level…. We must challenge ourselves to eat and digest, and allow society to call us too big. We will understand their message to mean too powerful" (84). What Chernik writes powerfully resonates with many of my students; however, I was shocked by the extent that it resonated with one student as well as how it informed the crux of her self-care project. *She wanted to eat.* Admittedly, I cried when I read her proposal, and I felt woefully unprepared to guide her through her project. After all, there is a difference between taking care of oneself by eating well and taking care of oneself by eating, period.

Within the Praxis Project Proposal prompt, I ask students to provide a theoretical underpinning for their projects. Essentially, I ask them to cite and analyze specific aspects of our readings within the context of their project. I ask them to do this so that the intentionality of their projects within the framework of our course is clear. Within their Praxis Project Proposals, I ask my students to state why they chose their project. This student simply stated, "I chose this project for myself," and in the very first line of describing the scope of her project, she wrote, "I need to learn to take care of myself." These first two sentences of her proposal made her intentionality more than clear. Instead of asking her to revise her project, I was thrilled to see that she was already "taking up space" by unapologetically centering herself and her needs within her project and its description. For this student, centering herself was revolutionary. However, for some students this centering comes naturally. For example, in this same class, two young men also chose to do self-care projects. One chose to get a massage and the other to walk and journal. While it is not my intention to belittle these young men or their projects, as some other young women have chosen similar options, despite my urging, they did not try to decenter themselves, or recognize and nod to the origins of self-care in a feminist context. Thus, they refused to contend with their own privilege, which could have been productive for themselves and others even while doing their projects and when reflecting on them.

While the actions students complete are important, their contextualization of these actions is really the point of the assignment. Thus, after my students complete their project, I ask them to write a Critical Reflection in order to contextualize their practice. Within this assignment, I ask them to describe specific steps they took to complete the "action" of their project and then to reflect on these actions again through the framework of our course. The aforementioned student began, "The project I did, was a self-care project. During this project I ate at least one meal a day for almost a month, from October 25th–November 27th. I know that doesn't seem like a self-care that people think of. However, for me it is something huge." She added, "This project opened my range of places I ate, and opened the range of what I ate, whether it was something on campus or if it was just something I packed. I ate a wide variety of foods during this project as well. I ate anything from an apple to grapes to a full Thanksgiving meal with pumpkin pie as dessert." Toward the end of her Critical Reflection, she cited the following excerpt from Chernik, calling it her "motivation": "Sitting in the hospital the summer after my college graduation, I grasped the absurdity of a nation of adult women dying to grow small. Armed with this insight, I loosened the grip of the starvation disease on my body. I determined to recreate my life based on an image of a woman warrior" (81). By contextualizing her self-care project within the framework Chernik provided, my student imagined every meal she ate and every bite she took as an act of warfare against the people and systems that had consistently force fed her the conflicting message that not only was she not enough, but that to be enough she had to make herself smaller. Through her self-care practice, my student began to understand that survival meant growth, figuratively and literally. Hentges writes, "Girls on Fire, and their struggles to survive and grow, can inspire us toward self-care…. Self-care is especially important for survival and healing as much as for transformation" (237). Therefore, what Chernik imagined as a "woman warrior" in her youth, we might now imagine as a Girl on Fire.

I do not know how this student is doing today. Thankfully, she was already seeking the help of a therapist, and she spoke often about the love and support of her friends. She also wrote about how much better she felt and how much more energy she had when she ate during her self-care project, and she said that she was going to try to continue to practice self-care. I like to imagine (and I hope) that she has continued to nourish herself in all the ways she feels she needs to. I would like to write that this student's story is unique. It is not. Hers is just one example of the gravity of the experiences with which young women walk into my—into our—classrooms. As such, sometimes supporting our students in ways that are meaningful and productive for them means letting them figure out and practice what they need to survive, to grow, or to burn.

Conclusion: "If we burn, you burn with us!"

As I write above, I have noticed that with increased frequency young women are asking, "How do we burn?" These young women speak and write often about how fearful they are for their younger sisters, their young nieces, themselves, and even their future daughters. They do not want girls and women younger than they are to navigate and endure what they and their mothers have. They ask repeatedly: Why were we not taught this sooner? What can I do? How can I help to change this? They are frustrated that despite the waves of feminism, and all the battles fought and won, they are fighting a complex and exhausting current that keeps them gasping for breath, so that finding dry land and igniting their flame does not seem possible.

When students ask me these questions, I give them practical steps they can take to become involved. However, as a teacher, I recognize that what they do and how they do it, or even if they want to do it, is entirely up to them. All I can do is work with them to create a classroom space where they feel heard, respected, and safe to speak or write aloud what they might not have before, and to support them as they begin to question and challenge the legitimacy of a system that has always told them they are powerful and yet makes them feel incredibly powerless. The majority of my students do not enter my classrooms feeling powerful, and they might not leave feeling that way either. However, I have found that by giving them space to make sense of their own lives and to engage the course in ways that are meaningful for them, they begin to burn. As one student wrote, "We have developed our understanding of feminism, learned so many things about ourselves throughout the process, and found an entire group of people that have similar values. Feminism has done so much for us women as a whole, and the course has surely lit a flame of empowerment with me."

Works Cited

Bae, Michelle S., and Olga Ivashkevich. "Introduction: Reimagining Girls' Resistance." *Girls, Cultural Productions, and Resistance*, edited by Michelle S. Bae and Olga Ivashkevich, Peter Lang, 2012, pp. 1–10.

Chernik, Abra Fortune. "The Body Politic." *Listen Up: Voices from the Next Feminist Generation*, edited by Barbara Findlen, Seal Press, 1995, pp. 75–84.

Gay, Roxanne. *Bad Feminist*. Harper Perennial, 2014.

Harris, Anita. *Future Girl: Young Women in the Twenty First Century*. Routledge, 2004.

Hentges, Sarah. *Girls on Fire: Transformative Heroines in Young Adult Dystopian Literature*. McFarland, 2018.

hooks, bell. *Teaching Community: A Pedagogy of Hope*. Routledge, 2003.

Ross, Loretta. "What Is Reproductive Justice?" *Reproductive Justice Briefing Book: A Primer on Reproductive Justice and Social Change*. https://www.law.berkeley.edu/php-programs/courses/fileDL.php?fID=4051.

Simmer-Brown, Judith. "Commitment and Openness: A Contemplative Approach to Pluralism." *The Heart of Learning: Spirituality in Education*, edited by Steven Glazer, Jeremy P. Tarcher/Putnam, 1999, pp. 97–112.

Valenti, Jessica. *Full Frontal Feminism: A Young Woman's Guide to Why Feminism Matters*. Seal Press, 2014.

It Starts with a Book

An Exemplary "Girl on Fire"
and Her Undergraduate Thesis
on Racial Social Justice

KATIE RYBAKOVA *and* SYDNI COLLIER

Rarely do professors and teachers see a young woman in their classroom and think to themselves—there is a Girl on Fire. Often these young women manifest as students who need more challenge or who may, at first, seem reluctant to participate in typical classroom activities. In this essay, I (Katie) co-author the trajectory of a mentorship between myself and a Girl on Fire— Sydni. This mentorship flourished in the setting of our first class together— Introduction to Literature. Throughout the essay, you will read my reflections along with Sydni's vignettes, set in italics. While my reflections (and later, my discussion of how they relate to current literature on mentorship and social justice) are an important justification for mentorship and teaching relevant texts, the primary purpose of this essay is to highlight Sydni—the Girl on Fire. In sharing her excerpts alongside my narrative, our goal is to encourage mentorship relationships that allow for Girls on Fire to succeed outside the four walls of a traditional classroom.

Context

My teaching philosophy centers around the question: How can you expect students to learn about the world if you shelter them from it? The context of this essay situates within a small (under 1,500 students), rural, private college where the majority of the student body are first generation college students. The Introduction to Literature course that was the initial touch-point with Sydni is a required course for all majors at the college. The majority of students take the course not to study literature but rather to fulfill a college requirement. They are used to sitting and getting information—being told how to interpret literature. In applying my teaching philosophy question to the course, we often push beyond finding text symbolism and metaphor and extend the discourse to include critical analysis of how the text matters today and why we should care, especially when reading canonical work. This is the way I have always taught literature, but admittedly this often makes me the proverbial black sheep amongst traditionalist literature professors. What I find is that students are often initially hesitant to share their opinion because they have *never been asked* to do so. They always look for the "right" answer— what is it that YOU, Dr. Rybakova, want to hear? I push back—it is not about what I think; it is about what you think, and why. Teaching students to not only share their opinion but extrapolate on why they feel that way is the first step. The second is to, as students gain confidence, have them apply more scholarly and critical analysis to texts to dig deeper and move beyond opinion. In an interdisciplinary fashion, we use different lenses to unpack texts, asking questions such as: How do elements of psychology surface in this text (psychoanalysis)? What would Karl Marx say (Marxist critique)? Different classes often gravitate towards a particular lens. These conversations and analyses help us to address course objectives that I have inherited and which tend to be broad, like "analyze a variety of texts."

In the course in which I met Sydni, students wanted to talk about power, identity, and mental health. Because this population also included many reluctant and unconfident readers (Wiggins 1), it was essential to scaffold various young adult literature (YAL) and contemporary texts into the traditional Western canon reading list—a strategy grounded in current scholarship on reading motivation and effective instruction (Cook 19; Rybakova 50). These were the books that engaged the students the most and led to the most powerful connections and conversations. We constantly asked ourselves—so what? Why should we care? We turned an especially critical eye towards the canon; what did these "dead white guys" write that matters to us today? How did stereotypes and the status quo, of, say, 1949 (the year Orwell wrote *1984*) situate the way the texts talked about (or omitted) contemporary topics such as racial and gender equality? This in turn leads to critical conversations regarding social justice, and makes the various texts come alive. While we read YAL, students build their confidence in using critical analysis so that when we get to more complex texts, we are able to more readily express notions of relevance. "Aha" moments often surface during these conversations about the canon. Instead of me leading the conversation in saying that we need to read these texts because they are timeless, we unpack them inductively, we connect them to issues of today, we talk about social justice—then, the students make the connection themselves. These text-to-world connections make the canon come alive for them; *they* make the conclusion that they are timeless and *they* are able to come away with more complex notions of events in daily life by extrapolating themes from literature and connecting them to the real world. For example, students in this class made the connection that literary time periods reacted to what was occurring in society at the moment, and so expected and anticipated more dystopian novels to get published in the future that push back against notions of racism, violence, and inequality. Even more powerful was that they recognized that these are not new ideas—the canon unpacked these notions fifty-plus years ago. Keep in mind, now, that most of these are students who claimed to have never finished a book from cover to cover when they entered my class.

While the reading list changes from year to year, in the fall of 2017, when Sydni entered my classroom for the first time, we began with Neal Shusterman's *Unwind*, a dystopian YA novel, as a scaffold into Bradbury's *Fahrenheit 451* and Golding's *Lord of the Flies*. We also used *Unwind* to practice applying the Marxist critical lens as a form of analysis. We would eventually cover other common critical lenses (e.g., Feminist, Historical, Biographical, Psychoanalytic, etc.) along with various poetry and texts like Green's *Looking for Alaska* and Kafka's *The Metamorphosis*.

Typically, students in the class initially are tentative to share their opinions about these texts and are often unsure of whether or not they are "correctly" analyzing them. Once they recognize that the course is not based on my own subjective viewpoint of the text but rather about meaning-making based on evidence and the reader's own experiences (Reader Response), more students are willing to take risks and share. Students start to recognize that *talking* about texts—critical discourse—is a powerful learning process. What I have found is that women in particular who initially seem disengaged can be Girls on Fire under cover. Girls on Fire tend to take fewer risks initially—they either have disengaged from material because it does not resonate with them or are used to getting A's with minimal effort. These are the students that need to be challenged.

I recognized the need to differentiate Sydni's instruction within the first month—she quickly took to conversations about oppression through the lens of Marxist critique, and seamlessly made both text-to-text and text-to-world connections. While many of the analytic papers I handed back to students required at least one revision, Sydni's work begged for more challenge. As a result of my approaching her after class and asking how we could adjust the course expectations to keep her engaged, learning, and challenged, the seed that would eventually become Sydni's thesis was planted.

At first, I was not a confident participant in Dr. Rybakova's course. I had just transferred from an institution where my grades were lower than they'd ever been, and I was beginning a new course of study—I worried that I would be intimidated into a passive role without even so much as an opportunity to gain any new information. Historically, I was a leader in my social groups, athletic pursuits, and extracurricular activities. In the classroom, however, I had a tendency to hesitate; I would reach a point of challenge and freeze. Naturally, when I transferred and changed my goals, I was afraid that precedent would be predictive of my future. Thankfully, this was not the case. As I began to speak up more and more, Dr. Rybakova pulled me aside. Initially terrified that I had done something wrong, I was relieved when she expressed that my feelings of complacency and boredom were noticed and acknowledged. Eventually, that conversation led to a dialogue regarding how we could best challenge me within the course as it stood, what my goals were at the institution, and how she could help me reach them, despite the fact that my interests existed outside of the traditional range of curriculum offered to me. In high school, I enrolled in six advanced placement classes and two college courses before I graduated. After I decided to transfer into Thomas, but before I finished my first semester of college, I was enrolled in a course that was an introduction to sports law. The topics of race-related barriers and paths of least resistance introduced in the course piqued my interest; however, I knew that Thomas didn't have any program sheet options that would align with what would become the focus of my academic and professional pursuits.

I could not tell you how I knew that Sydni was not being challenged. Perhaps it was a combination of body language and the insights that she was making—insights that others were not quite grasping yet so her comments often were either the end of the conversation or ignored. In my previous experience, I knew that students who did not feel heard or felt like their contribution did not matter would eventually disengage. I could tell that Sydni was used to getting positive feedback from teachers and was previously academically successful. She needed someone to push her boundaries so that she could learn something new rather than go through the motions of school—play the game of school, if you will.

A Mentorship Forms

We know several things about mentorship. Mentors help students to explore educational plans, connect to others, and can "provide instructional and emotional support" (Fergusen 212). Teacher-student mentorship is particularly powerful and effective when teachers mentor students who are socially and economically disadvantaged (Erickson, McDonald, and Elder 344). Fergusen suggested that while some research emphasized emotional connection as the foundation for a strong mentorship, other research emphasized the need for mentorship to grow from instructional practice (345). This ambiguity depicts the complexity of mentorship and speaks to the need for emotional as well as instructional support. Mentorship shifts and includes different roles. Sometimes mentors share their point of view from experience, and at other times they simply lend an ear. On still other occasions mentors act as coaches and advisors. Mentorship with a Girl on Fire is much more complex than the begrudging support of Haymitch as Katniss first enters the arena in *The Hunger Games*. Successful mentorship involves "voluntary interaction, expressive acts of service, reciprocal care and gratitude, and shared accomplishments" (Fergusen 217). These practices are further evidenced in interactions between me and Sydni as a mentoring relationship developed.

My initial individual conversation with Sydni in Introduction to Literature led to further individual conversations with her in my office. These conversations, while tangential in nature, were intellectually-stimulating and similar to conversations I would typically have with a graduate level student. Sydni would start off with a question about the course, which would then morph into a conversation about social justice, which in turn would end with a conversation about the current state of K–12 education (Sydni was an education major at the time).

While not the topic of the Introduction to Literature course by any means, social justice was inherently present in many of our discussions in the course as our examination of YAL that addressed contemporary issues begged the question, *so what*? Scholars such as Schieble, who critiqued the notion of whiteness through the use of YAL (212), and Barker, who underlined the need for action-based discussion on social justice using YAL (87) (as opposed to talking for the sake of discussion, not change), accentuated the ways in which my course structure underlined relevant and authentic topics with the use of contemporary literature. This topic often moved beyond the four walls of the classroom—hence why the office conversations that initiated Sydni's and my mentorship relationship centered around the topic of social justice.

Growing up, I was always someone who was excited to go to school. It felt like a safe place to me. I was smart; that was something I was always very aware of. Academics came easy to me, my family was supportive, and I never wanted for anything. I came from a community where I truly felt safe, and I never really considered the possibility that anyone would ever have an experience any different than mine. I wanted to help other people to feel the way that I had felt in school: smart, confident, and capable. I decided I wanted to become a teacher so that I could encourage students, like myself, to pursue what makes them happy; for me, it was learning. It was around the time that I began to narrow my scope of interest to education that I also became conscious of the narratives generated within my own rural, white community. I simply could not make sense of how, or, more critically, why other students in other communities would not be given the same opportunities I was. I didn't understand why my family members were so critical of other types of communities. As my knowledge grew, I began to understand that things like race, income, and gender affected how some people were treated and shaped their realities.

Though she was a college freshman at the time, I recognized in Sydni a zeal for learning that many graduate students I have worked with possessed. I have worked with many outstanding students—but Sydni stood out as a Girl on Fire. She was inquisitive and eager to learn.

I immediately felt safe with and supported by Dr. Rybakova. She understood me in a capacity that I had never been understood before. My parents, while always supportive, were not able to talk with me about my options, academic interests, and goals; I was interested in a field and level of rigor that was completely foreign to them. Dr. Rybakova saw something in me that I had always seen within myself, however, she had a level of expertise and knowledge that made her opinion extremely important to me. I wanted her to believe in me because I looked up to her, but also because I wanted to grow as a person and I felt that she was capable of helping me. Her support was different than any other instructor that I've ever had; she acknowledged my skill and challenged me to develop it further, rather than just validating my intelligence. She pushed me to be better.

Nurturing a Fire: The Road to an Undergraduate Thesis

Once a fire is started, it needs to be nurtured. In many ways building a fire is an almost perfect metaphor for mentorship, and Sydni's and my process resembles the building of a fire. A fire first needs to be ignited—this "lighting of the fire" occurred when I pulled Sydni aside in Introduction to Literature and asked her: *what is it that you need right now?* A fire then needs to be stoked—a large log would cause the fire to fizzle, but our initial free-flowing conversations acted as kindling. As Sydni gained confidence, more fuel needed to be added to her fire. This occurred in the context of more explicit and serious conversations about graduate school and the undertaking of an undergraduate thesis. As with any fire, external factors (or internal misgivings) can sometimes make the flames falter—it is the mentor's job to help reignite the fire to restore it to its previous strength, adding more kindling (conversations) and oxygen (encouragement).

Encouraging Sydni to consider graduate school involved a conversation about setting her up for success. First, we discussed *why* she wanted to eventually get a doctorate. She shared that she wanted to teach at the college level "like you and Dr. B" (Dr. B. was and still is another mentor of hers). I should have seen this as a sign that Sydni was not sure what she wanted out of a doctorate, but I took it as a compliment instead and began talking to her about options. But as with many college freshmen, she would change her mind, and her major, several times before feeling at peace with her decision. Several times in a later semester she came to my office frustrated and on the verge of tears—she was losing motivation in preservice teacher coursework and was not sure what she wanted to do. She labeled it an existential crisis; I saw a burned out student who was unsure what her calling really was.

I once walked into Dr. Rybakova's office with the intention to drop out of school. I felt overwhelmed with the concept of returning to the education program while the world around me was falling apart. Hate was being spread and encouraged through political office, environmental emergencies were emerging left and right, and I was pursuing a degree which would only allow me to aid in indirect ways. I wanted to make things better right then, and as an impulsive person, I saw no other choice but to leave school and work internationally. In a later semester, I sobbed about how I didn't want to be a teacher, but I didn't want to lose her as an advisor. I didn't want to disappoint her. I felt accountable to her like I felt accountable to my parents; they had all invested time and energy in my success, and I didn't want anyone to feel as though they had wasted it. I wanted to work under her, but not within her field. I had no idea where my energy was best directed, but I knew I didn't want to settle or push through something I wasn't passionate about. At the time, I felt incredibly helpless and lost.

Amidst Sydni's indecision, one thing was clear—Sydni wanted to go to a large, prestigious school, and for that to happen, she'd need a stellar writing sample. We started discussing a possible undergraduate thesis despite her not knowing what major would suit her best at the time. She was passionate about the topic of racial injustice in higher education. Our college, as a small, rural, and private college, had never had an undergraduate (or graduate student) complete an official thesis, so there were bureaucratic hurdles to jump over before beginning the process. As her advocate in this case, I spoke with our provost, coming up with a three-course independent study sequence called "Special Topics in Education—Research" that would eventually culminate in an undergraduate thesis defense. As we sat down again to come up with a more decisive plan and timeline, we opened the conversation back up—Sydni needed to figure out what major would be best for her. As her advisor and a professor in the teacher education program, she was worried that I would be upset with her if she chose not to major in education. I assured her that this was not about me—I would remain her advisor regardless of her decision, and ultimately it was about her success, not my ego.

By spring, Sydni was feeling better. Given that she was a unique student, we came up with a unique solution—she opted into a new degree plan offered by the college called an interdisciplinary degree. This opportunity allowed Sydni to mix content into her degree that was intentional in giving her the foundational knowledge and background she would need to explore the research question she planned to ask: How does race play a role in perceived academic success in a rural homogenously-white college environment? The degree path became a cross-walk of sociology, education, and English coursework and ultimately was beneficial for her thesis. However, her progress with her thesis began to falter. Her bigger plans of attending graduate school also had a certain direction but were neither fully formed nor actionable yet.

While working on my thesis, I hit wall after wall. I felt that my work was not coming together as it should; each chapter was foreign and intimidating to me. It did not come easily to me, which wasn't a concept I was familiar with; I began to lose my confidence. I took criticisms extremely personally. I knew I could do it, but for the second time I began to question if tackling a thesis was the right route for me. I feared that all my work would be wasted if my product didn't reach my expected potential. I was terrified that it wouldn't be good enough when it was finished, so I stopped trying to finish it. With research shuffled to the back of my list of priorities, I fell behind.

Mentorship of a Girl on Fire in this situation was unique in that Sydni was used to easily succeeding and meeting a teacher's expectations. Suddenly, her thesis drafts were coming back with 50, 60, 70 comments, most of them critiques. I was not being overly critical; my purpose was twofold. First, I wanted to prepare her for the sometimes brutal world of academia—in many ways *The Hunger Games* arena might even be symbolic of this career path. As scholars know, rejection is common, critique is harsh, and R1 institutions often function on the unwritten rule of "publish or perish." Thick skin is absolutely necessary, and helping Sydni to see past the critique to the possibility of revision and progress was essential. Secondly, these comments were revisions to the broad, overgeneralized language that she was accustomed to using in persuasive and analytical essays. Academic work, particularly thesis work, needs to be as unbiased as possible, particularly in the field of sociology, in order to showcase expertise in a subject rather than opinion. Autonomy (in other words, comments/critique that did not always explicitly give a "formula" for the writing) was also essential. Graduate work requires independence and initiative.

I had never been given so much freedom before. I almost forgot that, ultimately, I was supposed to produce something with it. Despite meeting, taking notes regarding my objectives, and beginning to understand the context that my research would be situated within, I still felt that my work was not progressing; I was coming up short. Dr. Rybakova, instead of restricting my freedom or structuring opportunities to manage, handed me a book on research methods. "Read this," she said, "and then come back with questions." I think this was a wake up call for me. I realized that asking for help wouldn't be enough. I would have to help myself. I was given everything I needed to succeed: resources, support, and freedom. Now it was time to see what I could do with it.

Sydni needed a boost in confidence. What better way to experience this boost than to present her work in a public venue? An opportunity to share her work would encourage progress since it would reach more than just my eyes and ears and would double as a great addition to her resume. First, she presented her work at a state conference for middle-level educators. She was among five other undergraduate students who showcased their work to educators across the state. This was practice for her debut on the national stage. She would go on to present the preliminary data from her research at the National Council of Teachers of English (NCTE) Convention, where she presented her thesis project as part of an undergraduate research session. It was called "The Future is Now." The Girl on Fire was back.

Sydni presented her findings in response to her research question, which centered around how race played a role in perceived academic success. She had collected focus group data and presented her results at the conference. During this presentation, the "hive-mind" of presenters and participants helped her work through why her work mattered and how it might become actionable with a written implications section. These implications included suggestions for teachers to incorporate texts that include racially diverse characters and situations with the intention of helping students examine how race shapes people's perceptions of a situation, despite the high percentage of white students in our classrooms. This gives a voice to students who identify as members of a minority group, and allows students in the dominant culture to critically examine their perceptions and assumptions of race.

Though I had attended NCTE before, this time was different. I was a presenter. I was... official? Despite the brief period of doubt, I felt like my research was important. I was excited and incredibly proud to be amongst intelligent people who cared about their work, wanted to make a difference, and were taking the steps to do so. I attended sessions tailored to my interests, I talked to people about their research, and to my surprise, they asked about mine. I felt validated, I was inspired, and, for the first time in a long time, I felt smart. After attending NCTE, I felt re-energized about my work. The passion I had undertaken my thesis project with, and lost for a while, was back.

The conference finalized Sydni's "life plan," as she called it. She wanted to complete a doctorate in sociology, eventually working for a nonprofit organization to help fight for social justice. She had already succeeded in bringing her work to a national conference, and in doing so, she took the seed we had planted in Introduction to Literature (through texts, conversations, and our initial mentorship relationship) and grew the proverbial flower of change. The Girl on Fire had been part of a larger dialogue and she now began to take steps towards actionable change. The fire was blazing bright with no sign of losing light or power.

Ultimately, I knew I wanted to help people. I wanted people to feel the power and control that I have always felt, regardless of socially constructed factors like race, gender, and socioeconomic status. I, as a person of privilege, have an opportunity and responsibility to fight inequality and advocate for justice, but I knew that fighting for what is right is most effective when you first know what's wrong. Within the context of the rural town where I grew up and pursued my undergraduate degree, there is little diversity. I wondered how this affected students of color within the rural education system and, as I began to research more and more, I realized there was little to no information regarding the barriers faced by ethnic minority scholars within rural contexts; there was even less regarding student perceptions of such barriers. After much consideration, back and forth, and narrowing down my scope of research, I decided that I would conduct my research on students' perceptions of academic barriers within rural contexts and the role that race plays in shaping said barriers. I felt that if I could help to shed light on an issue that, as a consequence of its "numerical insignificance," was seldom addressed, I could begin to establish myself within the field as a qualified, capable, and desirable candidate for continuing my education and eventually establishing a career path; I could begin to make things right.

At the time of this writing, Sydni continues to work on her thesis, finalizing her analysis and writing her implications section in preparation to defend her thesis in Fall 2019. I have had the pleasure of working with Sydni for two years now, and at the end of this year, she will be the first from our college to graduate with an interdisciplinary degree and a completed undergraduate thesis. As long as Sydni remains passionate about her goals and future career, she will continue to be a Girl on Fire at a top-tier graduate school—she is applying to schools like NYU and UC Berkeley. My role as a mentor in our relationship involved my nurturing the fire that was already present within her.

Lessons Learned; The Professor's Role

For a Girl on Fire to ignite, a mentor needs to take certain steps to provide kindling. Being a perfectionist does not bode well for a person undertaking the role of mentor. It is important to recognize that **mentorships morph with the needs of each individual student**. Sometimes Sydni needed simply an ear to listen to her "talk it out" so that she could reach a conclusion on her own after talking through a problem. As a solution-oriented person, I sometimes found it difficult to *not* impose my own solutions to her problems or concerns. On the flip side, there were also times when I needed to advocate for her, as was the case when I set up coursework so that she could work on her thesis with me and get credit for it. It was important to remain flexible, as the nature of the mentorship—and my role in it—changed as we continued to work together. Facing problems as a team was, in my eyes, the true power of this mentorship. Additionally, it is important to note that perhaps Sydni grew as a Girl on Fire because I embody components of a Girl on Fire myself. In many ways I exemplified my expectations not by telling Sydni what to do but by sharing what I do myself in my own research. This speaks to the need for a mentor to be a leader, and a powerful leader is one that leads by example, not by dictation.

This suggests that **mentorship cannot be forced**. I saw Sydni's potential, but never required or forced her to come and discuss alternatives to assignments or additional work. I never asked her to come talk to me in my office. I kept my door open, and I encouraged conversations with all of my students, and it just so happened that Sydni felt like I could be someone to help her be a Girl on Fire. As I worked with Sydni on her changing plan, her skill set and goals morphed into a topic and area that I did not have expertise in.

Mentorship doesn't mean that the student you work with is YOUR student. Sure, Sydni was assigned to me as an advisee, but I encouraged her to talk to other professors, particularly those with a sociology background, rather than insist that she work only with me. On the professor's end, there is a level of control that is at work here. Ultimately, her success was my success—but I had to live with the notion that she may have worked more productively or more effectively with another professor and our mentorship could have culminated with that. This leads to the next lesson that I learned as Sydni's mentor—sometimes showing students that you don't know everything, and that you are willing to learn with them, is a powerful lesson in and of itself. I felt confident that I could advise Sydni on how to prepare for a larger and more research-driven institution—I had gone to one myself—but I had little knowledge of sociology programs. We spent hours looking at these programs together. Sometimes I would look up sociology programs on my own time and send her an email with a few listings that she might be interested in.

Finally, and most importantly, **mentorship takes time**. Much like any human relationship, a mentorship is a give-and-take relationship, and it requires the effort of both parties for it to ultimately be successful. It is a hard topic to study empirically because it is so personalized. Anecdotal accounts like those I have shared in this essay might be the closest we can get to conveying the value of mentorship relationships that encourage Girls on Fire to keep burning.

Lessons Learned: The Girl on Fire

Despite the fact that I have only worked under Dr. Rybakova for two years now, I'm incredibly proud of (and grateful for) what we have accomplished together. I genuinely believe that my academic career, one that is representative of my abilities and potential, began the day she pulled me aside in Introduction to Literature. Through all my doubt, frustration, failures, and tears, she never faltered; she always made me feel capable. She believed in me when I didn't want her to, when I didn't believe she had reason to, and when I didn't believe in myself. Dr. Rybakova has introduced me to concepts, colleagues, and professional organizations, all with the intent to equip me with the tools necessary for me to succeed. I stumbled many times in my pursuit; I learned time management, self-discipline, accountability, the value of personal initiative, and the satisfaction that comes with proving those who doubt you wrong—even if that includes yourself. Through the process of writing my thesis, and ultimately becoming "The Girl on Fire," I have overcome fear, bureaucratic restrictions, and personal mountains that in hindsight are molehills. I've changed majors, areas of concentration, and career aspirations. I've gone back and forth and back again without any real plan, and I have at times felt like I could do nothing right. These thoughts, however, existed only in a vacuum. After every meeting with Dr. Rybakova, after every conference where I discussed my work, I felt supported, confident, and validated. I felt that my work had meaning because it didn't exist in a vacuum. It took me longer than I'm proud to admit to realize that my research was something that could go as far as I wanted; I wouldn't be micromanaged, I wouldn't be inhibited, and I wouldn't be coddled. Throughout the process of writing my thesis, I felt that I had power for the first time in my life and it was terrifying. I was so afraid of my potential to fail that I didn't even consider what it would be like if I were to succeed. The confidence I developed throughout this process was not something that Dr. Rybakova or any of my other mentors could help me acquire; it was something I had to build myself. As a student who personally knows how important student perceptions are, I think the most critical factor in creating a Girl on Fire is letting her carry her own flame, even if that includes the potential for it to be extinguished.

Conclusion

The prototypical Girl on Fire—Katniss Everdeen—was painted by the dystopian society that she lived in as dangerous. She was the spark that led to revolution in the districts. In many ways, Girls on Fire need mentorship, not only to fuel their spark into a burning fire, but also to help them navigate a society where being a Girl on Fire is not necessarily always positive. Particularly for Sydni, who wants to work in the realm of social justice, her journey to completing her degree and thesis successfully and beginning to evoke actionable change has not been easy, and she will continue to have to work diligently to strive for her career goals, pushing against the status quo, particularly in regard to how higher education institutions treat and help racially diverse students as they work to experience academic success. That being said, it has truly been an honor to work with a young woman that burns as bright as Sydni does. This essay serves as a culmination of our hard work and is a shared achievement that we will both be proud of. My only hope is that professors and teachers elsewhere have the privilege to mentor a Girl on Fire.

WORKS CITED

Barker, Lisa. "Promoting Social Justice: Rehearsing Discussion Leadership in a Young Adult Literature Course." *English Journal*, vol. 107, no. 5, pp. 87–90.

Bradbury, Ray. *Fahrenheit 451*. Ballantine Books, 1953.

Cook, Michael. "Using YAL to Question Stereotypes, Society, and Self." *Multicultural Education*, vol. 24, no. 1, pp. 19–24.

Erickson, Lance, McDonald, Steve, & Elder, Glen H. "Informal Mentors and Education: Complementary or Compensatory Resources?" *Sociology of Education*, vol. 82, no. 4, pp. 344–367.

Fergusen, Sherelle. "Ask Not What Your Mentor Can Do for You…: The Role of Reciprocal Exchange in Maintaining Student-Teacher Mentorships." *Sociological Forum*, vol. 33, no. 1, pp. 211–233.

Golding, William. *Lord of the Flies*. Faber & Faber, 1954.

Green, John. *Looking for Alaska*. Penguin Group, 2005.

Kafka, Franz. *The Metamorphosis*. Kurt Wolff, 1915.

Rybakova, Katie. "Using Young Adult Literature with First Generation College Students in an Introductory Literature College Course." *The ALAN Review*, vol. 46, no. 1, pp. 42–52.

Schieble, Melissa. "Critical Conversations on Whiteness with Young Adult Literature." *Journal of Adolescent & Adult Literacy*, vol. 56, no. 3, pp. 212–221.

Shusterman, Neal. *Unwind*. Simon & Schuster, 2007.

Wiggins, Janice. "Faculty and First Generation College Students: Bridging the Classroom Gap Together." *New Directions for Teaching and Learning*, vol. 127, pp. 1–4.

Teaching Octavia Butler's Diverse Body of Speculative Fiction

Genre, Race and the Radical Imaginary

BRYAN YAZELL

Since her death in 2006, Octavia E. Butler has become synonymous with the very best of what science fiction can offer. Long recognized as the only black woman in a literary field dominated by white men, Butler always reflects on the way power imbalances—between men and women, for example, as well as between white and black racial identities—shape the way we navigate our own world and even alternate versions of it (Canavan). Given her immense stature in the genre, along with the difficult social issues she touches on, teaching Butler provides immense opportunities and poses stark challenges. This essay derives from an undergraduate course dedicated to Butler's fiction, which I developed for the English literature program at the University of California, Davis in the winter of 2017. As fate would have it, the class appeared especially timely. Donald Trump had just recently moved into the White House and, not coincidentally, Butler's name was circulating in headlines. *The New Yorker*, for example, celebrated her predictive powers: here was the author whose 1998 novel, *Parable of the Talents*, predicted the "zealot" campaigning to "Make America Great Again" (Aguirre). But Butler's work is valuable for more than its predictive abilities. In my dual roles as an academic and a teacher, I constantly struggle to articulate the power of literature to transform the way readers see the world, or at least their role in it. When writing an academic essay, critics might be used to stressing a novel's capacity to subvert social norms; but how does such an approach translate to the classroom? My course on Butler's fiction provided an ideal opportunity to think through this major question alongside students who were, thanks at least in part to the political climate, eager to imagine social change as well.

Part of Butler's power to provoke draws from her adept ability to identify, and then subvert, the implicit cues and conventions that organize our world. Her careful attention to matters of race and gender exemplifies this approach. As Sarah Hentges notes, Butler is the ultimate Girl on Fire author because nearly all of her work casts young women as leaders rebelling against the social expectations set upon them (34). A keen appreciation of the marginalization of women of color motivated and sustained her imagination. "I began writing about power," she once declared, "because I had so little" (Davidson 35). By taking on power imbalances both in society and in genre fiction, Butler helped inaugurate a new generation of writers and social criticism. "In a hypermale sci-fi space where science and technology dominate," Ytasha Womack writes, "Butler provided a blueprint for how women, particularly women of color, could operate in these skewed realities and distant worlds" (110). As Womack suggests, Butler's legacy is especially evident in the recent generation of writers who continue to expand the representation of women and people of color in the genre. Nalo Hopkinson, Nisi Shawl, and Nnedi Okorafor are just a few of the prominent authors who have cited Butler as a major influence on their own, racially-diverse speculative writings (Canavan). I raise these points because they already indicate the extent to which Butler's power as a writer is tied to her capacity for exposing the hidden social and racial assumptions undergirding genre norms. How do these fictions typically address their readers? Who is visible or invisible in their visions of the future? The intersection between genre, race, and sexuality provided the groundwork for the conversations, close readings, and writing assignments in my own experience teaching Butler's radical fiction.

As a literature teacher, I am especially interested in approaching the various social issues in Butler's work by focusing on genre. When I speak of genre in my teaching, I am less interested in imposing labels than in thinking with students about our own investments in, and reactions to, these labels. In fact, genre theory helps explain how readers and authors alike share the work of interpretation: readers bring certain prior knowledge to a situation (e.g., what is typical for a zombie story), a text conforms to these expectations in some respects and bends them in others, and the contact between the two produces a "world" of meaning (Frow 7). It is important to note that, for genre theorists, this general formula applies not only in cases of reading fiction but in all cases where a reader, a text, and social situation come into contact: one approaches an argument differently when in a courtroom—how to present oneself, what tones to use, how to read subtle bodily gestures—than in, say, a dispute with a close friend (Herman 13). But one can also see this world making at play in the more conventional sense of genre. For example, readers expect cowboys in a Western and wizards in fantasy, and thus they are likely to intuit something provocative about a gun-slinging wizard or a spell-casting cowboy. I find that this particular understanding of genre helps to structure my courses on speculative fiction in more ways than one. Most immediately, it helps substantiate a point that any teacher of literature might be at pains to stress: a piece of fiction is not something we should examine as if it were behind museum glass, but rather something that invites us in to share in the world it makes. Moreover, this approach to genre means that students can draw from their own insights they have accumulated over time about fiction—whether from novels, video games, film, or television—and share their knowledge on day one of class.

Butler's sustained investigation into racism and sexism across all of her work is effective to the extent that readers (or students of her literature) immerse themselves in her work and recognize the overlap between her fictional worlds and their own. In the pages that follow, I provide several cases that showcase how her work invites scrutiny of both generic and social conventions alike. For literature teachers, these novels provide ample occasions to assist students in developing an analytical toolset for linking the social—evident in Butler's underlying interest in power dynamics—to specific formal and generic aspects of literature. For students, these conversations in the classroom encourage them to draw from and expand on what they already know. While students are unlikely to have a mental laundry list of all the conventions appropriate to, say, a vampire story or a young adult (YA) novel, they are likely to have some sense of when a given text conforms to or resists these categories.

As I stress throughout, a primary goal for this course is to aid students in decrying the various ways that genre conventions encode ways of interpreting the world, especially in regard to race and gender. As Hentges points out in *Girls on Fire*, even an ostensibly inclusive genre like YA fiction—which frequently foregrounds the experiences of young women—can too-easily rearticulate the hegemonic values of a white American readership (11). Butler's body of work, which draws on several generic traditions within any single text, is an ideal place to observe how literature begins to disentangle the imagination from the imaginative limitations Hentges notes above. One clearly important way Butler shakes up stale representations of gender and race is to center her stories on black women. For example, Lauren Olamina of the *Parable* series is a protagonist whose very being—a teenaged black girl who is the prophet of peace in a time of dystopia—stands in sharp contrast to the (typically male) white savior many might expect from speculative fiction. Lauren is thus an "original" Girl on Fire, one who helps to decenter whiteness from the speculative genre in general and from YA novels in particular (Hentges 49). This essay builds on this reception of Lauren by turning to other examples from Butler's fiction that similarly identify and disrupt the social assumptions that are often encoded into genre: *Kindred* (1979) incorporates elements of fantasy (in the form of time travel) and slave narrative; *Dawn* (1987) is an alien abduction narrative set in post-apocalyptic setting; and *Fledgling* (2005) refreshes the conventions of horror and the vampire story. The brief keywords listed here do little justice, of course, to the layered characters, plots, and moral ambiguities that are characteristic of Butler's work. But they provide an interpretative framework that, as I detail below, brings into view the assumptions we as readers bring to the world depicted both in and outside the pages of fiction.

Kindred: Whose Fantasy?

To be sure, my teaching experience largely consists of literature courses designed for students working toward a bachelor's degree in English. As a result, I expect that many of them will come to class ready to discuss extensively both literary texts and cases from popular culture alike. But I believe that teaching genre along the lines of what I outline below can be effective for a range of students with varying degrees of training, so to speak, in literary analysis. Part of the reason Butler's fiction is so powerful is because it gives ample occasions for readers to identify with the characters and situations she portrays: the Girls on Fire in her fiction are not faultless superheroes, but complex people who fight to survive in the face of violence from outside and self-doubt within. In addition to inviting readers to identify with her characters, Butler's use of genre conventions also calls out for recognition. To approach these linked concepts, I offered to my class the example of the American slave narrative in relation to Butler's novel, *Kindred*. As a specific literary form, the slave narrative conventionally denotes writing that relates the first-hand experience of subjects who escaped or were emancipated from slavery. Accordingly, these texts are bounded to a particular time and place: the narratives circulated in North America among abolitionist societies pressing to end slavery. After the Civil War, these accounts continued so that their traumatic memory would not be easily forgotten among subsequent generations. Students may also read relevant scholarly essays, such as Philip Gould's account of the slave narrative, to help drive home these distinctive features. To build on these early lessons, I ask my students to think about their previous encounters with slave narratives in any form. In doing so, I attempt to establish a dialogue with students early in the class about the usefulness of their own prior contact with literary genres—especially ones that, in contrast with something like fantasy or science fiction, they are not likely to recognize as a genre in and of itself.

The conversation should broach not only certain formal features that might define a genre, but also how genres circulate within popular culture. For example, many students identified film versions of slave stories and adaptation of slave narratives, such as *12 Years a Slave* (2013). The circulation of slave narratives on film in turn raises the questions of why these stories might need to be told today and why they might be particularly well suited for film adaptations. In my experience, students are usually quick to point out that the production of popular movies involving the slavery experience, from *Amistad* (1997) to *Django Unchained* (2012), reflects an abiding popular interest in the topic that has carried into the present day. Usually, the point is made that slave narratives have much left to say to audiences today who still confront the legacies of slavery, segregation, and other institutionalized forms of racial violence. Often, students will also note that these narratives tend to focus on men as central characters, a convention that might help explain which historical slave narratives have been adapted into film and which have not. To reiterate this last point, I provide excerpts from essays and blog posts identifying the lack of women protagonists in slave narrative films, such as Tamara Winfrey Harris's piece in *The American Prospect*. At this point, we have already begun to unpack our sense of a genre that students in the U.S. are likely to have encountered in some form or another.

Butler's *Kindred* builds on this in-class dialogue, which centers on recent depictions of slavery in popular media, and troubles some of its underlying assumptions. As noted above, historical slave narratives usefully contextualize the narrative form *Kindred* takes. The conversation then moves away from historical slave narratives to a "neo-slave narrative" like Butler's (Flagel 217). If we all acknowledge the need to recognize first-hand accounts of slavery, what does a wholly fictionalized account of slavery provide to readers? Published in 1979, *Kindred* is both a time-travel story and a slave narrative. The story involves Dana Franklin, a young black woman, who inexplicably travels back in time from Los Angeles in 1976 to a plantation near Baltimore in 1815. Once there, she eventually meets her ancestors: Alice, a young slave girl, and Rufus, the white son of the man who owns the plantation. Butler depicts Dana as a strong, self-assured woman who is set in a situation that is incredibly challenging in more ways than one. First, she has no control over when she travels back in time. She learns that she is essentially summoned across centuries whenever Rufus, her ancestor, suffers a life-threatening experience (*Kindred* 50). Even more complicated is the fact that her husband, a white man named Kevin, eventually travels back with her. At this point, she must struggle to survive in the dangerous situation she finds herself in while also keeping her interracial marriage secret—or else assuredly suffer from mob violence. Rufus's father enslaves Dana who, despite her literacy and general knowledge about the antebellum era, suffers horribly. Second, she struggles with guilt over her own involvement in the plantation system. As Rufus ages, Dana sees him slowly but surely conforming to the terrible slave-master archetype that his father has set for him, despite her repeated attempts at educating him to reject racism (*Kindred* 169). At the same time, she knows that her own birth depends on Rufus surviving into adulthood and fathering a child with Alice, the slave girl. *Kindred* thus stresses the troubling continuities between the antebellum period and the present when it comes to racism and, most literally for Dana, male control over women.

As this overview suggests, Butler's incorporation of both time-travel elements and the slave narrative genre raises questions that might otherwise simmer below the surface. Butler herself touches on these issues of genre in her explanation for what motivated her to write *Kindred*. The novel, she says, "was a kind of reaction to some of the things going on during the sixties when people were feeling ashamed of, or more strongly, angry with their parents for not having improved things faster, and I wanted to take a person from today and send that person back to slavery" (Kenan 496). She explains that, in contrast to most of her other work, *Kindred* should be understood as "fantasy" because it offers no attempt at explaining the science behind time travel; it is instead "a device for getting the character back to confront where she came from" (Kenan 496). Butler suggests that our understanding of historical events and institutions—even something as formative in U.S. history as plantation slavery—has the tendency to become overly reductive over time. *Kindred*'s simple fantasy device intersects with the slave narrative to thoroughly complicate our sense of this history. Time travel provides the basis for any number of scenarios that raise difficult moral questions. For their part, students were extremely attentive to what the time-travel device does, and might do, to lay bare the social issues in Butler's novel. For instance, one student wondered what might happen if Alice were to travel to the 1970s just as Dana traveled to the 1800s. Alice and several other slaves condemn Dana for her familiar relationship with Rufus, but how might their perspective change if they were to see Dana's world as well? The student concluded that this thought exercise helps to show how blackness in Butler's story, far from a concrete identity category, is instead fluid and responsive to social context.

As Butler explains, *Kindred* is a fantasy that immediately complicates any sense of wish fulfillment that we might expect from a time-traveling story. Dana is an independent black woman who finds herself enmeshed in the plantation system; Kevin, her husband, enjoys a level of freedom owing to his whiteness that she could never attain. Students were particularly interested in Dana's relationship with Kevin and its parallels with her relationship with Rufus. They consequently noted passages in the text that make this comparison clear throughout the story. For instance, Dana notices that Kevin, after spending some years in the nineteenth century, begins to sound "a little" like Rufus (*Kindred* 190). Elsewhere, Dana notes the similar "pale eyes" that both Kevin and Tom, Rufus's father, share (*Kindred* 90). The enduring privilege associated with whiteness comes across in both passages, students offered, even in the case of an otherwise sympathetic white character like Kevin. Butler's novel thus encourages questions of the type the student above raised in relation to Alice: we need not wonder—given the events in the story—what might happen if a white man were to travel to antebellum Baltimore alongside Dana, but we are encouraged to continue pondering the moral ambiguities the story poses well after it is finished.

In order to sustain this conversation, I paired our consideration of *Kindred* with another neo-slave narrative that indulges in wish-fulfillment of its own: Quentin Tarantino's film, *Django Unchained* (2012). Although the film contains no on-screen time traveling, it approaches the subject of slavery from a thoroughly modern perspective: a freed slave (Jamie Foxx) and his white mentor (Christoph Waltz) enact swift and hyperbolic violence on slavers and racists alike. There are several sources that can help students recognize the implicit narrative devices in Tarantino's film: Adilifu Nama describes *Django* as a "Gothic fantasy" (94), and Annalee Newitz's blog article treats the film as fantasy wish fulfillment, and contrasts it directly with *Kindred*. In view of Newitz's article in particular, students were better equipped to ask the question: whose fantasy is on display? Many commented on the disparate treatment of violence between Butler and Tarantino. Several students highlighted the moment in *Kindred* when Dana observes the plantation: she remarks that she is "almost disappointed" by the estate, which falls far short of the scale she had come to expect from watching movies like the 1939 film, *Gone with the Wind* (*Kindred* 67). In contrast, when she is brutally whipped shortly after, it is a pain that is inexpressible on the page (*Kindred* 107). The same students wondered in turn if the hyperbolic violence in *Django* might pose a problem that is conspicuously addressed in *Kindred*: Dana voices her own narrative and, consequently, she narrates scenes of violence (both observed and experienced), while Tarantino's film depicts heroic acts of vengeful bloodshed alongside horrific instances of plantation violence. As this last point indicates, our final discussion of *Kindred* touches on the conventions of not only fantasy and slave narratives but also film.

Kindred sets the groundwork for further classroom discussion about how Butler's fiction begins to unwrap questions of social justice from ones of genre and narrative. Most immediately, the novel introduces students to how narrative voice factors into Butler's stories. Dana narrates her own story and, consequently, the stark traumas she experiences firsthand. In this role, she underscores the importance of voice for Girls on Fire, who often narrate their experiences in a manner that brings readers "closer to the character's reality" (Hentges 113). The narrative voice in *Kindred* also gives students ample occasions to think critically about how the novel takes up and, alternatively, disrupts certain generic conventions. The comparison between the novel and *Django Unchained* underscores the value of voice in Butler's fiction: Dana not only notes what she sees, but also reacts in ways that register her disgust and—most intriguing for our class discussions—her disappointment. Ultimately, Dana must learn to recognize that which she has learned from popular sources like *Gone with the Wind*, whose rose-tinted depiction of the antebellum plantation falls well short of the reality she observes. At this point in the course, I encourage students to reflect on how *Kindred* uses narrative form (as in the case with Dana's voice) to invite our recognition before redirecting this attention inward. How much does fiction shape our understanding of the world, even in the case of slavery? What type of fiction might inspire better, more sensitive ways of seeing the world? By stressing its fantasy element, we can also appreciate how the novel encourages us to see the present in a new light. In short, *Kindred* assists students in understanding how formal literary techniques and social justice themes in a given novel together can orient our understanding of real-world events today.

Rethinking Alien Abduction in Dawn

The classroom conversations about fantasy and *Kindred* led to further consideration of Butler's work—and its presentation of complex moral quandaries—in the context of science fiction. *Dawn*, the first novel in Butler's Xenogenesis series (later published collectively under the title *Lilith's Brood*) exemplifies the author's use of a familiar genre toolset to address extremely complicated questions of race, sexuality, and maternity. From its earliest pages, *Dawn* meets familiar storylines from nuclear apocalypse stories and alien encounter narratives. Lilith Iyapo awakens in a strange alien spacecraft and learns that her abductors, a race of aliens known as the Oankali, have kept her in a state of sleep for 250 years. All human civilization has been wiped out by a nuclear event, and the Oankali have appointed themselves the task of repopulating the planet with the human survivors they have collected. But, as is the case with *Kindred*, Butler's protagonist must sacrifice much of herself in order to survive. The Oankali are primarily interested in genetic engineering: they crave alien genetic material, such as they find in humans like Lilith, in order to mix it with their own and create something new. Lilith has been selected to lead a group of survivors who are to return to Earth and rebuild civilization—which will eventually also consist of the Oankali-human hybrids. Lilith is in a difficult position in several ways. Most immediately, she is tasked with a responsibility that far outweighs any other human in the novel: the people she is supposed to lead resent her role and, because she is a black woman, this condensation is rife with racialized and sexualized overtones (*Lilith's Brood* 157). Moreover, she must also confront a profound xenophobia within herself: the Oankali are creatures whose tentacled forms disgust and terrify every human they encounter. Over the course of the novel, Lilith learns to overcome what she describes as "true xenophobia" in order to engage with—and even develop a deep affection for—specific Oankali characters (*Lilith's Brood* 23). As this last point suggests, *Dawn* is thoroughly invested in exploding the binaries, such as between an "us" and a "them," that might otherwise characterize alien encounter stories.

The way science fiction conventions propel Butler's commentary on binarism structured much of my class's discussion of the novel. As the plot summary already suggests, the text meditates on the question of consent throughout: can Lilith really ever say no to the Oankali if it means the end of humanity? But the most pressing way the novel deals with consent is in relation to Lilith's role as a potential mother to the Oankali-human hybrids. The work of the genetic exchange, readers learn, is to be completed via the use of a so-called third sex among the Oankali, the ooloi, who are readers of genetic material and can therefore know "everything that can be learned about you from your genes," including one's memories and desires (*Lilith's Brood* 23). For the Oankali, consent in the conventional sense is not an operative concern because bodies—or rather, our genes—tell them everything they need to know, even as humans like Lilith vocally refuse to comply. In order to best consider this nuanced subject, it is useful to first reiterate the way science fiction frames pressing social questions. For our class, the authority on this subject was Darko Suvin's famous overview of the genre in his 1979 book, *Metamorphoses of Science Fiction*. Science fiction by definition involves what he terms "estrangement and cognition," that is to say imaginative elements that are both like and unlike our own world (7–8). While science fiction might depict an alien society on a far-away planet, this presentation should provide us with the occasion to reflect on our own society and social conventions. Furthermore, what makes science fiction distinct from any other genre that imagines alternate worlds—from sword and sorcery fantasy to myths and even religious texts—is the presence of what Suvin calls a "novum," an invention or innovation within the narrative on which the estrangement rests and which is also given plausible explanation within the text itself (4).

The ooloi's depiction as third- or non-sexed subjects was without a doubt the element of the story that garnered the most attention from students and raised the most questions about Butler's story as a whole. *Dawn* reiterates the point that humanity has essentially brought destruction upon itself and, without the intervention of the Oankali, is doomed to repeat its cycle of destruction. However, the Oankali are motivated not by any moralistic or sympathetic concern but rather by their desire to retain the precious genetic material humans contain. The overall question Butler seems to be asking is: to what extent can humans ever reliably save themselves, given this presentation of the human condition as inherently flawed? In an article we reviewed in class, Hoda M. Zaki argues that in *Dawn* "human politics is not an arena for the exercise of choice or freedom, and it offers no opportunities for improvement of the human condition" (242). Zaki's firm position on this complex issue helped to ground our subsequent discussion. In order to show how Butler's treatment of the human condition scales down to specific scenes in the novel, one student volunteered a passage from the text that exemplifies the contrast between how humans and the Oankali understand agency. The passage details an encounter between Lilith, an ooloi named Nikanj, and Joseph, Lilith's romantic companion. The ooloi essentially see themselves as the conduit through which the genetic transfer takes place; rather than sexual intercourse in the conventional sense, an ooloi links with two humans and facilitates an "intimacy" that surpasses, in Lilith's recollection, the physical act of sex (*Lilith's Brood* 162). But while Lilith eventually becomes a willing participant in this exchange, Joseph is reluctant. In one instance, he protests directly to Nikanj:

> "You said I could choose. I've made my choice!"
> "You have, yes." It opened its jacket with its many-fingered true hands and stripped the garment from him. When he would have backed away, it held him. It managed to lie down on the bed with him without seeming to force him down. "You see. Your body has made a different choice" [*Lilith's Brood* 189].

Having presented this scene for consideration, the student raised the prospect that Butler's story questions human agency most forcefully in the case of sexual encounters. This in turn prompted more comments from students about how Butler reframes consent and rape. While no one in my class accused Butler of condoning rape in any sense—perhaps owing to their familiarity with her writing by this point in the course, especially in view of *Kindred*—they wondered aloud what the point of crumbling Joseph's consent in this scene might be.

As before, my teaching response to these important and difficult questions takes the form of reframing the inquiries to incorporate Butler's uses of genre. We therefore returned to Suvin's concept of the novum and applied it to the case of the Oankali. How does Butler's depiction of these genetic traders estrange our view of our own world, and what aspects of our world in particular does Butler invite us to scrutinize? For her part, Butler maintains that *Dawn*, along with the rest of the Xenogenesis series, casts a light on nothing less than the inherent fallibility of humanity. Reflecting on then-president Reagan's promise that the U.S. "could have winnable nuclear wars and how we'd all be safer if we had more nuclear weapons," Butler concludes: "I thought if people believed this, then there must be something wrong with us as human beings" (See 40). The Oankali cast into relief what it means to be human as Butler sees it: in other words, what it means to be brought up with values that are not conducive to peaceful cohabitation.

In ways that diverge from *Kindred*, *Dawn* gave students numerous occasions for discussing the ways literature can invite us to reevaluate our own understanding of complex issues related to, among other things, race and sexuality. Like Dana, Lilith fits the mold of the Girl on Fire not only because she is a strong woman protagonist, but also because she struggles with the weight of the tasks set for her. At the same time, the commitment to certain science fiction conventions means that the novel takes a different form than what students saw in *Kindred*. *Dawn* is told in a third-person narrative voice, which puts readers at a level of remove from both Lilith and the Oankali. In view of this narrative structure, several students remarked that *Dawn* already felt much more like a science fiction novel than did *Kindred*. Indeed, one student worried aloud whether she would enjoy the book as much, since she had never read a science fiction novel before. Teaching *Dawn* alongside the critical sources I mention above helps to situate Butler's generic innovations. But as I have stressed throughout, one need not be especially familiar with science fiction in advance in order to attend to how Butler refreshes the genre. Indeed, Lilith—like Dana—is a Girl on Fire who readers can identify with and, having done so, learn what she learns. Her strength lies not only in her leadership abilities, but in her ability to overcome her initial aversion to the Oankali. Butler presents xenophobia in a way that is more fundamental than what we think of as racism or sexism: the Oankali are fundamentally different than us in ways that we can barely comprehend. But at the same time, Butler does not merely enjoin us to love the Other. Instead, the Oankali's disregard of consent leaves the reader with a sense of disquiet. This notion of unease as a product of Butler's fiction is an important teaching outcome as well. As our classroom discussions attest, we know a social convention has been broken; but which one? How much leeway are we willing to grant someone in bending this unspoken rule? The fact that these questions can be aimed at Butler's invocation of both genre and social taboos further underscores the extent to which both are linked in her radical narratives.

The Vampires We Need: Fledgling

I have argued so far that stressing genre when teaching Butler helps clarify some of the nuanced moral questions encoded in her fiction. The last novel Butler wrote, and the last text we read for my course, is no exception. *Fledgling* is a vampire narrative that turns the conventions of this genre completely on its head. Most immediately, Butler refreshes vampire lore to provide a "science-fictionalized, biologically rational" explanation of the subject (Canavan). In *Fledgling*, a species known as the Ina drink the blood of humans, with whom they form symbiotic relationships. While they are longer-lived and physically more powerful than humans, they cannot survive in the sunlight. When we meet Shori Matthews, the protagonist of the story, she suffers from amnesia, and over the course of the story learns more about her powers as an Ina and her own complicated past. Moreover, while Shori physically resembles a ten-year old black child, she is actually a 53-year-old— and very powerful—example of an Ina-human hybrid, the result of genetic engineering to empower the Ina to walk in the daylight. Over the course of the novel, we learn that certain Ina factions see Shori as a threat to their way of life and attempt to kill her. She is aided on her journey to recover her memories and her role as a transgressive Ina by Wright, a man who becomes her first human "symbiont" and thereafter her constant companion. Already, Butler draws from and complicates what we might call the standard expectations from vampire stories. Characteristically for her fiction, the story focuses on a powerful Girl on Fire who leads others in the fight against oppressive forces. In doing so, she reverses the traditional gender roles in vampire stories, from *Dracula* (1897) to *Twilight* (2005), which cast mysterious, masculine vampire figures against vulnerable female characters. Shori's position as (what appears to be) a young black girl further inverts the power roles in this genre, inasmuch as it calls out the implied racial dynamic in these stories, which typically feature white protagonists battling ethnically-ambiguous vampires (Morris 148).

As was the case with *Dawn*, the uneasy scenarios in *Fledgling* produced extensive conversations among students about the intersection of genre and social values. From the earliest pages of the novel, Butler sustains Shori's ambiguous presentation as a pre-pubescent girl and powerful vampire. Shortly after she awakens with no memory, Shori wanders in a confused state near the road. Spotting her, Wright drives by and takes her into his vehicle to help. When she refuses to go to the hospital, Wright detains her as she attempts to escape. Narrating the scene, Shori notes the size discrepancy between the two as they struggle—at which point she bites him and draws blood for the first time in the novel (*Fledgling* 16). Here, the underlying sexual and power dynamic comes to the foreground:

> "It doesn't hurt anymore," he said. "It feels good. Which is weird. How do you do that?"
> "I don't know," I told him. "You taste good."
> "Do I?" He lifted me, squeezed past the division between the seats to my side of the car, and put me on his lap.
> "Let me bite you again," I whispered.
> He smiled. "If I do, what will you let me do?" [*Fledgling* 17–18].

Owing to our previous discussions, the fact that Butler presents an erotic relationship that cuts against convention came as little surprise to students. But as many indicated, the drastic difference in age between Wright and Shori (as she appears) immediately casts Wright, a major ally to Shori throughout the novel, in a suspicious light. While Shori has lived for over 50 years by the time of the encounter above, Wright can only assume he is dealing with a child. As is the case with *Dawn*, Butler raises probing questions about the nature of consent that sustain throughout the narrative. In *Dawn*, the Oankali claim to know humanity better than humans know themselves; they therefore look to the body to provide the consent that people are unwilling (or unable) to verbalize. In *Fledgling*, the Ina's bite turns humans into compliant symbionts due to a chemical reaction that results in physical addiction. As another symbiont explains, Ina venom is a powerful bonding agent that is hard to break: "It's like coke or something" (*Fledgling* 181). Far from being the victim of abuse, Shori instead enthralls her symbionts in a manner that blurs the lines between consent and compulsion.

Given the relatively long and persistent interest in vampire fiction, *Fledgling* brought to a head many of the preceding conversations about genre and their implicit codes for navigating the world. When dealing with the questions swirling around Shori's ambiguous relationship with Wright, I encouraged students to again reformulate their queries to account for genre. I have already mentioned above some of the scholarship attesting to the hegemonic coding of gender and race in vampire stories, which was also incorporated into our classroom discussion. To better assist in considering this claim, I played clips from several prominent film and television versions of vampire storytelling, including Francis Ford Coppola's version of *Bram Stoker's Dracula* (1992) and the pilot episode from Joss Whedon's television series, *Buffy the Vampire Slayer* (1997–2003). While examples of vampire lore are many, these cases nicely substantiate some of the genre's changing motifs alongside its more stable aspects. To provide an introduction to these examples, I cited Nina Auerbach's claim in *Our Vampires, Ourselves* that the "rapidity with which our Draculas date tell us only that every age embraces the vampire it needs" (145). In other words, vampire stories are continually retold in part because the shelf-life for the vast majority of vampire productions is short lived as a result of changing social mores. What appears like a cutting-edge reinterpretation one day—are vampires to be feared or admired?—looks out of date just a few years later. Whether or not one agrees with Auerbach's claim, it provides a useful way of framing teaching discussions around stories like *Fledgling*: namely, what does *this* vampire story *need* to say? There are numerous other examples of vampire lore that can provide productive points of comparison with the novel, such as *Let the Right One In* (2004), a novel (as well as Swedish and American films) about a young child vampire character, and the *Blade* films (1998–2004), which feature a vampire whose black skin empowers him, like Shori in *Fledgling*, to walk in the daylight. Given the diversity of vampire fictions, any addition to the canon must not only contend with what has come before but also, ideally, revise and refresh something that is in need of attention.

After reviewing these other examples, *Fledgling* may appear as disquieting as ever, but the social and generic rules it addresses come into clearer view. The novel's central relationship firmly rejects any attempt at imposing facile or conventional roles between the two subjects. Shori is at once a powerful vampire and also vulnerable. She appears not only to be a child but, more importantly for the other Ina in the story, a non-white child at that. As a result of the genetic modification, Shori possesses enough melanin in her skin to enable her to walk in the sun (*Fledgling* 66). For a rival group of Ina, she is an affront to their species, and her blackness marks her as the Other. Likewise, Wright is an ambiguous figure: he is a white man who is highly possessive of Shori, but he is also hopelessly linked to her via the symbiotic process that began with her first bite. While some students were willing to stake out a stronger position on the question Butler poses—can Wright consent? Is this relationship wrong, even though Shori is actually middle-aged?— it should be clear given this overview that the narrative for its part is less interested in providing answers than in provoking questions. Whatever the case, any attempt to descry agency in this narrative is especially challenging. Ultimately, Butler dramatizes how free choice is elusive for marginalized peoples in particular—feminized subjects, people of color, the young, and the poor. The novel elsewhere makes this point apparent. In one scene, Shori feeds on an older woman named Theodora, who in turn becomes her second symbiont. As Shori comes upon Theodora sleeping in bed, the scene recalls countless other vampire stories. Later, Theodora can't help but note her disappointment. "You are a vampire," she says to Shori, "you're supposed to be a tall, handsome, fully grown white man. Just my luck" (91). To return to Auerbach's quip, we are not necessarily getting the vampires that we want in this case, but we are getting the vampires that we need.

Overall, *Fledgling* assists students in thinking through the ways literature might nurture a raised social consciousness in ways that extend beyond the classroom. Most immediately, it demonstrates the extent to which Girls on Fire disrupt something of the imaginative monopoly even in many speculative and fantasy narratives. Putting Shori at the center of this new vampire story casts into relief the various gendered and racialized associations we as readers of fiction take on without necessarily realizing it. During the time of Butler's writing, women of color were largely invisible in the pages of speculative fiction. In contrast, Shori is a powerful presence that confounds any attempt to stereotype her. She is dangerous and also vulnerable; she is exceptional and also marginalized. By centering her fiction around powerful and complex Girls on Fire like Shori, Butler helps to reclaim a narrative presence for women of color in particular. In doing so, Butler helps us to connect matters of literature and culture to matters of social justice. Our classroom discussions following *Fledgling* repeatedly stressed this point: cultural sources are a critical area where norms concerning raced and gendered bodies circulate, harden, and become conventional wisdom. Students can see in Butler's work this process coming back into the light, where it can be scrutinized and, ideally, revised.

Conclusion: Butler's Radical Imagination

Butler's insight into race, gender, and popular culture extends well beyond the examples presented in this essay. What the preceding pages have tried to do instead is make legible some of the most apparent aspects of her radical imagination as they came up, and were extensively discussed, in my survey course on her literature. In my case, stressing Butler's generic innovations alongside her social thinking helped to situate the probing questions she poses on relatively stable ground. Thus, otherwise wide-ranging questions became more focused: what does this *generic innovation* or novel scenario enable Butler to say? How does her evaluation of consent change between the science fiction scenario in *Dawn* and the vampire scenario in *Fledgling*? Teaching genre and Butler's fiction along the lines presented here provides numerous occasions to identify and scrutinize the way literature prepares us to understand the world. To different degrees, we all bring a certain awareness of how genre affects the way we present ourselves and read others—whether it be when opening the pages of a thick science fiction tome or when we enter a university classroom—and what it might mean to subvert these expectations. To study genre closely in turn assists us in our scrutiny of the world at large because, as Mark Jerng explains, "we *participate in genres* in order to form and organize our sense of the world" (9, emphasis in original). Butler's fiction further underscores this framework because it touches on nuanced moral, racial, and gender issues that come with no easy solution. Instead, she encourages us to meditate on these subjects and to imagine what the world might look like if it assigned more voice and representation to radical Girls on Fire.

Butler implicates our own fallibility and complicity in the social institutions she criticizes; teaching her in a manner that draws students in and makes their prior knowledge assets to their learning will be in keeping with her fiction's overall aim. Doing so also reaffirms the value of Girls on Fire in the classroom. As Hentges explains, the Girl on Fire provides both a unifying theme and a unifying symbol to a course. Whether the class consists of a diverse collection of texts, or (like mine) a sustained survey of one author, students who enroll typically have a sense of what to expect. Hentges relates that in her own course students discussed what the symbol of the Girl on Fire meant to them while also extrapolating "what the Girl on Fire can be to young people, [and] how she can inspire and promote social justice" (206). Such conversations invite participants to share not only their own sense of how a given subject impacts them, but also how it circulates in the world more generally. Thus, a given classroom may comprise people of various backgrounds or interests, but discussions about how a given character or author—the Girl on Fire in this case—challenges social conventions asks us to imagine ourselves as part of a larger reading community. In other words, teaching Girls on Fire also necessarily involves discussions about genre. We might have much to learn from one book, but when we become well-versed in genre we better understand the strengths and limitations to any specific symbol or motif from across a vast body of works. As Butler asserts across her fiction, to understand conventions is difficult enough on its own because we are quick to take certain ideas—about race and gender to, say, space-traveling aliens—and turn them into cliché. But once we understand the rules of the world, both on and off the page, we are better equipped to change them.

Works Cited

Aguirre, Abby. "Octavia Butler's Prescient Vision of a Zealot Elected to 'Make America Great Again.'" *The New Yorker*, 2017, https://www.newyorker.com/books/second-read/octavia-butlers-prescient-vision-of-a-zealot-elected-to-make-america-great-again.

Auerbach, Nina. *Our Vampires, Ourselves*. University of Chicago Press, 1995.

Butler, Octavia E. *Fledgling*. Seven Stories Press, 2005.

_____. *Kindred*. Beacon Press, 2003.

_____. *Lilith's Brood*. Aspect/Warner Books, 2000.

_____. *Parable of the Sower*. Warner Books, 2000.

Canavan, Gerry. *Octavia E. Butler*. University of Illinois Press, 2016. *Modern Masters of Science Fiction*. E-book.

Davidson, Carolyn S. "The Science Fiction of Octavia Butler." *Sagala*, vol. 2, no. 1, 1981.

Flagel, Nadine. "'It's Almost Like Being There': Speculative Fiction, Slave Narrative, and the Crisis of Representation in Octavia Butler's Kindred." *Canadian Review of American Studies*, vol. 42, no. 2, 2012, pp. 216–245.

Frow, John. *Genre. The New Critical Idiom*, John Drakakis. Routledge, 2006.

Gould, Philip. "The Rise, Development, and Circulation of the Slave Narrative." *The Cambridge Companion to the African American Slave Narrative*, edited by Audrey Fisch, Cambridge University Press, 2007, pp. 11–27.

Harris, Tamara Winfrey. "12 Years a Female Slave—Not Coming to a Theatre Near You." *The American Prospect*, 2013, https://prospect.org/article/12-years-female-slave%E2%80%94not-coming-theatre-near-you.

Hentges, Sarah. *Girls on Fire: Transformative Heroines in Young Adult Dystopian Literature*. McFarland, 2018.

Herman, David. *Storytelling and the Sciences of Mind*. The MIT Press, 2013.

Jerng, Mark. *Racial Worldmaking: The Power of Popular Fiction.* Fordham University Press, 2018.

Kenan, Randall. "An Interview with Octavia E. Butler." *Callaloo,* vol. 14, no. 2, Spring 1991, pp. 495–504.

Morris, Susana M. "Black Girls Are from the Future: Afrofuturist Feminism in Octavia E. Butler's *Fledgling.*" *Women's Studies Quarterly,* vol. 40, no. 3/4, 2012, pp. 146–166.

Nama, Adilifu. *Race on the QT: Blackness and the Films of Quentin Tarantino.* University of Texas Press, 2015.

Newitz, Annalee. "Django Unchained: What Kind of Fantasy Is This?" *io9,* 2012, https://io9. gizmodo.com/django-unchained-what-kind-of-fantasy-is-this-5971780.

See, Lisa. "PW Interviews: Octavia E. Butler." *Conversations with Octavia Butler,* edited by Conseula Francis, University Press of Mississippi, 1993, pp. 43–48.

Suvin, Darko. *Metamorphoses of Science Fiction: On the Poetics and History of a Literary Genre.* Yale University Press, 1979.

Womack, Ytasha. *Afrofuturism: The World of Black Sci-Fi and Fantasy Culture.* 1st ed., Chicago Review Press, 2013.

Zaki, Hoda M. "Utopia, Dystopia, and Ideology in the Science Fiction of Octavia Butler." *Science Fiction Studies,* vol. 17, no. 2, 1990, pp. 239–251.

Teaching/Learning YA Dystopia's Girls on Fire in Denmark's Educational System and International Community

SARAH HENTGES, ELAINE BRUM,
PETRA ILIC *and* ROMAINE BERRY

While working on my book *Girls on Fire: Transformative Heroines in Young Adult Dystopian Literature*, I (Sarah) taught three incarnations of an upper-level, online topics course: "Girls on Fire: Gender, Culture, and Justice in YA Dystopian Literature" at the University of Maine at Augusta. I wrote extensively about this teaching experience in *Girls on Fire*, the book and teaching/research project that inspired this *Teaching Girls on Fire* edited collection and collaboration. They also inspired an elective graduate topics course that I taught in the fall of 2018 at the University of Southern Denmark (SDU) where I served as a Fulbright Distinguished Chair of American Studies at the Center for American Studies: "Girls on Fire: Young Adult Dystopia and American Futures." Not only does this teaching experience provide critical insights for teaching Girls on Fire in an international cultural and educational context, but it also provides profound readings of the Girl on Fire that I had spent so much time with before teaching and living in Denmark. My students provided me with a new spark on a topic that will never smolder, but most certainly could die down if we don't work to fan the flames.

This essay is a kind of meditation on my experiences teaching this course in Denmark to a group of mostly international students, and the role our different cultural backgrounds and perspectives played in challenging my perceptions of not only the course content, but also what it means to learn and "do school." I also want this essay to capture some of the essence of this course through the students' voices. Thus, three of my students are co-authors in this project that grew from our work together. (They are, perhaps coincidentally, not Danish; they are international students enrolled in the master's program in American studies at SDU.) In each section, I frame our conversation, centered around the activities that accompanied our discussion of *Girls on Fire: Transformative Heroines in Young Adult Dystopian Literature* and six novels: Octavia Butler's *Parable of the Sower*, Suzanne Collins's *Catching Fire*, Libba Bray's *Beauty Queens*, Sheri L. Smith's *Orleans*, Ambelin Kwaymullina's *The Interrogation of Ashala Wolf*, and Alaya Dawn Johnson's *The Summer Prince*.

I chose these books as representatives of different themes and tropes in YA dystopian novels and platforms for discussion of race, class, gender, sexuality, and nationality. I also chose them as more complex and nuanced examples of the genre and as books that can be read as stand-alone stories, as opposed to many books whose complexity relies upon drawing out the trajectory of a trilogy. I had been cautioned that Danish students don't read and don't come to class, but I found the reading completion and class attendance rates to be no different than the courses I teach at my home institution (granted, this was my first experience teaching a graduate-level seminar and these students were mostly not Danish). Students were engaged in our discussions whether they had finished the reading or not, and our conversations were often dynamic. We laughed, we argued, and we agreed to disagree.

What I did find to be different in the Danish context is the exam structure and the cultural attitude toward, and arrangement of, education. In Denmark, students are paid to be students. They can choose to go to class or not. At the end of the semester, they take an exam. If they pass the exam, they pass the class. If they don't, they can try to re-take the exam twice. The grading structure is rigid and a "good" grade is much lower than what my U.S. students would see as a "good" grade. Students are given the respect of adults who are tasked with engaging with their education on their terms, and all of this starts from an early age of specialization. Students in the MA program progress as a cohort, taking the same set of classes with a few elective choices and completing a thesis project in their last semester. My class was a third-semester elective course.

While variations on this structure exist—in the American studies program at SDU and elsewhere—this generalization is representative of the core difference I found between education in the U.S. and education in Denmark. In the U.S. education is a privilege; in Denmark, it is more of a right. So, what significance does the Girl on Fire hold in a country regularly cited as the happiest on earth, the first country to legalize gay marriage, a country increasingly cited for xenophobia and anti-immigration attitudes and legislation? What follows is a conversation, a set of topics that we each address:

the educational context of the course and the different educational experiences that each student brought to this course, three activities we completed in class, and what the students learned in the course. In part, this essay is a model for several in-class activities, with reflections by the teacher and the students. But more, in all of these reflections on the course and activities, we hope to demonstrate the ways in which the Girl on Fire speaks to us and inspires us across cultural differences and different educational foundations and experiences.

Educational Context for Teaching/Learning Girls on Fire

Sarah: I brought with me to Denmark two tried and true topics courses: Girls on Fire and a Hip-Hop America course. The latter failed miserably for a variety of reasons. But Girls on Fire proved to be an engaging course with a small group of students, many quite dedicated to the reading and discussion of these texts and the development of their own scholarly work. And then I threw them a few curve balls—the in-class activities that will be discussed here: an "Ode to Katniss" activity; a *Beauty Queens* meme project; and a "What Comes Next?" discussion about the ambiguous (or not-so-ambiguous) ending of *Orleans*. Not only did the students indulge my activities, they also created spontaneous brilliance that we all benefited from, and which I hope to portray here through the students' voices.

Students in Denmark, generally, and in the American studies master's program more specifically, are used to being taught through PowerPoint lectures and large group discussions. With nine students in class, two mostly taking the course at a distance, and four or five students attending almost all of the classes, we had many opportunities for in-depth discussions where all of the students participated—despite the awkwardness of our ill-fitting amphitheater-like room designed to hold 100 students. The MA program is taught in English and attracts not only Danish students, but also international students and immigrant students. Thus, our course was quite diverse, including students from Denmark, the U.K., Brazil, Germany (on exchange), Serbia, the Ukraine, and Slovenia.

Our class met once a week for thirteen weeks and consisted mostly of discussion that flowed from my sloppy, sometimes complicated, sometimes not-even-question questions and from the students connecting and extending comments made by their peers. We were able to cover an often exhaustive list of content in our two and a half hours of class. Twice I presented PowerPoints—as an introduction on the first day and in relation to *Orleans*, a presentation that connected several texts that we had discussed in relation to our class—Jesmyn Ward's *Salvage the Bones* and Beyoncé's *Lemonade*, as well as a film students were not familiar with, *Beasts of the Southern Wild*. One Danish student, Anna, did a presentation about the journey of the female heroine, a synchronous connection between her B.A. thesis topic and our class material. (She was also prepared to contribute an essay to this essay collection before the needs of family got in the way of her education, something that happens to my U.S. students often.) And a few times we connected the material to more creative endeavors through our activities, which I participated in along with the students. These activities are the focus of this essay. But before we discuss the in-class activities, some discussion of the educational contexts that students brought with them to the Danish classroom can help us to see the relevance of the Girl on Fire figure in their educations.

Elaine: In a lecture Dr. Sarah Hentges said: "In the U.S. education is a privilege," and so it is in Brazil. When I first moved to Denmark, I was surprised to learn that everyone has access to education and that the minimum requirement in the labor market would be a master's degree. I cannot explain how I felt when I was accepted to take the MA in American studies. I was dazzled by the opportunity to have access to brilliant professors and to international fellow students. I am still amazed by the number of books and articles we are expected to read per semester. Class attendance is not mandatory for many courses, which shows an impressive discipline and capacity for self-directed study by many Danish students and foreigners. On the downside, the integration with Danish students can be very difficult, as they tend to be reserved and prefer to interact with people they know, but I am still very grateful to the university and to our professors for giving me and other international students an opportunity to be part of a fantastic cultural encounter.

As part of the mandatory courses of the MA in American studies in Denmark, the students have the option to choose elective courses, which for me had great importance. Since the beginning of my education in Denmark I have felt a need to deal with cultural clashes and to improve "language and structure," which is still a great challenge for me. I also had the chance to choose interdisciplinary and intersectional courses such as "Human Rights" and "Gender and Sexuality" as well as "Girls on Fire," which definitely had a positive influence on my academic and personal development and contributed to my understanding of gender equality and the empowerment of women. When I first saw "Girls on Fire" on the elective courses list I thought that it would probably be a fun and less demanding course to take. But in fact, it is more complex than I imagined. In this course I learned how YA dystopian literature has the power to teach and inspire many readers to develop and/or increase self-consciousness about social justice and global socio-economic and political issues.

Professor Hentges has been very generous with all of the students. She has been motivating, listening to our opinions, allowing us to share ideas, and inspiring many of us to give our best effort despite our imperfections or failures. Overall, I must admit that I have become more interested and dedicated to studies where I can connect theoretical approaches to real life. All in all, I chose "Girls on Fire" and the other elective courses because I hoped that in combination, they would give me opportunities to discuss and practice different ideas, and maybe even provide a foundation for helping others in one way or another.

Petra: Gaining my bachelor's degree in Serbia and having the opportunity to start the master's program in Denmark at first seemed like an unreachable goal and later on an unbelievable turn of events, which undoubtedly filled me with an enormous amount of gratitude and made me feel extremely privileged to have such a chance. As a student in an ex-communist country with an old-fashioned educational system and an arguably failed attempt to modernize, you are taught to study hard and study by heart. Moreover, you are taught to embrace your professors' opinions and rarely express your own since it may not reflect what is found in the textbook or what your professors believe to be true. At least that was my impression during my four-year long bachelor's program in English language and literature in Serbia. Hence the shock and amazement with the educational system in Denmark when I first arrived here was immense.

I still vividly remember my conversations with my friends back in Serbia toward the beginning of my master's program in American studies. I remember being astonished because the professors in Denmark actually wanted us to express our opinions and did not get upset if those opinions were not in line with theirs. In addition, they would even ask us if we wanted to do certain activities, or watch documentaries, or discuss the topic of that class. It felt unbelievable and so easy and interesting, despite the large amount of material we had to read for each course.

Nevertheless, the exam period came and all of my fears and inexperience hit. I was supposed to write my first paper, with no previous knowledge about the form, the references, the style. However, as I suffered through the first paper, I also realized how fun it could be, and how I actually enjoyed writing and putting a piece of myself and my knowledge and opinions into a paper. To this day, that is the thing I enjoy the most about the Danish system. To be able to create something so professional, so academic, and still have your own voice in it, had seemed so distant to me before. Denmark gave me that opportunity and awoke my passion for writing and studying, which I thought would never happen again.

Besides that, the number and diversity of the courses I was able to take in these two years proved to me that university education could still be fun and enjoyable and give me the confidence and drive to pursue further accomplishments within the academic field. Being a great lover of literature, and especially classic literature, my first choices regarding the elective courses were always literature ones. Thus the natural choice for me was to take the "Girls on Fire" course, even though I had never been a big fan of either YA novels or the science-fiction genre. Once more the Danish system, but even more so Professor Hentges, proved me wrong and helped me realize that I should be more open-minded and less judgmental. The "Girls on Fire" course gave me the chance to express both my creativity and my opinions to the fullest, alongside the opportunity to get away from the realities of the world and imagine some other kind of life. The course combined all of the aspects of American studies I truly enjoy—cultural issues, gender issues, race issues, class issues—and Professor Hentges gave us the chance to develop our ideas in different directions, supporting, although maybe not necessarily agreeing with, all of them. It was truly an amazing experience, which unquestionably made me grow as a student and made me feel much more self-confident and proud of how far I have gotten since my beginnings in Serbia.

Romaine: By the time I had to make my course choices for semester three, I already knew that I would have to take these classes as distance/online classes and that greatly affected the choices I made. I decided to choose courses that I had an interest in and would be motivated to learn about on my own. If I had been residing in Denmark for this semester I might have opted to pick a subject that I was not familiar with, but as I had no face-to-face time with the lecturer or my classmates I realized I would be better off choosing a subject that I knew and loved, and decided on taking Dr. Hentges "Girls on Fire" course. I have always enjoyed reading the dystopian genre since before I even knew what it was; one of the first books I can remember reading as a child was *Z for Zachariah*. As a child and a young adult I always opted for books that had sci-fi/fantasy/post-apocalyptic themes, and I inherited my love of the supremely geeky television show *Star Trek* from my mum at an early age. Despite not necessarily understanding the nuanced subtext of these narratives, it was the re-imagining of a futuristic world that drew me to them: in the future you could be anything you wanted to be. *Star Trek* featured women as doctors and high-ranking officials while texts like *Z for Zachariah* taught that women can be self-sufficient and just as strong as men.

Since I only got the chance to attend one class I cannot really comment on my impression of how the course was taught, but the one class I did attend made me wish I was able to attend more often. The class was open to debate and discussion and no one was afraid to say something "wrong." In some of my previous classes people (myself included) would not risk speaking out or voicing opinions for fear of getting it "wrong," which in my opinion does not help anyone's understanding of a subject. I had taken a class the previous semester taught by Dr. Kim Warren, who was also a Fulbright Professor from

America, on the subject of "Gender and Sexuality" and felt that class would complement "Girls on Fire." I felt that the classes taught by both Fulbright Professors were slightly different to the ones delivered by Danish Professors. I personally felt that the American style of teaching was more similar to what I was used to in England in so much as there was a certain expectation that you would attend and participate in classes whereas the Danish style seemed to be a little more self-determined in that you didn't have to attend classes and you could turn in blank pages for exams.

Sarah: One thing that strikes me about the educational experiences my students share here is how diverse they are and how they share challenges across their diverse circumstances. These were not the students or the challenges that I expected to encounter when I came to Denmark to teach American studies. These students are representative of the diversity of the students in this Girls on Fire class, and this diversity contributed to the rich conversations that we had in class. In addition to our formal class discussions, we also had a lot of conversations, mostly on breaks (which are plentiful in the Danish classroom) but also during class time when the characters' struggles could be compared to the students' challenges. Because many of us were navigating an unfamiliar system, we developed some camaraderie in our classroom, which also contributed to our in-class activities. Finally, I will note that I chose not to edit the students' use of my name in this essay. In the egalitarian society of Denmark, students and professors are on a first-name basis, the same as I am with my students in the U.S. Despite the fact that I ask all my students to call me Sarah, I find that students from more traditional educational systems are usually more comfortable calling me Professor or Dr. Hentges.

"Ode to Katniss": On-the-Spot Poetry

Sarah: I had done versions of this activity in past classes, like College Writing and Introduction to Women's Studies. In these classes, my students came up with amazing, creative poems in about 15 minutes and they all read their poems aloud (with the option to have me read their poem if they were too shy, but not the option to opt out). The original version of the assignment was cribbed from The Breakbeat Poet's writing workshop that I had attended on my home campus (in conjunction with a Hip Hop class I was teaching at the time). Kevin Coval would be happy to see this assignment find new and diverse homes. But I was not sure how this activity would turn out, not only in this new context, but also in this new form.

The original assignment asks students to list random things in answer to questions like: what's something you never leave home without? (One of the best poems ever to come from this assignment was in response to the answer: "anxiety."); what color would you paint a room?; favorite food; activity for a summer day, etc. Students then choose a word from the list, get a bit of instruction in the poetic form of the Ode, and write a poem on the spot.

In my redesigned activity, students were asked to list responses to questions like: something Katniss will never lose; someone Katniss loves to hate; a symbol of home; and something Katniss will never get past. Students wrote poems in an unfairly short amount of time and all but one read their poem aloud in class (no doubt because of his anxiety; thus, I did not push him to share as I might with other students). One student, Barbora, had been annoyed with Katniss throughout our class discussion and so we all enjoyed the ironic turn when she was then asked to write an "Ode" to Katniss (which was done quite well!). The students' poems were fun and enlightening—mine couldn't hold a candle to theirs!—and the two included below are both written by multi-lingual writers whose first language is not English. To be fair, I wrote three poems in the same time frame (with no prep). This one's my favorite:

> A handful of berries
> can bring down the Capital
> can make someone a hero or a martyr.
> A handful of berries
> can end the suffering
> or begin a whole
> new world of pain.

Elaine: All of our "Girls on Fire" class meetings were both instructive and entertaining, boosting not only our critical thinking but also our creative development. Personally, I found it really hard to create a poem in a short time and in a foreign language, as I guess it would have been easier for me to express my emotions or impressions in Portuguese, my native language. Besides, I would have preferred to write about other characters that I fell in love with or had great thoughts about, such as Fen and Daniel from the book *Orleans*. Certainly, Katniss is a "Girl on Fire," but the Hunger Games movies changed my ideas about this character, although I find the series pretty cool. I wrote the Ode anyway and although I thought the rhyming and my end-result was not too impressive, at least it gave us some good laughs.

Ode to Katniss Everdeen

Was she a beautiful girl in a starvation world?
Pretty little Katniss, loved her daddy, her jacket, and her birds,
But it was for her mother and sister that she gave the most.
She just wanted to hunt her meals,
But then, the President Snow forced her into a bad deal.
Gale became nervous, when Peeta got closer,
But her heart was broken by Haymitch, the drunkard.

Her nightmares pushed her out of her bed.
Poor Katniss! She did not want to be so bad.
The Hunger Games rose her like the Mockingjay.
And she became the heroine and the symbol of a rebellion case.
Katniss is a girl on fire, a survivor.
And she can get whatever she desires.

Petra: One of the things I really enjoyed about taking the Girls on Fire course was that it made me feel very relaxed, since the atmosphere in class was very friendly, and it still provided me with the necessary knowledge regarding crucial issues in American studies. However, when the time came for us to write the poem, or more specifically, the Ode to Katniss, I have to admit I felt uneasy. One of my first thoughts was: I am not doing this. Firstly, I do not like writing poems. Secondly, I do not in particular like Katniss and I am not sure what I would even say about her that would praise her. Mostly out of respect for Professor Hentges did I start to write my poem, wondering how to start, what to say, and how to actually write an ode. It took me a long time to put my first verse on the paper, but then it became much easier and the final product turned out to be very satisfactory to me. I was once again proved wrong and reminded that I should not approach things with judgment, but have trust in the process and let myself go. This activity showed me that my creativity could come out even from the most unexpected and uncomfortable places and the end product was the feeling of pride in myself, but also the feeling of self-accomplishment, because I proved to myself that I could do even the things I thought I did not necessarily like. In addition, I ended up liking my poem and I can say I take pride in it. The following is my humble contribution to the world of poets and to the world of Katniss, our ultimate Girl on Fire.

Ode to Katniss

To all the victims of The Hunger Games,
for people we lost,
let's not forget their names.

To Rue, lying in the bed of flowers,
for life means nothing,
just look at Wiress.

To Mags' final dance
in the thickest fog,
for blistered and wounded,
here is the ode.

To recognize the Capitol's sin,
Let's all raise the Mockingjay pin!

Romaine: I did attempt to write something about this, but unfortunately didn't submit what I had written. I've never written an "ode" before and have never been particularly good at creative writing, but I also felt a disconnect from the class. I have since deleted what I wrote, but I focused on the theme of nature, the role it played in the narrative and just how important it was for Katniss. As I had no idea the form it should take I based the rhythm and shape on Keats' *Ode to a Grecian Urn*. I found this task a challenge and I feel like it helped me focus on elements of the text that I hadn't necessarily found important or interesting from a superficial reading of it. It helped me to look at the narrative from a different angle that I hadn't seen by just reading the text and looking for the obvious. Katniss is a reluctant heroine, one that is simultaneously a survivor/victim and a participant trapped by the Panem political machine that controls its citizens' lives. Her relationship with nature is one of the only things that allows her to feel free and escape the nightmare that is her life.

Sarah: Whenever I introduce creative assignments, like this Ode to Katniss activity, I expect resistance. The whole time the students were working on this activity, I was worried that I had made a mistake. They did not look happy; a few looked almost angry. But once we were sharing and laughing, the tension lifted. Challenging students to think differently about texts and characters can bring new perspectives on Katniss as the Girl on Fire, but it can also (and perhaps more importantly) bring new perspectives to education and to the ways in which students understand themselves. And the students' reflections here are good reminders: Petra was adamant that she did not want to do this assignment, but she did, and it gave her a connection to her classmates. Romaine felt alienated by the assignment because she did not have the opportunity to participate in the activity with us in class. I also did not follow up with her quickly enough to attempt to reinforce her participation. Despite the fact that I had left the door open for her to submit any of her activities or reflections related to class, she never took me up on the offer until preparing for the final exam paper. This is the unfortunate experience of a distance student in a system that is not set up to serve distance students.

Beauty Queens *Meme Project: Capturing Diversity in Text and Image*

Sarah: Originally this assignment was a *Beauty Queens* collage, but as I thought about how to do a collage as a collective project in our classroom, I morphed this idea into the creation of a meme that would represent one of the (diverse) characters in the novel. I asked students to choose a character from the novel and to find a representative quote and image to create a meme. A meme is relatively simple compared to a collage—only one image is needed instead of many. It is also an assignment that asks students to pair an image with text, opening the door for discussion of the kinds of images that are chosen to represent Girls on Fire and how these images help to shape our understanding. Finally, the creation of a meme is low tech compared to creating a collaborative digital collage in a classroom with little technical support (and I didn't have the arts and crafts kind of supplies I often have on my home campus). Students could create a meme on their phone, which is all the tech they needed. I hoped that this assignment would lend itself to helping us talk about the ways in which these characters are simultaneously stereotyped even as they act to defy stereotypes. When a few students chose other characters besides the beauty queens, I let them roll with it to see what they came up with. And, of course, their grasp of technology for such an activity was better than mine. Students immediately utilized the "meme generator" available online and Petra tapped into more savvy technology to include animation. Unfortunately, none of our memes are high resolution enough for publication, so our descriptions will have to suffice. I have never assigned this activity before, but I certainly will in the future, and I enjoyed the activity at least as much as the students. My meme was about Mary Lou. I found a picture of a variety of fruit (Mary Lou is a vegetarian) and added the quote: "But I feel so much—it's like I want to eat up the world…. Why is that wrong?"

Elaine: Some days you are inspired, other days not at all. I did not have that much to express for this activity, but I must agree that Petra and Anna's memes were fantastic! And overall, I was really impressed by my classmates' creativity and abilities.

Petra: Libba Bray's *Beauty Queens* is definitely a novel that does not leave anybody indifferent. I believe that each and every one of us in class had our own opinion on this book and while some of us loved it, others did not. (I personally loved the novel and its use of satire.) When Professor Hentges assigned us the meme project I was very excited to get down to it, even though I was not sure how I could present one very complex character through just one picture. One of the scenes that most vividly stuck in my mind while I was reading the book was when the girls accidentally ate the hallucinogenic berries and, quite inebriated, started telling their childhood stories. My meme, I hope successfully, tried to depict Tiara's childhood memory, with her dinosaur toy—Mr. Wiggles—which she one night found under her bedsheets, at an inappropriate place. Berries in the meme are in motion, putting the emphasis on her current mental state and the alien stands as a sign that Tiara is hallucinating. I also wanted to capture Libba Bray's satire, pairing the image with Tiara's tagline: "Ohmigosh."

I truly enjoyed this activity and I was really excited to see what my classmates created and all the memes in the class were wonderful. What I believe was great about the project was that all of us had a chance to express ourselves and use our wit and creativity to depict the characters, and as a result, by giving our personal touch to it, we to a certain extent became a part of Libba Bray's world of *Beauty Queens*.

Romaine: I created a meme of Miss Montana when she responds to the question "are you on the rag or something?" by exclaiming, "No. I'm just pissed off right now" (150) because I find it so true that men are allowed to be angry and it's justifiable, whereas when women try to express their anger they are emotional, hysterical and are often rendered unable to express themselves. In the picture, Miss Montana is attacking a cowering man with a bouquet of flowers. *Beauty Queens* was an empowering and inclusive text that challenged gender and racial stereotypes at every opportunity.

I used the *Beauty Queens* text in my final exam as I felt that it expressed many issues that both females and males face due to societal expectations based solely on gender and race. Although this novel is mainly about what it is to be female and modern western ideals of beauty, it also speaks to how men are often restricted by the same gender structure. Young men can be just as trapped by gender constructs as women if they do not ascribe to society's standard of manliness. Men can express their anger without it being attributed to their hormones, however, they are not always able to express other facets of their personality due to society's expectations of what it is to be a male, resulting in what's known as "toxic masculinity" which can lead to mental health issues.

Sarah: While Elaine claims that she was uninspired, I remember her meme being just as good as the other memes! It was clear in class how much Petra enjoyed this activity—a different form of creativity was needed for this assignment, compared to the Ode assignment and perhaps the Ode helped to get her thinking outside the box. But she was also inspired by Bray's use of sarcasm and her ability to balance the stories of so many diverse characters. Romaine was also inspired by this novel and not only completed the meme assignment, but also shared it with me. She felt more confident in this assignment than she had in the Ode assignment. While the students mostly agreed that the novel was a little bit too long-winded, they appreciated what Bray was trying to do and what I was trying to do—provide a girl-centered text that challenges the whitewashed stories and characters of most popular YA novels. When I assign this activity in the future, I will specify that students must choose one of the beauty queens, not one of the other characters in the book—the intent was to create a kind of collage of representations that reflect the diversity of the characters in the novel as well as the diversity of the Girl on Fire more generally.

"What Comes Next?": Imagining New Futures for Orleans

Sarah: I had considered asking the students to do some in-class writing for this in-class activity, but we spent so much time discussing the novel that we were running out of class time. Instead, I asked students to think about what comes next in this story. Is it a sequel? An epilogue? Whose story is it? Is Fen dead? What happens to Enola? To Daniel? To Orleans and The Outer States?

Our conversation around the students' visions for what comes next was lively. We had many laughs, especially since every possible outcome from Chris's perspective could be explained in mass extinction. But in addition to our laughs, the students came up with insights on the story that opened our conversations in new directions. Elaine and I insisted—sometimes dramatically—that Fen could not possibly be dead. And Oddur rattled off the story that we all wanted to read. We wished that Sherri L. Smith had been listening!

Elaine: Please Sherri L. Smith, give a future to Fen, Daniel and Enola! As previously mentioned, I completely fell in love with the book *Orleans*. It is simple and authentic! It played with my imagination from the very beginning to the very end and I share Professor Hentges's positivity and refuse to believe that Fen's story ends at this point. Some of my classmates agreed that Fen died at the end of the novel, but other alternative possibilities were also discussed. I imagined Fen as a powerful and twisting hurricane that is capable of changing the world or, like some other protagonists, of coming back like a Phoenix, more powerful than ever. As I connect stories to reality, it is natural for me to connect Daniel's behavior and comments to many of the tourists who go to Rio de Janeiro in Brazil ready to see the local ghetto areas, *favelas*, on so-called "jungle tours," which I think is a very limited and stereotyped way to get to know a new place and local people. I wish the author could write a sequel to *Orleans* where Fen survived and got the chance to give Daniel a better understanding of her world and joined the fight against the adversaries by raising baby Enola, who could become the best cultural encounter ever, combining Fen's wild abilities and Daniel's intellectualism. Enola could also become a scientist, develop Daniel's research and eventually discover the cure for the Delta virus. Can you imagine a woman as a scientist who saves the world? I can, and I think it would motivate many young readers to think about this possibility.

Petra: Sherri L. Smith's *Orleans* was definitely my favorite novel in the Girls on Fire course and I would gladly read it again. It captivated me from the beginning, both in terms of the language and different dialects used in the book and in terms of the extremely exciting and interesting plot. Unfortunately, I was not able to attend the class where Professor Hentges and my classmates discussed the continuation of the story, but I absolutely had my own ideas and I really hope the book will have a sequel. Since for the final paper we were given the opportunity to choose what we would like to write about, my paper "The Importance and Influence of the Male Protagonists on the Female Characters in YA Dystopia Fiction Written by Women" dealt mostly with gender representation and gender inequality in the books, and *Orleans* proved to be a great source of inspiration for me during the project. My main argument was that the men in the YA novels still largely controlled the narrative, despite the increased number of female protagonists in the novels. As we can see in *Orleans*, Fen de la Guerre definitely epitomizes the Girl on Fire: she is brave and intelligent and has a goal to save baby Enola and by any means provide a better life for her. Nevertheless, it is hardly possible to imagine her succeeding in her endeavors without having the young scientist Daniel by her side. Although she is unarguably in control throughout the novel, Fen finally decides to put Enola's life into Daniel's hands and most likely dies. What we as readers see on the last pages of the novel is Daniel holding a baby and leaving Orleans, which in my opinion signifies that Fen passed the control of the narrative to Daniel and men in general. However, I would still love to see the sequel and see where Daniel and Enola are now and maybe challenge Sherri L. Smith to prove me wrong by possibly giving all the control and voice to Enola, or even give it back to Fen, if it turns out that she is still alive.

Romaine: I didn't partake in this exercise, but I like to think the ending of the book is open to interpretation so that there is still an element of hope.

Sarah: The end of this novel, even if we don't imagine what happens next, provides a springboard for discussions of the Girl on Fire and her central role in these novels—or her not-so-central role. Two students chose to write about the role that boys play in these novels; specifically, they argued that the Girl on Fire is ultimately undercut by the boys in the novels who actually control the narrative. Petra reflects this idea in her analysis of *Orleans* here (and in the next section where she describes her final exam paper). Where we might see Fen's partnership with Daniel as an example of teamwork, Petra sees the passing of Enola from Fen to Daniel as a passing of narrative control that reflects on the Girl on Fire's lack of agency. Elaine, on the other hand, passionately disagrees with Petra's viewpoints. In taking up this novel in her master's thesis, she was able to further explore this novel, as well as *The Summer Prince* and *Parable of the Sower*, particularly in terms of how these books represent black girls as Girls on Fire—as agents of change in fiction as well as in real life struggles for social justice. The Girls on Fire burn the brightest, but they also recognize the need for coalitions.

The Girls on Fire

Sarah: Four of us—none of the students contributing to this essay—concluded our Girls on Fire course on a cold rainy day on couches near the campus Starbucks, drinking hot chocolate or coffee and eating the home-baked goods two of the students made for us (in Danish: *kage*—everything is cake in Denmark and no event is complete without some kind of cake). It was a proper Danish ending to our class as we talked about the students' final paper ideas and my Girls on Fire dreams—this *Teaching Girls on Fire* edited collection and a much more unconventional mind/body fitness dance event (discussed in the conclusion). We also just talked, riffing off of the relationships we had built throughout the course, and commiserating about the dreary day as well as the possibilities that the future might hold.

In this final section, I've asked my students to reflect on what they learned over the course of the semester—about themselves and about our Girls on Fire subject matter. It might also be worth noting three other important comparative contexts for this course: (1) Because we had Elaine, a student from Brazil, in our course, we had insights on *The Summer Prince* that gave us a further layer for our comparative studies. (2) We also had conversations related to *The Summer Prince* that touched on some of the more insidious elements of the Danish immigration system. One student's 15-year-old daughter had been denied citizenship because she was thought to be too old to assimilate. She had already gained the required level of fluency in Danish and had completed a year of school where she made friends and plans for her future. (3) The exam format allowed for students to write a paper with an original argument about the course subject matter, developing their own analyses and their own voices as scholars. In several classes we discussed the students' ideas for their exam paper topics and arguments, each adding new insights to our understanding of the Girl on Fire.

Elaine: Our classes were very productive and enlightening. We read a few novels that I probably would not have had the possibility to read if it was not because of this course. These readings highlight intersectional aspects such as race, gender, sexuality and class, emphasizing political statements and providing knowledge about history, culture, language and self-consciousness. I think that in some ways the authors are re-writing history, as they are including diversity, ethnic and cultural miscegenation to their stories, empowering girls/women and validating people's voices, identities, traditions and most of all, their existence.

When I first read *The Summer Prince* my first reaction was to appreciate how the author wrote beautifully about the Brazilian history and culture, but I also became really frustrated with the stereotypes. Nowadays, I am analyzing this book for my thesis, and as an afterthought, I must admit that what really bothered me is confronting the idea and reality that even after centuries of submission, many Brazilian women still suffer from oppression, psychological abuse, and sexual violence. Although there are many problems in my country, I want to focus on solutions. How can we change it? Many of us are already resisting, fighting for our rights, getting educated, changing our history and trying to make a better future for the generations to come.

Recently, I have learned that not everyone is tolerant of diversity in Denmark and the immigration policies here have become even more restrictive, but I still appreciate the social democracy and women's empowerment. With the MA in American studies, I have learned about historical and cultural differences, and above all, how education and knowledge are keys to one's freedom and self-determination.

For our final exam we were allowed to choose a topic and our own arguments, which I think really helped us in our own journey to self-consciousness and academic development. I decided to write about the forms of knowledge that I found in the YA dystopian literature we read in class. Approved by Professor Hentges, the title of my assignment was changed to "Knowledge is Power in the Quest for Survival in Dystopian Worlds," as I discussed education and knowledge as powerful instruments in the quest for survival portrayed in young adult dystopian literature and American culture. I tried to describe and examine examples of how characters in the books we read use their knowledge in the quest for their own survival and/or in their communities. Besides, in the process of this assignment I found it interesting to cite the speeches of the former president Barack Obama on race and the Pakistani Malala Yousafzai on education. I consider Malala a "Girl on Fire," a survivor and transformative heroine with a real-life story in our contemporary dystopian world, because of her activism for the rights to education and females' rights, and for inspiring young people globally.

I have learned that many authors of YA dystopian literature are writing transformative narratives, bringing alternative and empowering "intersectional" characters and stories leading readers to self-awareness and reflection on their own reality, social responsibilities and injustices. These narratives are full of concepts that many readers are not familiar with and can teach and inspire them to become transformative agents engaged in changing their own communities.

Petra: Recent years have proven that gender inequality in the world is still a huge and omnipresent issue. Although we are mostly aware of females' struggles in undeveloped nations, it has been shown that even the so-called "modern" countries have not established equality and the recent movements of women raising their voices has confirmed this. I believe that YA dystopian fiction is a very important, but unfortunately often disregarded, tool for fighting this problem. These strong, independent and intelligent female protagonists could be so beneficial for young girls, who are often the readers of the genre, and could inspire them to fight and be aware of their worth and possibilities in the world. Here again, however, we are faced with the oppression and stereotypes that authors, such as Octavia E. Butler, have been trying to fight for many years now and although progress has been made, there is still a long road ahead of all of us before equality is achieved.

What the Girls on Fire course offered me was the opportunity to gain more consciousness regarding the important issues in American studies. It also inspired me to think more in terms of focusing my academic career on fighting for female rights and equal female representation in the world. With this in mind, I wrote my paper arguing that male dominance is still largely present in the YA dystopian novels, hoping to contribute to the improvement of female representation in YA literature and hoping to make the readers of the genre aware of the issues and encourage them to pursue the fight for equality. Some of the books assigned during our course, such as Alaya Dawn Johnson's *The Summer Prince*, abound in scenes where arguably the male character is the protagonist and the female is complying with his wishes and requests, blindly trusting him in the process. Although in most cases the Girls on Fire end up as the winners and the ones with control over the narrative, it is questionable whether they would be there without the male to help them. This is not to say that there should be a clear line between the two, completely dividing the male from the female, but rather that we, as females, should be heard and should be trusted and given the control we most certainly deserve, both in literature and in reality.

Finally, although I was a bit uncertain whether the Girls on Fire course would fulfill my expectations regarding the content of the books and although I most certainly approached it with a fair amount of judgment, the great leadership of Professor Hentges and her unusual approach to teaching the course made me realize how beneficial and mind-opening this whole experience was. Despite the fact that I was not amused by all of the books we had to read during the course, I am glad that I came around to novels such as Smith's *Orleans* and Butler's *Parable of the Sower*, which I would probably never have come across were it not for this course. I came out of this experience not only as a student aware of her capabilities, analytical thinking, creativity and stance over different issues in American studies, but also as a student with new ideas and an open attitude not only for YA dystopian novels, but other literary genres that I have not encountered before. I believe that Professor Hentges's idea for this course was to spark that Girl on Fire in all of us and she undoubtedly succeeded in that task with me.

Romaine: I really enjoyed this class even though I was unable to actively participate with the group. The texts were interesting and gave me more of an insight into the novels I had previously read when I was younger, reading them more for pleasure than for analysis. I enjoyed reading the theory text by Professor Hentges and it gave me lots to think about in terms of my final exam, in which I decided to write about Hollywood's interpretation of young adult dystopian novels and discuss why some of these texts were adapted and others were not. The course also served as inspiration for my final master's thesis, which will look at the role of Hollywood adaptations in comparison to the source texts.

In my mind, Girls on Fire are not just about females getting their fair share of representation in novels or Hollywood blockbusters, although this is important. Girls on Fire serve a much greater purpose in encouraging people, both males and females, to question our current social structures and to ultimately challenge our preconceived notions of gender and race. Hopefully these young adult dystopian novels can enable their readers to reimagine the world and redefine what it means to be male, female, non-white, white, and disabled. At a time when movements such as Black Lives Matter and #MeToo are enabling people who would not normally have a voice to speak out, these types of narratives are even more important as they show us alternatives to the structures that currently not only define us but also confine us.

Sarah: In these final reflections, we can see the Girls on Fire qualities that each of these women embody and the ways in which these qualities play out in their educations. As Elaine notes above, "Many of us are already resisting, fighting for our rights, getting educated, changing our history and trying to make a better future for the generations to come." It is, perhaps, also worth mentioning that both Elaine and Romaine took up Girls on Fire topics for their master's thesis work in the semester following our course. Two other students in this course also asked me to advise their thesis work based upon their experience working with me in this class. In part, we had developed a working relationship, but they were also interested in writing about topics that are outside of the scope of much of their American studies education. (For instance, one of the students chose to write about Beyoncé's *Lemonade* and Janelle Monáe's *Dirty Computer* and the feminist theory and practice that these texts negotiate.) Despite the gender equality found in Denmark, I have found that the women I have worked with still feel the effects of gender inequality and thirst for the opportunity to study feminist theory and practice. My Girls on Fire course provided an opportunity to continue their education about gender and race that they had begun with the American Fulbright they had worked with the year before. But more, the Girl on Fire provided a salient model and metaphor for their work as well as a source of inspiration.

Conclusions

Sarah: The opportunities for American scholars to have comparative conversations in international contexts are too few and far between. I am privileged to be able to take part in this Fulbright and to be able to work with this group of international students and my many other Danish students and international students in my other classes. I always learn at least as much as my students and this was an opportunity for authentic, engaged, joyful, playful, insightful conversations about texts and contexts that I love, texts and contexts that I have invested much time and consideration into reading and writing and thinking about, and a subject matter that I advocate for as transformative, in and out of the classroom.

I regularly tell my students that I am optimistic and students can quite easily recognize my passion for teaching. At a "Meet Your Professor" event early in the semester, one student asked me how I can be so optimistic when I study dystopia, a version of the most common question that I get about my work. My first response is always a joke about how there's always hope that tomorrow will be an opportunity for something better. But my more sincere response stems from my faith in the power of the myth and symbol of the Girl on Fire—the collective power of Girls on Fire—and the ways in which my students fan the flames of my optimism.

Connecting with my students in Denmark only further stokes this fire as the Girls on Fire seeds are spread further away from my American studies home than I have ever ventured. Getting an "Other" perspective is always a valuable teaching/learning experience and this particular incarnation demonstrates the power of YA dystopia's Girl on Fire to build community and sow love while pushing back against the systems and forces of oppression that threaten our collective future. Denmark is an egalitarian society that teaches children independence and values people and aims to provide a certain standard of living (for instance, healthcare for all and mandatory vacation time). But Denmark is also a rather closed society that can be hard to break into if you are a foreigner and its education system is rigid and challenging. Even the most utopic spaces have room for improvement. Perhaps my conclusions are as romantic as the novels that we study; regardless, my students' voices are the forces that keep the fire burning.

WORKS CITED

Bray, Libba. *Beauty Queens*. Scholastic, 2011.

Collins, Suzanne. *Catching Fire*. Scholastic, 2009.

Hentges, Sarah. *Girls on Fire: Transformative Female Protagonists in Young Adult Dystopian Literature*. McFarland, 2018.

Johnson, Alaya Dawn. *The Summer Prince*. Levine-Scholastic, 2013.

Kwaymullina, Ambelin. *The Interrogation of Ashala Wolf*. Candlewick, 2012.

Smith, Sherri L. *Orleans*. Penguin, 2013.

Conclusion

"[Girls on Fire]: Tear This Wall Down!"
International and Imaginative Contexts
for Teaching Girls on Fire

Sarah Hentges

Being a Fulbright scholar opens up opportunities to teach (and learn) beyond our home contexts as well as beyond our classrooms. We have the opportunity to learn about new places and to meet new people, to find new perspectives on our teaching and scholarship, and to experience new ideas and practices. As Sean and I have been collaborating on this edited collection, I have also been extending and expanding the idea of Girls on Fire in an international location—the physical place of Odense, Denmark, as well as the more amorphous space of my international community in and beyond Denmark. In other words, in addition to the formal academic teaching Girls on Fire context that I (and my students) write about in the previous essay, I was able to expand, deepen, and extend my Girls on Fire work through a variety of conferences, presentations, and activities, on and off campus. These opportunities gave me new, fruitful lenses on a topic that I have written about and taught about in a variety of U.S. contexts as I explored and shared ideas about: the role and meaning of Girls on Fire monuments, connections to the fall of the Berlin wall, connections to American politics, and extensions of creative/critical pedagogies. I wish for every scholar, teacher, and student to have such opportunities and because I have had this privilege, I feel I also have the responsibility to share the insights I have gained as a result of this experience.

My Fulbright work also brought opportunities to teach about Girls on Fire in several international spaces beyond Denmark (Bergen, Norway; Porto, Portugal; and Aristotle University of Thessaloniki, Greece) and reach out to students from a variety of non–American locations—Danish students, Nor-

191

wegian students, Portuguese students, Greek students, and international students from around the world. And, of course, the idea of the Girl on Fire resonates in all of these spaces; she is a symbol we all need in our contemporary (and often dystopic) world.

The final context I will discuss here—an event celebrating International Women's Day at the University of Southern Denmark—brought Girls on Fire outside of academic contexts into recreational fitness/dance spaces, an idea I also extended into a summer school program in Greece on the theme of health, culture, and healing. Thus, in conclusion to this collection of essays about teaching Girls on Fire, I want to offer a few examples that have helped to not only internationalize my American studies work and reignite the importance for me of feminism and intersectionality as central theories and pedagogies for teaching Girls on Fire, but also speak to some of the ongoing struggles of Girls on Fire (especially those who continue to be marginalized). These observations and analyses provide some important connections to the essays in this collection and to future Girls on Fire projects. What unites Girls on Fire across time and location is our shared oppression as well as our shared global future, but this global future is shared by Girls on Fire and our allies as well as by those who fail to recognize (or continue to push actively against) the power and importance of the contributions of girls and women in social and political (and academic and popular) contexts. What empowers Girls on Fire is ignited by these same forces.

Building New Monuments

After the "Monuments: Reminding and Warning" panel ended at the Nordic Association for American studies' "Monuments" conference in Bergen, Norway, I turned to the Finnish scholar next to me and began to ask her about her work. I was quickly interrupted by the panel moderator, an older white man who had just delivered a resounding masterpiece comparing his generation's experience of Vietnam as understood through an analysis of Sam Peckinpah's *The Wild Bunch*. The paper he read was an ode to Peckinpah as he described the impact of the film as "a monument" that defined his life. It was a moving piece and performance. It was in stark contrast to my presentation about the role and meaning of monuments in young adult (YA) dystopian literature and the power and potential of Girls on Fire. As the applause faded, he dramatically plopped down on the other side of our Finnish colleague, leaned in close, and profusely apologized for mispronouncing her name, interrupting our conversation before it began. This small move is representative of my experiences at academic conferences and in other patriarchal American spaces; (some) men, consciously or unconsciously, perform ideas and control spaces so that they are the center of attention and they treat women like appendages and after-thoughts. I shrugged it off. I had seen worse at a plenary talk the previous day when an older white man had verbally attacked and shamed a woman who was talking about guns and sex toys because she had not properly contextualized a problematic video. It was an extreme example of a commonly seen patriarchal attitude. After her talk, I made sure she knew I saw that dynamic in action.

I was then approached by a (male) Russian academic—a fan of dystopian literature who was eager to talk. As he talked about his interest in dystopia and shared a few interesting Girls on Fire resources, a young woman stood nearby patiently waiting to talk to me. As I politely detached from the cloying conversation and turned my attention to the young woman, she lit up. She thanked me for my presentation and told me she had not really read any YA or dystopian literature. But the Girls on Fire ideas I talked about intrigued her. She then asked me if I had seen the *Captain Marvel* movie (I had not) and launched into a thoughtful analysis, applying the ideas about Girls on Fire to the Captain Marvel protagonist. As she talked, her passion for the subject matter shined through. I told her she was right on in her analysis and encouraged her to run with her ideas. I got her email, gave her a few book recommendations, and reinforced my previous encouragement. This girl was on fire. She wasn't my student; she wasn't a student at all, but she was inspired to continue being a life-long learner. I gave her, I hoped, a spark that she might be able to further ignite.

These are the opportunities that sustain my work (and perhaps all teachers' work) and get me through academic conferences. Any time I attend a conference, I am reminded of what I love about academia (passion, ideas, awkward personalities) and what I hate (posturing, pushing agendas, talking without listening). But then there are also moments to make genuine connections. I contextualize this moment of connection within the actions of the men in this conference space because this context exemplifies some of the structural challenges of promoting Girls on Fire as stories that shape the future in new ways. Everywhere I go, women immediately connect with the idea of Girls on Fire. But what I have shared so far is also only part of the story.

The young woman I connected with told me that the reason why she hadn't read dystopian stories is because when she tried to read them they reminded her too much of the real world of her home country, India. I told her that a student I worked with from Brazil had made a similar observation and that these correlations are an important part of dystopia's power to help us understand our world. Thinking about these texts that had previously disturbed her through the lens of the Girl on Fire had given her a new way of thinking about these stories. Rather than see dystopia as stories about the future, she began to see them as stories about our present.

I made some similar connections with young women when I presented another incarnation of my Girls on Fire work to American studies students at my home base of the University of Southern Denmark (SDU) the following week. At SDU, I have found that my American studies students are intensely interested in politics (elections, policies), which has been a challenge because my interest has always been in *cultural* politics. But, this is one of the ways that my students have helped me to grow, personally and professionally. In this "American Studies Day" talk I made connections to identity politics, utopian visions, and dystopian realities, but really I barely talked about Girls on Fire. I only used this idea to frame the possibility of transformational social and political change. After my talk I connected with a woman who had finished her MA in American studies a couple of years ago, but she came back to campus for "American Studies Day" to continue her learning. She told me that she was originally from Guatemala and that she had avoided books like *The Hunger Games* before because they reminded her too much of the realities of her home country. Again, I had only briefly connected contemporary politics to the Girl on Fire of YA dystopia, but the hope of the Girls on Fire had sparked something in her as well. And, again, I sent her an email with a few more resources and book suggestions to help her continue informal education as a life-long learner.

The fact that these brief connections in the scope of rather ordinary academic presentations were with young women of color is an important element to the theory and practice of teaching Girls on Fire. In my Girls on Fire work, I write about the problems of segregation in academia, and I am frustrated that these dynamics I critique are somewhat replicated and modeled here in this *Teaching Girls on Fire* book. Perhaps our Call for Papers did not reach into spaces where scholars and teachers are engaging with ideas of "Othered Girls on Fire" or Girls of Color on Fire, what I consider to be the cornerstone of my book and scholarly work on the subject. Or, maybe the Girl on Fire idea does not translate into these spaces because there are other texts and contexts that resonate more with students of color. Or maybe our tight timeline did not give us the opportunity to circulate our call for papers widely enough. Whatever the reasons, making sure that the Girl on Fire is recognized not only for her gender, but also for her "otherness" is important. The Girl on Fire, I argue, is Othered by a variety of forces and is a multidimensional and intersectional character (58–59). So, besides structural patterns of white supremacy, why do so many of us continue to imagine the Girl on Fire as "white"? Does whiteness make her seemingly more "universal"? If the masculine or gender-neutral attributes of Katniss make her more appealing to male readers, as some have argued, then does her imagined whiteness make her—and Girls on Fire, by extension—less appealing? These are some of the questions we need to keep asking.

As further demonstration of the importance of reaching out beyond segregated spaces, the context I have provided about my connection with the young woman at the Monuments conference in Bergen is still incomplete. Before the panel had begun I had met this same woman. She was standing in the entryway at the hotel conference location, looking lost. When she saw me heading toward the bathroom, she began asking me for directions. When I told her I only spoke English, she quickly shifted. She was looking for the chair of my panel; I thought she was another presenter. I gave her directions to the room where we'd be presenting. It turned out that she was not a presenter, but was just there to attend this panel. After the first two presentations and question and answer sessions concluded, the moderator took the floor. He told us some context for his presentation that day, including the fact that he had better do a good job since his wife and one of his dear former students were in attendance. He did not mention them by name, just nodded in their direction. As in so many patriarchal contexts, they were his props. His wife, a kind and beautiful woman, had been obviously engaged in my presentation and had shared a connection she found to my work during the question and answer portion. The former student was the young woman I connected with. She was there for the moral support of her former teacher, a former Fulbright in Norway. She fulfilled this role, but she also found a new way of thinking about monuments and joined the Girls on Fire fold.

These connections I made with young women of color are representative of the ways in which the idea of the Girl on Fire can plant new seeds of ideas and how it does so in the patriarchal soil where we are all mucking around, so to speak. One of the things that surprised me about living, teaching, and learning in international contexts during my Fulbright year is the ways in which patriarchy is still alive and well in places that I had assumed to be more enlightened than the U.S. They are more enlightened in many ways, but even in places where equality is found more readily in society at large, women's lives and opportunities are still shaped by some of the same sexist patriarchal assumptions and structures. As a result of this shared structural force, the female students that I worked with were often hungry for opportunities to learn about women, to read feminist texts and apply feminist lenses. They often verbalized their appreciation of the opportunities my teaching gave them. This too is an example of the power and potential of Girls on Fire.

Minds and Bodies and Collective Trauma

In the spring of 2019, I was invited to give a plenary talk at the annual conference for the Portuguese Association for Anglo-American studies. It was the 40th Anniversary of the organization and they provided a list of anniversaries that contributors to the conference program might connect with. At first glance, I didn't think that I could make a connection, but then I thought of the most obvious connection of all—the role and meaning of walls in YA dystopian texts and the fall of the Berlin Wall in 1989. This conference not only gave me another opportunity to think about Girls on Fire and YA dystopia texts in new ways; it also extended the work I had begun to develop in my "American Studies Day" talk where I connected contemporary politics to dystopia and Girls on Fire. Further, by thinking about walls as more than just physical manifestations of social control, I was also able to extend my work in the realm of mind/body fitness, particularly the connections between trauma and individual and structural transformations.

In YA dystopia, the wall is a powerful and multifaceted symbol. In my *Girls on Fire* book, I write about the ways in which walls are used to keep people safe and protected ... and controlled. Of course, these walls are illusions of safety and Girls on Fire have no problem circumventing these walls when they need to. Further, it seems the inevitability of such walls is that they are almost always going to be torn down. The news at the moment when I was thinking about my conference presentation was all about The Wall that President Trump wants to build—the wall that Trump promised to build, the wall that rallied fear and white supremacy, the wall that the shut down the U.S. government. This wall is a symbol of the past and a distraction from the scandals that build their own walls between left and right. It is a wall that divides the population as well as the nation's physical borders. I started to think more about the symbolic power of walls that I had begun to develop in my Girls on Fire book.

Thinking about the mental/emotional walls in YA dystopia, and the role that these walls play in the stories of Girls on Fire opened up new and interesting connections that I will continue to unpack and extend, in and out of the classroom. From the wall that is violently toppled in Octavia E. Butler's *Parable of the Sower*, to the walls in *Eve* that imprison Eve and her peers in their school, to the fence around District 12 that is electrified to contain and control Katniss, to the wall that separates Orleans from the Outer States (in *Orleans*), to the tiered walls of Palmares Tres in *The Summer Prince* that protect and contain the city and separate the classes, the examples in YA dystopian texts abound. In addition to examples from YA dystopia, the history of the fall of the Berlin Wall, and connections to contemporary U.S. politics, I made a connection to Roxane Gay's book, *Hunger: A Memoir of (My) Body*; she writes: "I no longer need the body fortress I built. I need to tear down some of the walls, and I need to tear down those walls for me and me alone, no matter what good may come of that demolition. I think of it as undestroying myself" (303). Gay is a fan of The Hunger Games books and films and in her book *Bad Feminist* she writes about her inability to objectively critique these books—the subject matter is too near and dear to her heart. This connection also deepens our readings of texts like The Hunger Games books as we consider the multiple traumas that Katniss endures and survives, and is haunted by long after the Games have ended. It helps explain the walls that Cia describes in a trauma-induced dream in *Independent Study* (the second book in The Testing series): "One wall meets another. Then another./A cage that cannot be seen is no less there than if the walls were made of steel. …/ And I realize—the walls are constructed of my terror. To escape, I will have to not only face, but defeat, my fear" (264). Cia does just this. And while trauma nearly breaks Katniss, and certainly leaves her forever scarred, Cia is empowered to become one of the leaders because she knows that "the only way to be sure The Testing we had never happens again is not to trust our leaders. It is to be one of them" (*Graduation Day* 290–91). She explains further, "Despite what I have learned and what I have done, I am still the girl from Five Lakes who wants to lead and help my country. And there is still so much for me to do" (292–93). Rather than return home to the familiar safety of Five Lakes, like Katniss returns to District 12, Cia leaves home (and the boy she loves, though she hopes he'll follow) with a sense of responsibility and purpose.

Perhaps the best example of the power of walls—both physical and mental/emotional—is from *Requiem*, the third book in the Delirium series. While the wall in *Parable of the Sower* is torn down by the collective forces of the oppressed outside the wall, the tearing down of the wall in *Requiem* illustrates the need for collective action in order to tear down both kinds of walls. Lena calls for the reader to "Take down the walls …. All of you, wherever you are…. Find it, the hard stuff, the links of metal and chink, the fragments of stone filling your stomach. And pull, and pull, and pull" (219). I offer these examples not only as illustrations of this theme within YA dystopian books about Girls on Fire but also as an example of some of the connections that we can help students make in our classrooms. These literary texts can be supplemented by sources and discussions related to the historical and contemporary political examples I describe above, but also with the ever-growing number of sources exploring trauma and PTSD and the ways in which trauma is (quite literally) stored in the body. This connection and discussion can further lead to a discussion about the importance of collective action in struggles for social justice, as well as the need for self-care so that Girls on Fire can continue to burn instead of just burning themselves out (Hentges 234–38), an idea that I will return to in another section below.

In addition to expanding my scholarly work and teaching in new ways, this conference presentation provided several unexpected and empowering connections. First, after a long week with little sleep, an early flight, and a growing pile of work (as is typical of the over-committed academic), I was not looking forward to participating in another academic conference (though I was excited about the content of my presentation as described above). After a flight delay that caused me to miss most of the conference, I was exhausted and just wanted to eat and crash. Instead, I agreed to attend the conference dinner and was pleasantly surprised to find a group of warm and welcoming Portuguese colleagues and rather than engaging in painful small talk, I learned about a project that several of them were involved with—a study of foodways and utopia (see Index, *Alimentopia*). Not only was I intrigued by this project, I was sure that my talk the next day—the last thing before final remarks—would resonate with many of the conference attendees. For once, I had an audience that was familiar with many of the texts I was talking about and the question and answer period raised countless excellent questions about: the "exceptional" character of so many of the Girls on Fire and whether I found this to be problematic; what I thought about Theresa in The Maze Runner series; what I thought these books meant to teenage readers who would be inclined to push back against such heavy-handed adult instruction; what I thought about the turn toward resistance in the latest season of Hulu's *The Handmaid's Tale*; what I thought about the arguments that YA is too simplistic; and whether these books are arguing for individual or collective empowerment. As if I wasn't already moved by these questions, I was approached by many students before and after my talk.

Because there were so many faculty who were interested in utopia/dystopia, there were many students who were as well. Some wanted to know about resources; some shared resources with me. One young woman (whose presentation I had unfortunately missed) told me about her thesis about YA literature and how excited she was for my talk; after, she was gushing in her praise and thanks for everything she had learned from my talk. One undergraduate young man, whose presentation about queer utopia in Shakespeare I had been able to attend before my talk, was excited to learn more about YA texts that he might consider in his master's work. Several thanked me for bringing attention to texts that are so often dismissed by scholars and critics. And one young woman thanked me and told me I was right about what these texts mean to young readers. She told me that she and her sister had both read many of the books and that they had found hope and refuge among these texts. From the students as well as from my hosts, I received so much love that I was a bit overwhelmed. It was my first keynote invitation; it was the first time I really felt that my work mattered beyond the conference. I felt empowered. But, again, it proved to me that this idea—this symbol of the Girl on Fire—has power that we are only beginning to tap into.

Black Girls on Fire: Dismantling Academic, Social and Cultural Segregation

As I discuss in the previous essay, the texts I selected for my MA course on Girls on Fire were the books that centered more on "Othered" Girl on Fire protagonists. Thus, my students in Denmark got a different picture of Girls on Fire than if we had read a majority of texts that had white or ambiguously-raced protagonists. Given the texts discussed in this collection of essays, I would have to assume that the YA dystopian texts that center girls of color—like *Beauty Queens*, *Orleans*, and *The Summer Prince*—are taught less often than the texts that are popular with young readers (like The Hunger Games novels and films) and texts that address issues that are more "universal" to the social and cultural experiences of all girls (like the texts discussed in part two of this book that provide a way to talk about the #MeToo movement). These text choices make sense given the various restrictions placed on teaching at every level, but they also do not do justice to the spirit of the Girl on Fire. This deficiency is part of what I address in my *Girls on Fire* book when I argue that both popular culture texts and academic inquiries suffer from segregation, as I also note above. Toward a remedy to this structural ill, I offer two examples that I hope will serve as models for other teachers who would like to challenge status quo and highlight real-life issues and concerns like climate change and police brutality.

The first example was mentioned in the previous essay—one of the two Power Point lectures I did in my graduate-level Girls on Fire course, and a topic I further developed for a presentation at a small symposium of American studies scholars at Copenhagen University: "(Othered) Girls on Fire: Dystopia, Reality, and Imagination in American Culture and (New) Orleans." In this class lesson and presentation, I brought together four texts that speak to each other in interesting layers, providing a kind of continuum—from girlhood through adolescence to womanhood, from survival through sacrifice to empowerment, from fantasy to reality to imagination, and from the past to the present to the future: the film, *Beasts of the Southern Wild*; the contemporary novel, *Salvage the Bones*; the YA dystopia novel, *Orleans*; and Beyoncé's album and film, *Lemonade*. All of these texts are tied together by geographic location—the South, and more specifically, New Orleans. And all of these texts model the diversity and strength of black women and girls, culminating in Beyoncé's powerful representation of Black, Southern women that gives them visibility, voice, and individual and collective power. The film version of *Lemonade* gives us a diversity of representations of black women— represented by famous faces like Serena Williams, Amandla Stenberg (Rue from *The Hunger Games* film), Quvenzhané Wallis (from *Beasts of the*

Southern Wild), and Beyoncé's daughter, Blue Ivy. Mixed in among these pop culture icons are the mothers of young men shot by police, holding framed pictures of their sons, and home video footage of Beyoncé's family (including Jay-Z's grandmother and Beyoncé's parents). *Lemonade* also provides social, cultural, and political critiques and the many faces, looks, and personalities that a woman like Beyoncé can choose to embody and enact and, in part, encourage other women to do the same. Perhaps most important to my arguments here, within this collection of texts, *Lemonade* is the most explicitly feminist text, and can be used to revisit ideas and themes explored in the other texts where the feminist aspects are present but not centered.

Some of the instructional frames that teachers can provide for these texts include the many themes that play out in them in different kinds of ways, for instance: poverty, gender, race, sexuality, survival, coming of age, climate change and environmental disaster, voice and agency, motherhood(s), fathers/family/care-givers, trauma and survival, empowerment, redefinition, community, and empowerment. While these themes get varying degrees of treatment in these texts, the theme of motherhood highlights the multidimensional aspects and challenges of these texts, and perhaps does not get as much treatment in YA literature (which often includes absent parents and fathers more often than mothers). Together, these texts explore motherhood, mothers, and mothering; absent mothers; expanded definitions of mother, including adopted mothers, fathers as mothers, and mothers as leaders; mother as survivor; mother as protector; mother as (uncontrollable) nature; mother as role model; mother as mover; mother as mentor; and mother as making room for Girls on Fire.

While these were all ideas that were presented to students who were then left to engage with these ideas mostly outside of class, and to my peers who were mostly unfamiliar with all of these texts, there are many ways that these texts could be used together to expand and diversify our approaches to teaching Girls on Fire. These texts could be used together as a unit or set of lessons within a variety of courses, including high school and college literature classes, women's studies classes, sociology classes, and history classes, for instance. Through the power of words and images, the examples and connections that students can explore are myriad. Further, these textual connections can be explored through connections to contemporary issues by asking students to research one or more of the contemporary issues that these texts present—from the roles and representations of women and girls in politics and popular culture, to the impacts on girls and their communities post Hurricane Katrina, to the recent (and ongoing) police shootings of black men and boys. And still further, these texts and students' research can be used as impetus for civic engagement projects or "action" projects (Hentges 209–14). The authors throughout this collection of teaching Girls on Fire essays give us all kinds of models and examples of these kinds of projects.

My second example here also grows from my work in Denmark. After my "American Studies Day" presentation, another young woman approached me and made a connection with a YA novel she had recently read, *The Hate U Give*. While she recognized that *The Hate U Give* is not a dystopian novel, she made connections to the kind of dystopic conditions that drive the protagonist of the novel, as she argued, to engage in activism. Her connections made me think about the importance of explicitly including the voices and experiences of "Othered" Girls on Fire, and girls of color more generally, in all classroom spaces. In the newest incarnation of my Girls on Fire class, I plan to teach *The Hate U Give* as a way of connecting not only to the idea of the Girl on Fire in YA dystopia, but also to the real-life "dystopic" conditions that drive some girls to activism out of necessity. Further, the 2019 Netflix film, *See You Yesterday*, provides a perfect companion text—and science and science fiction elements—for considerations of this novel and of the related social justice issues. In fact, the following texts could be provided for a deeper examination of the themes of police brutality and state violence highlighted in Beyoncé's *Lemonade* (mostly through visual representation).

The smart, sassy Black girl character, C.J. Walker (a nod to Madam C.J. Walker, the first African American millionaire), is the protagonist of *See You Yesterday*, rather than occupying the sidekick role she is so often relegated to in books, films, and TV shows (if she appears at all). C.J. is a brilliant science prodigy at The Bronx High School of Science and she and her sidekick and best friend, Sebastian, are working on creating a "temporal relocation" device that will be their ticket to a scholarship at a prestigious university. When her brother is shot by a police officer, only the latest casualty of state violence, C.J. is certain she can change his fate by going back in time. Of course, as science fiction fans know, when we start messing around in the past, the consequences of the future are out of our control. Both of these texts offer many connections to Black culture and contemporary social justice struggles like the #BlackLivesMatter movement, sometimes in heavy-handed ways. And both of these texts extend our imaginations, not only in regard to the possibilities of the future, but also in regard to who we consider to be a Girl on Fire. Ultimately, not even science—or science fiction—can change the material circumstance of the lives of Black people in America; to do that will necessitate our making structural and systemic changes. These stories, explored in scholarship and in the classroom, I hope, can model the necessity of making intersectional connections as well as explicit connections to the experiences of Black girls and girls of color, in and out of fiction. But, of course, we all have to make a conscious effort to teach not only what we think our students will most connect with, but also what we know they might not otherwise be exposed to outside of their education, whether these are texts, contexts, theories, or interpretive lenses. Further, as educators it is our responsibility to give students tools for critical interpretations and for texts that are unfamiliar as well as for those (mainstream, popular) texts that they are most exposed to in spaces where critical attention is not encouraged. By diversifying our classroom spaces, we might be able to begin (or continue) the process of dismantling academic, cultural, and social segregation.

Harnessing the Bravery of the Girls on Fire Through Creative/Critical Pedagogy

The last context for Teaching Girls on Fire is the most unconventional. On the last day of my graduate Girls on Fire class, I showed the three students who made it to class on that dreary winter day a draft of my poster for a Girls on Fire inspired event—Girls on Fire: Mind/Body Fitness Dance. I had debated with myself about whether I was going to offer this event in Denmark. My attempts to bring mind/body fitness dance to people in academic settings had crashed and burned several times before. It didn't do all that well in fitness settings either. The students were a bit skeptical, but still supportive. I left class that day unsure whether I would offer this event. But I decided to embody the Girl on Fire; in Denmark, I had nothing to lose. In addition to inviting the students from my Girls on Fire class, I loosely connected this event to my spring MA class about "Bodies, Minds, and Movements," in order to illustrate the "in practice" work we were asking students to do while inviting students to also be brave. (None of them were, but this might be less about bravery and more about the date, time, and location.) I made posters and a Facebook event and wrote a blog. I also made a connection with the International Students office to tap into a wider pool of interested participants at SDU. I connected the event to International Women's Day on Friday, March 8 and held it in the Winter Garden—an open space with skylights—on the SDU campus.

This event and incarnation of Girls on Fire is rooted in my work as a fitness and yoga instructor, a side job I have held throughout my years in graduate school and into the present, a side job that has become an intricate part of my academic work, which I have presented twice at the annual conference for the National Women's Studies Association. (I write about this work extensively in my book *Women and Fitness in American Culture* and my blog on www.cultureandmovement.com.) This work meshes well with the symbolic power of the Girl on Fire and combines inspirational music and mindful movement that offers both the structure of choreography and the opportunity for "free dance." I open the event (and include on the handout I make available) with a brief introduction to the theme:

The "Girls on Fire" theme takes us on a journey through music and movement as we experience a story of the world on fire and we become protagonists in our own story. We're grounded and connected to earth even as we play in in the clouds. We're warriors who fight with our minds and our bodies.

And a Girl on Fire story:

> The story that frames our movement: *We stand on top of the wreckage of a fading world—a dying planet, corrupt governments, poverty, hunger, disease. Looking toward the horizon, we see hope. We see love and the cleansing power of fire. We gather our tools—the mental, the physical, the mystical—and prepare for battle. We are not alone. This is our story. This is where the future begins.*

The playlist and choreography carry forth this story and invite participants to embody the power of the Girl on Fire. The playlist begins with Alicia Keys's "Girl on Fire" song (of course) and includes other Girl on Fire artists like Beyoncé, Janelle Monáe, Ani diFranco, and Lorde. We fight battles, we fall in love (maybe with ourselves), we claim our strength, and we gather our comrades. This work is also undergirded by the critical/creative theories I explore in *Women and Fitness in American Culture*.

I was also able to bring this idea (in a much smaller dose) to a summer school program on "Health—Culture—Healing" in Greece. This two day teaching opportunity at the University of Aristotle included lectures and discussion as well as hands-on activities. Amidst the topics on mind/body American fitness, I used the symbol and story of the Girl on Fire as an example of how to use storytelling and movement in classrooms and community spaces. Again, as a symbol, the Girl on Fire is powerful and empowering; coupled with a form of mindful movement, this symbol resonates in new ways. In this workshop, and in my graduate "critical themes" course about bodies, minds, and movements, I further used the symbol of the Girl on Fire to help students think about self-care. As I discuss in my *Girls on Fire* book, in *Shadows Cast by Stars*, Madda gives Cass a wealth of advice about how to take care of herself, particularly by staying balanced and connected to the earth (237–38). I share this example of mind/body fitness dance as inspiration for Girls on Fire projects that take the symbolic power of Girls on Fire out of the classroom and out of the box, so to speak. Moving the body in new ways also moves the mind in new ways and moving the mind in new ways might move us toward new ideas for a better future for us all.

Teaching to the Future

After a semester of sabbatical and a Fulbright year in Denmark, I will return to my home institution in Bangor, Maine, and my Girls on Fire work will continue to evolve. I'll be teaching a new online class, revised from my original Girls on Fire course. This new Girls on Fire course is subtitled "Feminism, Activism, and the Future" and I am still in the process of working out the best curriculum to bring together the Girls on Fire of YA dystopia with the real-life Girls on Fire. The essays in this collection speak to new directions, new contexts, and new lenses as well as examples that lend themselves in practical and theoretical ways in our classrooms. Working with Sean and these authors, and presenting my work in the contexts described here, I have been re-inspired by the power and potential of the pedagogy of Girls on Fire. An imagined incendiary extrapolation. All of these examples—while perhaps reaching and hoping—exemplify the power of the Girl on Fire as a tool for teaching and learning.

All of the connections I outline in this conclusion internationalize and diversify Girls on Fire ideas and (I hope) create an ember of a new idea and applications that can positively impact individual lives and communities. This is part of the power of Girls on Fire that comes through teaching. It is important that these connections are with women and about women as agents of change, but also that we find new ways to engage boys and men as well—after all, our future is a shared future. The men in my classes remind me how very important this work is as they struggle to unlearn toxic masculinity, challenge themselves to be allies, address and dismantle structural confines, and work to make sure their daughters have the resources and opportunities they need to burn brightly and that their sons have respect for themselves as well as for girls and women. Further, through my collaborations on this book and other Girls on Fire projects I am reminded that men like Sean and Bryan are doing the critical feminist work that is too often attributed only to women and too often used to teach girls and women empowerment without remembering to foster, for instance, the emotional intelligence of boys and men. As I write about in *Girls on Fire*, the love interest for female protagonists often acts as the "boy as consciousness" (132–38), the "key that unlocks the body of the Girl on Fire as much as her mind" (134). Girls on Fire, and the women they grow up to be, need to return the favor and foster our boys and men as much as we do girls and women. As Katniss reminds President Snow in *Mockingjay*, " If we burn, you burn with us!"

Finally, in this conclusion I want to highlight one last example of teaching Girls on Fire that might lend itself to intersectional analysis and new explorations of the Girl on Fire. Fortunately, with the growing number of Girls on Fire making space in popular culture, like *Captain Marvel* and *Star Trek: Discovery*'s Michael Burnham, for instance, we have no shortage of texts to connect, consider, and teach! Without the distractions of home and with only YouTube and Danish Netflix to entertain me, I started watching *The 100*, a CW Network television show based on the four-book series by Kass Morgan. (Kass Morgan also holds writing credit for 80 episodes.) These books didn't make it into my initial study of Girls on Fire in YA dystopian literature for no good reason. I don't remember these books coming up in my searches though I remember hearing something about the TV series when it premiered. Perhaps I omitted them knowing that I didn't have time to tackle the book series and the television series within the scope of the project and I decided to focus on film representations instead. (At the time, I did not yet have access to the show's network.) Further, the books are most often described online as science fiction while the TV series is described as dystopian or post-apocalyptic (which it definitely is). Regardless of the reasons, I certainly missed an opportunity to engage with this pop culture manifestation of YA dystopia and Girls on Fire. I now have these books on my reading list and have been binge-watching the show.

The basic premise of this story is quite complicated, with multiple story lines, characters, communities, and conflicts. At the start, there are two narratives that parallel each other—the action happening with the adults on the space station (the Ark), and the narrative happening on the ground where the leaders of the Ark have just sent 100 "criminal" children to what may or may not be an inhospitable earth. One of the most interesting elements of this show is the myriad characters that we might consider to be Girls on Fire. In addition to the obvious, beautiful, blond star of the show and center of the story, Clarke, we have the Commander of the Grounders, Lexa; the mechanic on the engineering crew who becomes disabled in battle, Raven; the illegal second child who lived in hiding for much of her life and then becomes a warrior, Octavia; the girl who follows in the footsteps of her mother who was a revolutionary and helps the prisoners in Sky Mountain, Maya; and more. Along with these girls, there is a diverse cast of boys and men as well as many women with influential roles and positions. Further, Clarke's sexuality is not given a label, but she loves and has sex with both men and women and there are other instances where the identity politics of todays' world are portrayed in intersectional ways. In addition, the show tackles a variety of topics that can create a springboard for conversations in relation to other texts and critical issues. For instance, what is the difference between a "criminal" and someone who breaks the law? How do we build and sustain communities when faced with impossible odds? Should the needs of the few outweigh the needs of the many? What makes someone a "good guy"? What role does violence play in struggles to build a better world? How do communities create a sense of belonging? What does race and gender mean when the human race has been threatened with extinction?

I hope that teachers, scholars, readers/watchers, and students will bring the ideas of Girls on Fire to critical analysis of this show since there is much material to consider here—in the books and films alone, as well as in the ways this YA series is adapted for a television audience. For a variety of reasons, this show is an example of a smart and successful adaptation of a YA book series to the small screen, in its sixth season at the time of this writing. Hollywood's treatment of Girls on Fire texts, as one of my graduate students in Denmark (Romaine) explored in her MA thesis, do not always translate the Girls on Fire to the screen. Then again, readers/watchers and social movers can always take these texts in new, and transformative, directions.

* * *

When I return to Maine, I'll also be sharing *Teaching Girls on Fire* with colleagues through workshops and the development of an online resource that I hope to develop from students' praxis work as well as from other opportunities—like workshops for teachers—I hope to create from a meager mini-grant I received for this project. Perhaps this work will be taken up by other teachers, in other locations. Perhaps I will provide a blueprint; perhaps I will not need to. Perhaps the fire will spread, the networks will grow; we will burn without burning out. As I regularly remind those who are listening to me share ideas about Girls on Fire, YA dystopia is not a pessimistic genre. In the individual and collective stories there is always hope, but the most important message is our collective stake in the future and the power of empathy, community, consciousness, and love.

Works Cited

Beasts of the Southern Wild. Directed by Benh Zeitlin. Performances by Quvenzhané Wallis and Dwight Henry. Cinereach, 2013.

Beyoncé. *Lemonade*. Parkwood Entertainment, 2016, www.beyonce.com/album/lemonade-visual-album/.

Gay, Roxane. *Bad Feminist: Essays*. Harper Perennial, 2014.

_____. *Hunger: A Memoir of (My) Body*. HarperCollins, 2017.

Hentges, Sarah. "Girls on Fire: Political Power in Young Adult Dystopia." Theconversation.com The Conversation US, 20 Mar. 2015. Web. 23 Apr. 2017.

_____. "Othered Girls on Fire: Navigating the Complex Terrain of YA Dystopia's Female Protagonist." *Children's and Young Adult Literature and Culture: A Mosaic of Criticism*. Ed. Amie Doughty. Cambridge Scholars, 2016.

_____. *Pictures of Girlhood: Modern Female Adolescence on Film*. McFarland, 2006.

_____. "This Class Is on Fire! (and Online): Teaching YA Dystopia and the Girl on Fire Through Themes, Contexts, and Action." *SIGNAL Journal* XXXIX.1 (Fall 2015/Winter 2016): 41–53.

_____. *Women and Fitness in American Culture*. McFarland, 2013.

The 100. Developed by Jason Rothenberg. Seasons 1–6. The CW, 2014.

See You Yesterday. Directed by Stefon Bristol and produced by Spike Lee. Netflix, 2019.

Smith, Sherri L. *Orleans*. Penguin, 2013.

Thomas, Angie. *The Hate U Give*. HarperCollins, 2017.

Ward, Jesmyn. *Salvage the Bones*. Bloomsbury, 2011.

About the Contributors

Nicole Ann **Amato** is a Ph.D. student in the language, literacy, and culture program at the University of Iowa. Prior to this, she was a high school literature teacher for ten years, teaching in Greenville, South Carolina, and Chicago. Her research interests include young adult literature, critical youth studies, critical literacy, culturally sustaining and relevant pedagogy, and teacher education.

Arianna **Banack** is a doctoral student at the University of Tennessee, Knoxville, in the literacy studies program with a specialization in children's and young adult literature. Her research focuses on the connections between reading engagement and YAL. Prior to enrolling at UTK, she was a high school English teacher in Connecticut. She serves as coeditor of *The ALAN Review*.

Romaine **Berry** has a master's degree in American studies from the University of Southern Denmark. She previously received a BA at Plymouth University in the United Kingdom in history and American studies.

Elaine **Brum** is a Brazilian journalist with a BA in social communication, a postgraduate degree in art and culture from Universidade Cândido Mendes (UCAM), and a master's degree in American studies from the University of Southern Denmark (SDU). She is interested in film and television production, sports, social media, cyberculture, human rights and intersectional studies.

Sydni **Collier** graduated magna cum laude with a BA in interdisciplinary studies from Thomas College. Her areas of concentration included English, education, and sociology and her thesis centered around student perceptions of academic barriers within rural contexts with a specific focus on race. She plans to pursue a doctorate in sociology.

Sean P. **Connors** is an associate professor of English education at the University of Arkansas. His scholarship and teaching focuses on the application of diverse critical perspectives to young adult literature. He is the editor of *The Politics of Panem* and the host of *The Storyteller's Thread*, a monthly podcast devoted to children's and young adult literature.

Wendy J. **Glenn** is a professor of literacy studies, the chair of Secondary Humanities, and the co-director of Teacher Education at the University of Colorado Boulder. Her research centers on literature and literacies for young adults. She is the former

President of the Assembly on Literature for Adolescents of the National Council of Teachers of English (ALAN) and outgoing senior editor of the organization's peer-reviewed journal, *The ALAN Review.*

Amanda **Haertling Thein** is the Associate Dean for Academic Affairs and Graduate Programs and a professor at the University of Iowa. Her research focuses on socio-cultural and socio-emotional aspects of literary response, critical approaches to multicultural literature instruction, and the intersection of critical youth studies and young adult literature. She is the coeditor of *English Teaching* and co-author of four books, including *Teaching to Exceed the English Language Arts Common Core State Standards.*

Sarah **Hentges** is an associate professor at the University of Maine at Augusta. She teaches a variety of courses in women's and gender studies, American studies, inter-disciplinary studies, and English. Her books include *Pictures of Girlhood, Women and Fitness in American Culture, Universal Interdisciplinarity,* and *Girls on Fire.* She also teaches fitness classes in her community and on her campus and maintains a website at www.cultureandmovement.com.

Petra **Ilic** is a graduate student with an MA in American studies from the University of Southern Denmark and a BA in English language and literature from the University of Nis, Serbia. Her main interests include gender and race studies. She teaches Chinese and Japanese students online, focusing on the English language and British and American culture.

Kate **Lechtenberg** is a doctoral candidate in language, literacy, and culture at the University of Iowa, where her research focuses on text selection and classroom dialogues about literature.

Caitlin **Metheny** is a doctoral student at the University of Tennessee, Knoxville, in the literacy studies program, with a specialization in children's and young adult literature. Her research involves the visibility of diverse populations in young adult literature. She serves as coeditor of *The ALAN Review.*

Tessa **Pyles** completed her Ph.D. in 2020 in the American culture studies program at Bowling Green State University. In every classroom, she strives to foster a space of openness and acceptance, and she supports students as they use their lived experiences and knowledge as tools to interrogate larger systems and structures of social, cultural, and political power.

Amanda **Rigell** is a first-year doctoral student in literacy education at the University of Tennessee, Knoxville. Her research interests include reading motivation, YA literature, and the reading-writing connection. She is a licensed reading specialist and has thirteen years of experience as a middle and high school classroom teacher.

Gretchen **Rumohr** is an associate professor of English and department chair at Aquinas College, where she teaches writing and language arts methods. She has published, presented, and reviewed for various NCTE efforts. She has also written poetry for *Language Arts Journal of Michigan* as well as *The Paterson Review.*

Katie **Rybakova** earned a Ph.D. in curriculum and instruction from Florida State University and is an assistant professor of education at Thomas College. She is certified to teach 6–12th grade English in Florida and holds a K–12 teaching students with exceptionalities certification as well. Her research interests include young adult literature and digital literacies. She serves as the executive director of the Maine Association for Middle Level Education.

Katie **Sluiter** is a junior high school ELA teacher and a doctoral student in the English education program at Western Michigan University. Her professional presentations and publications center on reading and writing alongside the young adults she teaches. She is a member of both NCTE and ALAN and is a National Writing Project Fellow.

Jenna **Spiering** is an assistant professor in the School of Library and Information Science at the University of South Carolina in Columbia, where she studies youth literature, school libraries, and adolescent literacies.

Lissette Lopez **Szwydky** is an assistant professor at the University of Arkansas where she teaches and publishes in the areas of 19th-century literature and culture, gender studies, adaptation and media studies, and professional development for liberal arts majors. She has published on the early adaptation histories of 19th-century texts, and specializes in Frankenstein's 200-year multimedia cultural history. She is working on a book titled *Transmedia Adaptation in the Nineteenth Century.*

Roberta Seelinger **Trites** holds the rank of Distinguished Professor of English at Illinois State University, where she has taught since 1991. She is the author, among other works, of *Waking Sleeping Beauty, Disturbing the Universe, Twain, Alcott, and the Birth of the Adolescent Reform Novel, Literary Conceptualizations of Growth* and *Twenty-First-Century Feminisms in Children's and Adolescent Literature.*

Bryan **Yazell** is an assistant professor at the University of Southern Denmark. His research focuses on the ways literary sources inform popular understandings of welfare politics from the late 19th century to the present. His scholarship on the political imaginary in speculative fiction appears in *Studies in the Fantastic* and *The Routledge Companion to Transnational American Studies.* His work appears courtesy of the Danish National Research Foundation (grant no. DNRF127).

Index

Abelson, Jenn 104
activism 1, 6, 7, 9, 15, 20, 49, 50, 80, 83, 86, 87, 101, 106, 109, 186, 201, 204
advocacy 9, 20, 71, 75, 80, 84–6, 87, 88, 89–90, 92, 93, 95, 96, 100, 101, 103; *see also* ally
Afrofuturism 170; *see also* Womack, Ytasha
agency 7, 9, 10, 49, 56, 58, 60, 63, 66, 106, 109, 112, 113, 114, 116–19, 163, 167, 184, 200
Aguirre, Abby 154, 169
Ali, S.K. 74, 90; *see also Saints and Misfits*
Alimentopia 13, 15, 198
ally 5, 9, 12, 29, 59, 76, 80, 81–2, 93, 95, 100, 103, 166, 192, 204; *see also* advocacy
Amato, Nicole Ann 10, 105, 207
American 6, 12, 13, 14, 33, 53, 67, 79, 91, 124, 154, 156, 157, 166, 177, 186, 188, 189, 191, 192, 201, 202–3; *see also* United States
The American Prospect 158, 169
American studies 11, 12, 169, 171–2, 173, 174, 175, 176, 179, 186, 187, 188, 189, 192, 194, 195, 196, 199, 207, 208, 209
Amistad 158
Amorosano, Ken 28, 33
Anderson, Laurie Halse 15, 71–2, 75–6, 82, 90, 97, 103; *see also Speak, Shout*
Anderson, M.T. 65, 67; *see also Feed*
Ansbach, Jennifer 3, 15
Appleman, Deborah 118–19, 120
Asking for It 9, 10, 16, 105, 107–8, 109, 110–12, 113–19, 120; *see also* O'Neill, Louise
athlete 8, 12, 19–20, 22–4, 25, 26–8, 30–2, 33, 36, 37, 38, 42, 81, 82, 144
The Atlantic 102, 103
Atwood, Margaret 107; *see also The Handmaid's Tale*
Auerbach, Nina 166, 167, 169

Bad Feminist 126, 139, 197, 206; *see also* Gay, Roxane
Bae, Michelle S. 126, 127, 128, 139; *see also Girls, Cultural Productions, and Resistance*
Baker, Carissa Ann 64, 67

Banack, Arianna 9, 12–13, 71, 207
Barker, Lisa 145, 153
Barnes, Mary 21, 26, 33
BBC News 79, 90
Beasts of the Southern Wild 174, 199, 206
beauty 37, 47, 48, 109, 110, 111, 113, 117, 118, 130, 134, 135, 178, 182, 205
Beauty Queens 172, 173, 180–82, 189, 199; *see also* Bray, Libba
Bee, Samantha 87
Beers, Kylene 96, 103
Berlin Wall 191, 196
Berry, Romaine 12, 171, 207
Beyoncé 174, 188, 199–200, 201, 203, 206; *see also Lemonade*
Biles, Simone 27, 79, 91
Birthmarked 11, 15; *see also* O'Brien, Caragh
#BlackLivesMatter 3, 188, 201; *see also* hashtag movements
Blade 167
Blank, Hanne 132
Blood Water Paint 100, 103; *see also* McCullough, Joy
Blue Ivy 200
body image 127, 132
Boehm-Schnitker, Nadine 49, 50
Bohnenberger, Jann E. 86, 91
Bower, Jody Gentian 15; *see also Jane Eyre's Sisters*
boys 12–13, 30–2, 33, 37, 38, 42, 43, 50, 68, 72, 79, 81–2, 84, 90, 91, 105, 106, 110, 111–12, 129, 184, 200, 204, 205; *see also* males
Bradbury, Ray 143, 153
Bradley, Laura 90
Bram Stoker's Dracula 166; *see also* Coppola, Francis Ford
Brave New World 117
Bray, Libba 172, 181, 182, 189; *see also Beauty Queens*
The Breakbeat Poets 177
Brown, Mackenzie 28, 33–4
Brum, Elaine 12, 171, 207

212   Index

Buehler, Jennifer 21, 33
Buffy the Vampire Slayer 42, 166
Burke, Tarana 73, 92–3; *see also* #MeToo
Butler, Octavia 5, 11, 14, 15, 154–70, 172, 187, 196; see also *Dawn*; *Fledgling*; *Kindred*; Olamina, Lauren; *Parable of the Sower*; *Parable of the Talents*; Xenogenesis (book series)

Canavan, Gerry 154, 165, 169
canonical 1, 7, 8, 11, 13, 38, 72, 117, 142–3, 167
Captain Marvel 193, 204
Carillo, Nadia Martinez 34
Casper, Monica J. 108, 120
Castillo, Ana 81, 90
Catching Fire 15, 55, 56, 58, 60, 62, 67, 172, 189; *see also* Collins; *The Hunger Games*
Chernik, Abra Fortune 132, 137, 138, 139
Childs, Ann M.M. 56, 67
Christensen, Linda 93, 101, 103
Clark, Leisa A. 68
classism *see* intersectionality
classroom 1, 7, 9, 11, 12, 13, 14, 33, 48, 54, 73, 75, 77, 81, 89, 119, 124, 125, 126, 131, 138–9, 141, 144, 145, 156, 160, 167, 168, 169, 180–1, 197, 201–2, 203, 204; high school 49, 72, 73, 80, 83, 88, 94, 97, 101, 102, 103, 104; university 10, 123–4, 128, 129–30, 132, 141, 149, 153, 154, 168, 174, 177, 189; *see also* jigsaw (activity); secondary education; teachers
Cleveland, Erika 71, 90
climate change 1, 3, 13, 199, 200
Clinton, Hillary 62
CNN 79, 91
Coffee, Patrick 25, 33
Colantonio-Yurko, Kathleen C. 71, 72, 73, 74, 90
Colbert, Steven 87
college *see* university
Collier, Sydni 11, 141, 207
Collins, Suzanne 4, 8, 15, 19, 22, 23, 24, 25, 26, 29, 32, 33, 35, 51, 52, 53, 62, 64, 67, 106, 107, 113, 120, 172, 189; see also *The Hunger Games*
coming of age 131, 200
Common Core State Standards 72, 96, 98, 103, 208
community 4, 5, 9, 11, 13, 25, 26, 49, 56–7, 61, 66, 83, 84, 86–8, 89, 92, 94, 100, 101, 105, 108–9, 110, 111, 112, 114, 117, 124, 125, 127, 131, 136, 139, 145, 146, 169, 189, 191, 200, 203, 206
Connors, Sean P. 1, 3, 4, 7, 8, 12, 15, 35, 37, 50, 61, 64, 67, 68, 191, 204, 207
Conrad, Daniel 87, 90
Cook, Michael 142, 153
Coppola, Francis Ford 166; see also *Bram Stoker's Dracula*
Coval, Kevin 177

critical 1, 7, 10, 11, 12, 14, 33, 36, 38, 40, 41, 50, 68, 90, 123, 138, 142, 143, 153, 164, 169, 202, 203, 204, 205; consciousness 14; educators 48, 191, 207, 208; thinking 20, 52, 66, 178
Critical Trauma Studies 108, 120
Currie, Dawn H. 37, 41, 50

Davidson, Carolyn S. 155, 169
Davies, Bronwyn 21, 27, 33
Davis, Wynne 31, 33
Dawn 157, 161–64, 165, 166, 168; *see also* Butler, Octavia E.
Day, Sara K. 4, 15, 50, 67, 68; see also *Female Rebellion in Young Adult Fiction*
DeCarvalho, Lauren J. 34
Delirium (book series) 11, 15, 197; *see also* Oliver, Lauren
Denmark 12, 14, 171–7, 185–6, 188–9, 191–2, 194, 199, 201, 202, 203, 206
Descartes, Rene 57
Diaz, Natalie 27, 33
diFranco, Ani 203
Dirty Computer 188; *see also* Monáe, Janelle
diversity 14, 41, 87, 150, 167, 177, 180, 182, 185, 186, 199
Django Unchained 158, 160, 161, 170; *see also* Tarantino, Quentin
Dracula 165
Dumbledore 66
Dunn, George A. 68
Durand, Sybil 71, 90
dystopian 13, 26, 32, 107, 108, 113, 118, 119, 152, 156, 170, 186, 189, 192, 193, 194, 196, 198, 199, 201; literature 1, 3–4, 5, 7, 8, 11, 12, 13, 15, 27, 36, 37, 38, 49, 50, 65, 67, 68, 89, 106, 107, 108, 109, 117, 118, 119, 120, 125, 130, 139, 143, 169, 171–2, 174, 176, 184, 186, 187–8, 189, 193, 194, 196, 197, 199, 201, 204, 206

ecocriticism 64, 65
ecofeminism 63, 64, 65, 67, 68
Edwards, Haley Sweetland 90
Elder, Glen H. 144, 153
embodiment 6, 7, 9, 41, 52, 55, 57, 58, 59, 60, 61, 66, 72, 76, 77, 78, 84, 85, 87, 89, 90, 93, 113, 157, 188, 200, 202, 203
empowerment 3, 20, 33, 34, 38, 54–5, 66, 68, 86, 101, 106, 124, 139, 174, 186, 198, 199, 200, 204
English Language Arts Standards 72, 90
Erickson, Lance 144, 153
Esckilsen, Erik E. 32, 33
ESPN-W 27, 28, 33, 34
Eve 196
Everdeen, Katniss *see* Katniss
Exit, Pursued by a Bear 100, 103; *see also* Johnston, E.K.

Facebook 13, 15, 113, 114, 202; *see also* social media

Fallon, Jimmy 87
family 24, 26, 29, 32, 38, 41, 43, 46, 47, 58, 64, 78, 97, 105, 106, 108, 111, 114, 115–6, 117, 132, 133, 135, 145–6, 174, 200; *see also* parents
fantasy (genre) 156, 157, 159, 160, 161, 162, 167, 170, 176, 199
fathers 30, 46, 55, 112, 116, 158–9, 160, 200; *see also* family; parents
Feed 65, 67; *see also* Anderson, M.T.
Female Rebellion in Young Adult Fiction 4; *see also* Day, Sara K.; Green-Barteet, Miranda A.; Montz, Amy L.
feminism 8, 10, 13, 36–7, 41, 49, 50, 51–57, 61, 65, 66, 67, 68, 80, 81, 83, 125–7, 135, 136, 139, 140, 170, 192, 204, 209; first wave 53, 54; intersectional 37, 80; material 52, 58, 60, 68; second wave 53, 54, 66, 134; third wave 51, 56–7, 58, 66, 83; *see also* feminist; intersectionality; postfeminism
feminist 8, 9, 10, 36, 38, 42, 43, 47, 50, 51, 52, 53–4, 56–7, 61, 63, 65, 66, 67, 68, 80, 81, 106, 107, 116–17, 118–19, 120, 127–8, 134, 137, 139, 143, 195, 200, 204; anti-feminist 113; criticism 53, 57, 65; discourse 36, 126; literature 56, 65, 137; methodologies 8, 52; movement 83; pedagogy 127, 128, 132; philosophy 42, 43, 57; protagonists 106, 113; theory 54, 63, 65, 124, 188; *see also* feminism
Fergusen, Sherelle 144, 145, 153
Flagel, Nadine 158, 169
Fledgling 157, 164–68, 169, 170; *see also* Butler, Octavia
food 13, 15, 23, 24, 27, 58–9, 63, 102, 198
Ford, Christine Blasey 72, 75, 76, 78, 79, 88, 90, 91, 106
Foucault, Michel 55, 67
Francis, Lauren 68
Frankenstein 8, 41, 50; *see also* Shelley, Mary
Friedan, Betty 53, 67
Fritz, Sonya Sawyer 35, 50
Frow, John 155, 169
Full Frontal Feminism 135, 140; *see also* Valenti, Jessica
Future Girl 36–8, 50, 125, 139; *see also* Harris, Anita

Gamerman, Ellen 72, 90
Garriott, Deidre Anne Evens 67, 68
Gay, Roxane 126–27, 139, 196, 206; see also *Bad Feminist*; *Hunger: A Memoir of (My) Body*
gender 11, 19, 31, 36–7, 38, 39, 41, 43, 44, 45–7, 50, 52, 53–7, 66, 68, 80–1, 83, 89, 98, 117, 118, 119, 120, 126, 130, 134, 142, 155, 156, 165, 166, 168, 174, 182, 184, 186, 188, 194, 205; cis-gender 51
genre *see* dystopian; fantasy; literature; science fiction; speculative fiction; young adult literature
Giardina, Michael D. 20, 33
Gibney, Sharon 32, 33
Gill, Rosalind 46, 47, 50
Girl on Fire 1, 5, 6, 66–7, 77–9, 89–90, 115, 119, 124, 128, 138, 141, 150, 169, 171, 172–4, 182, 185, 188, 189, 192–3, 194, 195, 198, 201, 202–3, 204; collective category 3, 5, 72–3, 76, 88, 94, 188–9, 192; definition of 6, 106, 125, 128, 168–9; (fictional) character(s) 6, 36, 38, 39, 74, 80, 83, 85, 94, 97, 109, 119, 131, 156, 157, 160, 164, 167–9, 184, 187, 189, 192, 199, 206; Katniss as 106, 152, 178–80; real-life example 25, 28, 75, 79, 83, 141, 143, 152, 146–52, 155, 169, 186, 202; spirit of 7, 9, 12, 48, 72, 75, 76, 78, 82, 88, 93, 187, 188, 199; stories about 109; traditional 109, 112, 117; trope 103, 106, 107, 108; YA heroines 39, 41, 46, 48
"Girl on Fire" (song) 73, 203; *see also* Keys, Alicia
Girls, Cultural Productions, and Resistance 126, 139; *see also* Bae, Michelle S.; Ivashkevich, Olga
girls of color 5, 14, 170, 184, 194, 199–201
Girls on Fire (book) 5, 11, 14, 15, 50, 120, 125, 139, 169, 171, 189; *see also* Hentges
Glenn, Wendy J. 8, 12, 19, 33, 207
Golding, William 143, 153
Gone with the Wind (film) 160, 161
Gould, Philip 157, 169
Graduation Day 197; *see also* The Testing series
Green, John 143, 153; see also *Looking for Alaska*
Grigoriadis, Vanessa 90
Grosz, Elizabeth 57, 67
Grundy, William 28, 33
Gruss, Susanne 49, 50
Guanio-Uluru, Lykke 68
Green Valentine 13, 16; *see also* Wilkinson, Lili
Green-Barteet, Miranda A. 4, 15, 50, 67, 68; see also *Female Rebellion in Young Adult Fiction*

The Handmaid's Tale 107; television show 198
Hanna, Julian 103
Hansen, Kathryn Strong 68
Haq, Husna 35, 50
Harde, Roxanne 64–5, 67
Hardin, Marie 34
Harré, Rom 21, 27, 33, 34
Harris, Anita 36, 39, 40, 50, 125, 139
Harris, Tamara Winfrey 158, 169
Harry Potter (book series) 5, 35, 42, 50; *see also* Rowling, J.K.
Harry Potter Alliance 5–6, 15

Harvey, David A. 61, 67
hashtag movements 2, 3, 9, 12, 71–4, 75–6, 78, 82–3, 87–90, 91, 92–3, 96; see also #BlackLivesMatter; #MeToo; social media
The Hate U Give 201, 206; see also Thomas, Angie
Hedin, Diane 87, 90
Heinecken, Dawn 31, 33
Heldring, Thatcher 32, 33
Hentges, Sarah 1, 3, 4, 5, 6, 7, 8, 11, 12, 13, 14, 15, 37, 50, 93, 106, 107, 109, 110, 113, 115, 119, 120, 125, 128, 130, 136, 138, 139, 155, 156, 160, 168, 169, 171, 174, 176, 177, 179, 181, 183, 184, 186, 187, 188, 189, 191, 197, 200, 206, 208; see also Girls on Fire; Pictures of Girlhood; Women and Fitness in American Culture
Herman, David 155, 169
Hesse, Karen 65, 67; see also Out of the Dust
heteronormativity 5, 23, 51, 66
high school 3, 4, 12, 48, 76, 94, 104, 113, 129, 132, 144, 200, 201; see also secondary
history 8, 10, 12, 25, 31, 33, 38, 41, 42–3, 44, 45–6, 49, 50, 51, 54, 62, 63, 64, 67, 73, 83, 119, 124, 158–9, 185, 186, 188, 196, 197, 200; historical bad girl 36, 38, 39, 41, 43, 46, 47, 48–50
Hobbes, Michael 132
Hochschild, Arlie Russel 30, 33
homophobia 1, 123, 124
hooks, bell 124, 139; see also Teaching Community: A Pedagogy of Hope
Hopkinson, Nalo 155
Hunger: A Memoir of (My) Body 196, 206; see also Gay, Roxane
The Hunger Games 4, 6, 8, 15, 19, 20, 22, 24, 2, 27, 28, 30, 31, 33, 35, 50, 51–2, 53, 54, 56, 58–9, 61, 62–3, 64, 67, 68, 106, 113, 145, 148, 178, 179, 194, 196–7, 199; see also Collins, Suzanne; Johanna; Katniss; Rue
The Hunting Ground 99, 103
Hurricane Katrina 200

identity 19, 20, 22, 23, 28, 30, 32, 46, 49, 50, 80, 81, 123, 126, 127–8, 130, 142, 159, 194, 205
ideology 20, 39, 105, 128, 170
Ilic, Petra 12, 171, 208
Independent Study 197; see also The Testing series
interdisciplinary 7, 11, 72, 142, 148, 150, 174
international (contexts) 10, 12, 30, 39, 43, 44, 45, 46, 62, 85–6, 89, 100–1, 171–2, 175, 186, 189, 101, 191–2, 193, 194, 195, 202
The Interrogation of Ashala Wolf 172, 189; see also Kwaymullina, Ambelin
intersectionality 4, 14, 37, 39, 40, 46, 71, 80, 108, 123, 124, 126, 134, 174, 176, 185, 186, 192, 194, 201, 204, 205; see also feminism; race

intertextuality 96, 99, 100
Ivashkevich, Olga 126, 127, 128, 139; see also Girls, Cultural Productions, and Resistance
Iyapo, Lilith 161–64; see also Butler, Octavia; Dawn; Lilith's Brood

Jane Eyre's Sisters 13, 15; see also Bower, Jody G.
Jenkins, Henry 5, 15
Jerng, Mark 168, 170
jigsaw (activity) 78, 79, 88, 96, 98, 103; see also classroom
Johanna 54, 55, 56; see also The Hunger Games
Johnson, Alaya Dawn 65, 67, 172, 187, 189; see also The Summer Prince
Johnson, Mark M. 57, 67
Johnston, E.K. 100, 103; see also Exit, Pursued by a Bear
Jones, Whitney Elaine 67, 68
justice 6, 29, 66, 82, 84, 93, 94, 96, 97, 98, 100, 101, 103, 104, 105, 108, 118, 133, 140, 150; see also social justice

Kafka, Franz 143, 153
Kantor, Jodi 91
Katniss 4, 5, 8, 19–20, 22–5, 26–9, 30, 32, 35, 51, 52–3, 54, 55–7, 58–60, 62–3, 64, 67, 68, 89, 106, 107, 113, 145, 152, 178–80, 194, 196, 197, 204; as Girl on Fire 152, 178–80; as Mockingjay 55, 56, 58, 179; "Ode to Katniss" (activity) 173, 177–80, 182; see also The Hunger Games
Kavanaugh, Brett 75, 78, 106, 119
Kelly, Deirdre M. 37, 50
Kelly, Michael 103
Kenan, Randall 159, 170
Keys, Alicia 4, 73, 91, 203; see also "Girl on Fire" (song)
Kiely, Brendan 100, 103; see also Tradition
Kindred 157–61, 163, 164, 169; see also Butler, Octavia
King, Ynestra 63, 67
King-Watkins, Danielle 19, 31, 33
Knutsson, Catherine 15; see also Shadows Cast By Stars
Kolodny, Annette 63, 67
Kwaymullina, Ambelin 172, 189; see also The Interrogation of Ashala Wolf

Lakoff, George 57, 67
Landis, Dylan 131; see also Rainy Royal
Langton, Rae 63, 67
Lechtenberg, Kate 10, 105, 208
Legend 37; see also Lu, Marie
Lemonade 174, 199, 200, 201, 206; see also Beyoncé
Let the Right One In 166
Lilith's Brood 161, 162, 163, 169; see also But-

ler, Octavia; Iyapo, Lilith; Xenogenesis (book series)
literature *see* canonical; genre; young adult
Looking for Alaska 143, 153
Lord of the Flies 143, 153
Lorde 203
Lu, Marie 37; see also *Legend*
Lysistrata 94, 100, 103

Maconi, Caryn 28, 33
Macri, Nick 29, 34
males 25, 31, 49, 53, 63, 65, 74, 182, 188; *see also* boys
Malo-Juvera, Victor 72, 74, 91
Manter, Lisa 68
masculinity 12–3, 19, 41, 47, 48, 51, 53, 54, 68, 79, 81, 83, 165, 182, 194, 204
Mathieu, Jennifer 15, 80, 81, 88, 89, 91; see also *Moxie*
Matthews, Shori 165–8; see also *Fledgling*
The Maze Runner (book series) 198
McCullough, Joy 100, 103; see also *Blood Water Paint*
McDonald, Steve 144, 153
McGowan, Rose 79, 88, 91
McRobbie, Angela 37, 38, 41, 50
Meeusen, Meghann 68
men 12, 30–1, 36, 41, 43, 51, 54, 55, 63, 66, 82, 84, 97, 98, 105, 107, 110, 111, 113, 123, 125, 129, 133, 137, 154, 158, 176, 182, 184, 192–3, 200, 204, 205
menstruation 58, 133
mentors 11, 30, 144–8, 150–3, 141, 200; mentor text 81, 87, 101
Metamorphoses of Science Fiction 162, 170
Metheny, Caitlin 9, 12–3, 71, 208
methodology 8, 52, 54, 66, 94
#MeToo 3, 9, 12, 71–4, 75–6, 78, 82–3, 87–90, 91, 93, 96, 103, 104, 119, 188, 199; *see also* hashtag movements
Metz, Jennifer L. 20, 33
Michaud, Nicolas 68
Milano, Alyssa 71, 90
Miller, Henry 71, 72, 73, 74, 90
misogyny 10, 94, 100, 108, 116, 118, 119, 124
Mockingjay 4, 51, 55, 56, 59, 60, 62, 63, 67, 107, 120; *see also* Collins, Suzanne
Moghaddam, Fathali 21, 26, 34
Monáe, Janelle 188, 203; see also *Dirty Computer*
Montz, Amy L. 4, 15, 50, 67, 68; see also *Female Rebellion in Young Adult Fiction*
monuments 191, 192, 195
Moore, Maya 27, 33
morality 21, 22, 26, 27–9, 33, 34, 37, 41, 94, 157, 159, 160, 161, 162, 164, 168
Morgan, Kass 204; see also *The 100*
Morgan, Megan 102, 103
Morris, Susana M. 165, 170

mothers 11, 22, 43, 45–6, 47, 49, 55, 56, 58, 59, 63, 99, 110, 112, 116, 126, 139, 162, 178, 200, 205; *see also* family; parents
Moxie 9, 12, 15, 72, 79–83, 88–9, 91; *see also* Mathieu, Jennifer

Nama, Adilifu 160, 170
Nassar, Larry 78, 79, 91
National Council of Teachers of English (NCTE) 103, 149
National Sexual Violence Resource Center (NSVRC) 92, 104
Negra, Diane 47, 50
neoliberalism 8, 36, 37, 38, 39–41, 43, 44, 46, 47, 49, 50, 52, 61–2, 63–4, 65, 66, 67
The New York Times 62, 79, 82, 91
Newitz, Annalee 160, 170
Newsela 96, 103, 104
Nightline 79, 91
Nike 25, 33, 34
1984 (novel) 107, 142
Noah, Trevor 87
The Nowhere Girls 9–10, 16, 72, 83–6, 88, 91, 93, 94–101, 103, 104; *see also* Reed, Amy Lynn
Nussbaum, Martha 63, 67

Obama, Barack 186
O'Brien, Caragh M. 15; see also *Birthmarked*
Ocasio-Cortez, Alexandria 9
O'Donovan, Emma 105–19; see also *Asking for It*
Okorafor, Nnedi 155
Oliver, Lauren 15; see also *Delirium, Pandemonium, Requiem*
Olamina, Lauren 15; see also Butler, Octavia; *Parable of the Sower*
The 100 204–6; *see also* Morgan, Cass
O'Neill, Louise 10, 16, 105, 107, 108, 110, 114, 115, 120
Oppel, Kenneth 12, 16, 36, 38, 41–3, 46–8, 49, 50; see also *This Dark Endeavor*
oppression 3, 5, 39, 64, 106, 108, 109, 126, 134, 143, 186, 187, 189, 192
Orleans 11, 16, 65, 67, 172, 173, 178, 183–4, 187, 189, 196, 199, 206; *see also* Smith, Sherri L.
Orwell, George 107, 142
othered 5, 14, 164, 167, 194, 199, 201, 206
Our Vampires, Ourselves 166, 169
Out of the Dust 65, 67

Palumbo, Donald E. 68
Pandemonium 15; *see also* Oliver, Lauren
Parable of the Sower 5, 15, 169, 172, 184, 187, 196, 197; *see also* Butler, Octavia; Olamina, Lauren
Parable of the Talents 154; *see also* Butler, Octavia
parents 43, 45, 51, 93, 103, 108, 112, 132, 133,

135, 146, 147, 159, 200; *see also* fathers; mothers; parents

patriarchy 13, 60, 62, 63–4, 106, 108, 113, 116, 126, 137, 192, 193, 195; ideology 105; society 27, 106, 108, 109, 113; structures 5, 8, 10, 44, 56, 64, 65, 108, 118, 119, 195

Paul, Lissa 56, 67

Peckinpah, Sam 192; see also *The Wild Bunch*

pedagogy 10, 14, 124, 127, 128, 132, 139, 191, 192, 204; *see also* classroom; feminist

Pellizzoni, Luigi 64, 67

Pepper, Christopher 87, 91

Pew Research Center 71, 91

Pharr, Mary F. 68

Pictures of Girlhood 206; *see also* Hentges, Sarah

poetry 27, 75–6, 81, 87, 97, 101, 103, 124, 143, 177–9

police brutality 199, 200, 201

political economy 39, 61

politics 3, 4, 5, 6, 9, 13, 24, 26, 34, 37, 39, 41, 46, 48, 53, 62, 87, 107, 108, 125, 127, 130, 132, 133, 134, 136, 147, 155, 163, 174, 180, 185, 191, 192, 194, 196, 197, 200, 206; gender 3, 45; identity 49, 50, 194, 205

Pomerantz, Shauna 37, 41, 50, 62, 67

popular culture 4, 5, 6, 8, 10, 35, 37, 47, 49, 50, 67, 107, 157, 158, 168, 199, 200, 202, 204

positioning theory 20–2, 26–7, 33, 34

postfeminism 8, 36, 38, 39–41, 43–4, 46–7, 50; *see also* feminism

poverty 56, 102, 167, 200, 203

power 21, 22, 24, 26, 27–8, 30, 31, 33, 53, 59, 60, 62, 63, 66, 67, 76, 82, 95, 98–9, 101, 142, 150, 154–5, 156, 165, 196–7; "girl power" 20, 36–7, 50, 124; of literature and stories 6, 80, 118, 130, 154–5, 170, 174, 189, 193, 200; structures 29, 80, 82, 83, 124, 130; as toward social change 1, 4, 6–7, 8, 11, 21, 54–6, 96, 101, 126, 131, 136, 152, 186, 189, 192, 195, 198, 199, 202, 203, 204, 206

praxis 136–9, 206

Primorac, Antonijia 47, 50

Prince Charming 51

privilege 21, 31, 45, 46, 134, 138, 150, 160, 172, 174

Probst, Roberty E. 96, 103

Proulx, Natalie 87, 91

Prout, Chessy 100, 104

Pyles, Tessa 10–11, 123, 208

Quidditch 31, 33, 34

Raby, Rebecca 37, 50, 62, 67

race 10, 14, 37, 67, 80, 135, 144, 146, 148, 149, 150, 155, 156, 161, 164, 166, 168, 169, 170, 176, 182, 186, 188, 199, 205; *see also* intersectionality

Race on the QT 170

Racial Worldmaking 170

racism 1, 14, 39, 40, 108, 123, 124, 126, 134, 143, 156, 159, 160, 164; *see also* white supremacy

Rape, Abuse, and Incest National Network (RAINN) 74, 91, 100, 104

Rainy Royal 131; *see also* Landis, Dylan

Raisman, Aly 79, 88, 91

Reagan, Ronald 39, 163

Red Brigade Lucknow 85–6, 90

Reed, Amy 16, 83, 84, 85, 91, 93, 94, 99, 103, 104; see also *The Nowhere Girls*

Requiem 15, 197; *see also* Oliver, Lauren

Rigell, Amanda 9, 12–3, 71, 208

Riot Grrrls 36, 80, 81

romance 6, 30, 47, 68, 130

Ross, Loretta 133, 140

Rowling, J.K. 5; *see also* Harry Potter

Rue 24, 28, 29, 53, 55, 56, 58, 60, 179, 199; see also *The Hunger Games*

Rumohr, Gretchen 9–10, 92, 208

Ruthven, Andrea 68

Rybakova, Katie 11, 141, 153, 209

Saints and Misfits 74, 90; *see also* Ali, S.K.

Salvage the Bones 174, 199, 206; *see also* Ward, Jessmyn

Sarkeesian, Anita 52, 67

Scharff, Christina 46, 50

Schieble, Melissa 145, 153

Schmidt, Samantha 91

Schulten, Katherine 87, 91

science fiction 154, 157, 161, 162, 164, 168, 169, 170, 201, 205

secondary education 72, 94, 96, 117, 118; *see also* high school

See, Lisa 164, 170

See You Yesterday 201, 206

segregation 158, 194, 195, 199, 202

self-care 136, 137–8, 197, 203

service learning 72, 87–9, 91

sex 48, 53, 74, 76, 80–1, 82, 89, 94, 97, 98, 99, 100–1, 102–3, 110, 111, 115, 118, 130, 133, 136, 163, 205; education 83; roles 53; third sex 162

sexism 1, 39, 40, 45, 46, 52, 53, 54, 66, 82, 91, 106, 108, 123, 124, 126, 156, 164, 195

sexual assault 9, 10, 12, 71, 72, 74–86, 87, 88, 90, 91, 92–4, 95, 96, 97, 99, 100, 101, 102, 103, 104, 105, 106, 107, 108, 109, 111–12, 113–18, 119, 127, 131–32, 163; *see also* trauma; violence

sexual harassment 79, 82, 91, 93, 96, 97

sexuality 38, 41, 109, 111, 117, 118, 125, 130, 134, 155, 161, 164, 200, 205

Shadows Cast by Stars 11, 15; *see also* Knutsson, Catherine

Shawl, Nisi 155

Shelley, Mary 41, 42, 43, 46, 49, 50; see also *Frankenstein*

Shout 9, 15, 72, 75–6, 78, 81, 87, 90, 103; *see also* Anderson, Laurie Halse
Shusterman, Neal 65, 67, 153; see also *Unwind*
SIGNAL Journal 1, 15, 67, 206
Simmer-Brown, Judith 128, 140
Simmons, Amber 4, 15, 48–9, 50
Slack, Andrew 6, 15
slave narratives 157–61, 169
Sleeping Beauty 113
Sluiter, Katie 9–10, 92, 209
slut-shaming 109, 111, 120
Smith, Alexandra Nutter 34
Smith, Sherri L. 16, 65, 67, 172, 183–4, 187, 189, 206; see also *Orleans*
social justice 4, 9, 10, 11, 13, 14, 136, 141, 142, 143, 145, 149, 153, 160–1, 168, 169, 174, 184, 197, 201; *see also* justice
social media 4, 53, 75, 80, 83, 87, 88, 102, 108, 112, 114; *see also* #BlackLivesMatter; Facebook; hashtag movements; #MeToo
Speak 9, 15, 71–2, 76–9, 82, 88, 90; *see also* Anderson, Laurie Halse
Speak Out 89, 91
Spears, Brittney 4
speculative fiction 11, 155, 156, 169
Spiering, Jenna 10, 105, 209
Sproull, Patrick 108, 120
Star Trek 176
Star Trek Discovery 204
Stark, Rachel 52, 68
Stenberg, Amandla 199; see also *Lemonade*; Rue
structural 14, 39, 40, 44–6, 47, 106, 130, 194, 195, 196, 199, 201, 204
The Summer Prince 65, 67, 172, 185, 186, 189, 196, 199; *see also* Johnson, Alaya Dawn
Suvin, Darko 162, 163, 170
Sweeney, Brian N. 109, 120
Szwydky, Lissette Lopez 8, 12, 35, 209

Tan, Siu-Lan 21, 26, 34
Tarantino, Quentin 160, 170; see also *Django Unchained*
Taurasi, Diana 27
teachers 1, 3–4, 5, 7, 8, 9, 10, 11, 14, 20, 35, 36, 38, 40, 41, 46, 49, 52, 62, 66, 71, 72–3, 74, 75, 77–83, 86, 88, 89–90, 93, 95, 96, 97, 100, 101, 102, 103, 117–9, 129, 135, 139, 141, 144, 145, 147, 148, 149, 153, 154, 155–6, 173, 191, 194, 195, 199, 200, 205, 206; *see also* classroom
Teaching Community: A Pedagogy of Hope 124, 139; *see also* hooks, bell
teens 3, 22, 35, 41, 42, 50, 62, 65, 66–7, 72, 82, 86, 94, 96, 97
Terry, Alice W. 86, 91
The Testing (book series) 197; see also *Independent Study*
Thaller, Sarah 52, 68

Thein, Amanda Haertling 10, 105, 208
This Dark Endeavor 12, 16, 36, 38, 41–8, 50; *see also* Oppel, Kenneth
Thomas, Angie 206; see also *The Hate U Give*
Tilton, James 52, 68
Time's Up 87, 93, 104; *see also* hashtag movements; social media
To Kill a Mockingbird 177
Tradition 100, 103; *see also* Kiely, Brendan
transformation 3, 4, 5, 7, 11, 35, 55, 62, 93, 112, 130, 138, 154, 186, 194, 196, 206
trauma 4, 9, 52, 64, 66, 71, 77, 78, 95, 106, 108–9, 113–14, 118, 128, 157, 160, 196, 197, 200; PTSD 52, 197; sexual 10, 106, 107, 112, 114–17, 118, 119; *see also* sexual assault; violence
Trikha, Ritika 52, 68
Trites, Roberta Seelinger 8–9, 36, 37, 50, 51, 58, 59, 61, 65, 66, 67, 68, 113, 120, 209
Trump, Donald 107, 154, 196
12 Years a Slave 158
Twilight 54, 68, 165
Twitter *see* social media
Twohey, Megan 91
Tyler, Julie Elizabeth 67, 68

The Unapologetic Fat Girl's Guide to Exercise and Other Incendiary Acts 132; *see also* Blank, Hanne
Underlined 76, 90
UNESCO 30
United States 39, 53, 95, 106, 107, 159, 163, 172, 174, 177, 191, 195, 196; *see also* American
U.S. Department of Health and Human Services 20, 74, 91
US Quidditch *see* Quidditch
Unwind 65, 67, 143, 153; *see also* Shusterman, Neal

Valenti, Jessica 135, 140; see also *Full Frontal Feminism*
The Vampire Chronicles 42
Villa, Walter 28, 34
violence 1, 4, 10, 64, 77, 82, 96–7, 102, 107, 108, 109, 116, 117, 120, 127, 130, 131, 143, 157, 160, 205; gun 101; racial 158; sexual 10, 72, 73–4, 75–6, 82, 92–3, 96, 102, 104, 106–7, 108, 111, 112, 116, 119, 127, 130, 131–32, 186; slow 110; state 109, 201; systemic 109, 112, 113, 117, 118, 119; *see also* sexual assault; trauma
voice 3, 10, 29, 56–7, 59, 77–8, 91, 94, 106, 113–15, 118, 119, 123, 125, 149, 160–1, 164, 168, 175, 184, 188, 199, 200

Waking Sleeping Beauty 68, 113, 120
Walker, C.J. 201
Wallis, Quvenzhané 199, 206; see also *Beasts of the Southern Wild*; *Lemonade*

218   Index

Ward, Barbara A. 35, 50
Ward, Jesmyn 174, 206; see also *Salvage the Bones*
Warren, Karen J. 63–4, 68
Weinstein, Harvey 78, 79, 90, 91
Wertheimer, Eric 108, 120
Whedon, Joss 166; see also *Buffy the Vampire Slayer*
White, Brian 98, 104
white supremacy 5, 14, 194, 196; see also racism
whiteness 134, 145, 153, 156, 159–60, 194
Whiteside, Erin 20, 23, 30, 34
Wiggins, Janice 142, 153
The Wild Bunch 192; see also Peckinpah, Sam
Wilhelm, Jeffrey D. 95, 98, 104
Wilkinson, Lili 16; see also *Green Valentine*
Williams, Kyndall 53, 68
Williams, Serena 25, 27, 199
Wilson, Julie A. 39, 50
Wolfson, Susan J. 50
Wollstonecraft, Mary 43, 50
Womack, Ytasha 155, 170; see also *Afrofuturism*
Women and Fitness in American Culture 202, 203, 206; see also Hentges, Sarah
women of color 3, 14, 27, 133, 155, 167–8, 194

women's studies 10, 11, 123, 124, 129, 136, 177, 200, 202
Wonder Woman 66

Xenogenesis (book series) 161, 163; see also Butler, Octavia E.; *Lilith's Brood*
xenophobia 124, 162, 164, 172

Yancy, George 82, 91
Yazell, Bryan 11, 14, 154, 209
Ylönen, Marja 64, 67
Young, Terrell A. 35, 50
young adult literature (YA or YAL) 7, 8, 10, 19, 20, 35, 36, 37, 40, 41, 42, 43, 44, 46, 48, 52, 62, 65, 67, 71, 72, 74, 75, 83, 86, 89–90, 93, 102, 106, 107, 109, 124, 142, 145, 182, 184, 187, 198, 200, 201; dystopian 3, 4, 7, 13, 35, 36, 89, 106, 107, 119, 130, 142, 143, 156, 172, 174, 186, 187, 189, 192, 194, 196, 197, 199, 201, 204, 205, 206; neo–Victorian 36, 38, 41, 43, 49; realistic fiction 72, 83, 117–18, 119
Yousafzai, Malala 186
YWCA 97, 101, 102, 103, 104

Z for Zachariah 176
Zaki, Hoda M. 163, 170
zines 83, 90